LIABILITY AND LAW

IN RECREATION,

PARKS, AND SPORTS

LIABILITY AND LAW IN RECREATION, PARKS, AND SPORTS

Ronald A. Kaiser, J.D.

Texas A&M University

Prentice-Hall, Englewood Cliffs, New Jersey 07632

Library of Congress Cataloging-in-Publication Data

Kaiser, Ronald.
  Liability and law in recreation, parks, and sports.

  Includes bibliographies and index.
  1. Tort liability of recreation agencies—
United States. 2. Tort liability of parks—United
States. 3. Liability for sports accidents—United
States. I. Title.
KF1290.P5K35 1986   346.7303′2   85-19233
                        347.30632

Cover designer: Ben Santora
Manufacturing buyer: Harry P. Baisley

© 1986 by Prentice-Hall
A Division of Simon & Schuster, Inc.
Englewood Cliffs, New Jersey 07632

10 9 8 7 6 5 4 3 2 1

ISBN 0-13-535089-1   01

Prentice-Hall International, Inc., *London*
Prentice-Hall of Australia Pty. Limited, *Sydney*
Editora Prentice-Hall do Brasil, Ltda., *Rio de Janeiro*
Prentice-Hall Canada Inc., *Toronto*
Prentice-Hall Hispanoamericana, S.A., *Mexico*
Prentice-Hall of India Private Limited, *New Delhi*
Prentice-Hall of Japan, Inc., *Tokyo*
Prentice-Hall of Southeast Asia Pte. Ltd., *Singapore*
Whitehall Books Limited, *Wellington, New Zealand*

TO MY PARENTS AND FAMILY

RONALD A. KAISER, a practitioner in the recreation and sports field, has taught courses at Michigan State University and Texas A&M University and delivered numerous lectures on the subject. A professor at Texas A&M University, Mr. Kaiser also practices law and is a partner in a sports agency firm.

contents

table of cases

Principal cases are in capital letters.

preface

The first thing we do,
let's kill all the lawyers!
–Shakespeare, Henry VI

Protection of lawyers is not the intent of this book, rather the purpose is to help students and professionals in the fields of parks, recreation, sports, and leisure to understand and manage legal risks. These fields have experienced unprecedented growth over the last twenty years in user participation and in injury litigation. In the 1960s lawsuits were an anomaly for the manager, today they are ubiquitous. This book provides a valuable tool for managers who must deal with a variety of legal concerns on a routine basis.

The manager's role is to efficiently administer recreation programs and not to second guess the attorney. The lawyer's task is to protect clients–to keep them out of court and to represent them when in court. In partnership, both parties must minimize legal risks, therefore each must understand the other's job and not try to usurp it. The intent of this book is not to train lawyers but to inform and educate managers about the legal risks pervasive to parks, recreation, sports, and leisure services. Often the student and manager in discussing a legal problem with an attorney is presented with a barrage of legal jargon or a litany of citations to cases drawn from a reservoir of lawbooks. This book is structured to part the mystical shroud that surrounds the law and to explain in layman's language the legal aspects of management decisions. It incorporates the case method of teaching the management of legal risks which is superior to simply citing general rules that are always easy to illustrate. Through the study of cases, the reader can learn from the unfortunate results of poor decision making by others.

Where possible, the most recent cases have been used. However, a 1930 case dealing with a specific point of law may still be valid today unless overturned by the court. In some of the older cases the language is formal and difficult to follow and so these cases are used only when a more recent case is not available. All of the cases have been edited and only the pertinent rules of law discussed. Rules of law important to attorneys but not germane to the manager have been deleted.

The body of law described in this book is derived from many sources and jurisdictions. It is important to recognize that the law may vary from state to state. This variance is attributable to differences in state statutes and case law, making it impossible to explain all the exceptions to the rules of law. It is often said, "the average lawyer knows the general rules of law and a good lawyer all the exceptions."

Many people have directly contributed to the preparation of this book. Special thanks are in order to Lois Beach for editorial assistance, to Hope Peart and Mildred Musick for hours of typing and proofreading, to Rusty Reid for creative ideas on the graphics, and to the faculty and students in the Texas A&M University Department of Recreation and Parks for many ideas and suggestions on the subject.

A book, like its author, contains the imprints of mentors, teachers, colleagues, and friends. Although they have not directly contributed to writing this text their influence guided the pen and I would like to recognize some of them—Joseph Seavey, Louis Twardzik, John Fitzgerald, former Justice of the Michigan Supreme Court, James Beers, Gale Jamsen, Lynn Kindinger, Leighton Leighty, Patricia Russ, Mark Bonn, Raleigh Barlowe, Milton Steinmueller, William Upina, John Greenslit, Roy Singleton, Jim Fletcher, Ed Heath, Sharron Brown, Dick Hanson and Blanche Hockett.

one

legal liability: an overview

Recreation and leisure have never been more important to the American public. It is paradoxical that record numbers of citizens are visiting parks and participating in recreation, sports, and leisure activities and are also suing the providers of these services for all types of injuries. Litigation has become the nation's secular religion and it is practiced regularly against public and private park, recreation, sports, and leisure enterprises.* As a result, law and liability have become synonymous terrors to the managers of these services. In the last ten years providers of recreation and leisure services have experienced a dramatic increase in the number and seriousness of legal liability claims asserted against them, their directors, administrators, and employees. By any measure the range of recreation and sports litigation is astonishing. Consider

  ✳ The father of a Little League ball player sued the manager of the team, contending he failed to provide a proper role model for the boy.[1]
  A Houston YMCA was ordered by the Texas Supreme Court in 1981 to pay $133,000 in damages to a man blinded in one eye when hit by the mechanical arm of a pitching machine in a home-run batting contest.[2]
  ✳ A visitor at Six Flags Over Texas Amusement Park sued the organization when she was butted by a small billy goat in a petting zoo.[3]

  *Enterprises include the public and private sector of the leisure industry.

1

✗ A man in Washington D.C. sued and recovered $4.6 million from the operator of a pool. He claimed the diving board was too flexible, and it caused paralysis when he dove into the pool.[4]

✗ A Bristol, Connecticut, high school girl sued her gym teacher and the city after she broke a finger trying to catch a pop fly in a school softball game. She alleged that her teacher not only failed to instruct her in the art of catching but also failed to warn her of the inherent dangers in playing the outfield.[5]

✗ A man confined to a wheelchair sued the New York City Road Runners Club for discrimination when it refused to permit him to participate in the 1977 New York City Marathon.[6]

A taxpayer challenged the City of New York's acceptance of $600,000 from the family and friends of Adele Levy to erect a $1.2 million recreation facility in a park as a memorial to Levy. The taxpayer claimed the amount was insufficient to complete the facility.[7]

An umpire was assaulted by a fan after a baseball game because he supposedly ejected the home team's manager from the game in the ninth inning. The umpire sued the baseball team, the manager, and the spectator who struck him.[8]

✗ A college hockey player whose skull was fractured when a puck penetrated the gap of his three-sided helmet sued the manufacturer of the helmet, the sporting goods store that sold it to the school, and the school he attended. He charged negligence and was awarded $85,000 in damages.[9]

The parents of a fourteen year-old-boy sued the National Park Service for injuries sustained when the boy left a path area, crawled to the edge of a thermal pool, fell in, and was severely scalded.[10]

Critics charge that these lawsuits and the millions of others filed annually amount to a legal explosion, a judiciary out of control. The impulse to sue is attributed by many to greed. The glut of recreation and sports litigation runs deeper than greed; it is a signal of changes in our society and of events that have gone wrong. It may be a little thing—like the refusal of an agency to abide by a promise—or it may be a major failure—like the deprivation of a person's constitutionally guaranteed right of privacy. Those who look for easy solutions to reducing litigation are myopic in vision because a variety of complex legal and societal changes account for the increases in recreation and sports litigation. A brief discussion of these factors is necessary for an understanding of the complex and volatile legal patterns now evolving.

Significant changes in procedural and substantive laws have led to democratization of our legal system. At least in theory these changes permit everyone to sue for everything and bode of a revolution in the making.[11] The rigid procedural rules of court have been liberalized through adoption of federal rules of civil procedure and their state court counterparts. Class action lawsuits spread widely after a major change in the federal rules in 1966. Standing to sue has been read less rigidly and mootness of certain classes of cases has narrowed. These rule changes required the courts to overlook putative defects in legal forms and consider the substance of claims. Legislatures have also made changes in court rules. Many statutes provide, contrary to the normal rule, that a successful plaintiff can recover the cost of attorneys' fees from the losing defendant. This may have encouraged litigation.

Substantively, courts and legislatures have whittled away or repealed old restrictive rules that insulated wrongdoers. The rapid demise of the dogmatic doctrine of sovereign and municipal immunity is certainly an important factor in the increase in lawsuits against public park and recreation agencies. A study of claims against sixteen California cities showed a 200 percent increase in claims paid between 1970 and 1975. During this period average losses climbed from $40,000 to $162,000.[12] The United States Supreme Court opened the floodgates of litigation against cities in 1978, when it declared that municipalities were persons and could be sued for damages under provisions of the Civil Rights Act of 1871 now known as Section 1983.[13] Through the end of 1981, there were 13,000 cases pending against municipalities based on alleged Section 1983 violations.[14]

Sovereign immunity protects public agencies and by its terms does not protect public officials and employees from lawsuits. Although many public officials had limited protection when performing official duties, no official or employee was ever absolved for liability from torts committed outside the scope of official duties. Legislative and judicial aversion to sovereign immunity carried over into the official immunity enjoyed by public employees. Courts have developed a distinction between an official's *discretionary* and *ministerial* acts. Discretionary acts are those requiring personal deliberation, decision, and judgment. Ministerial acts involve mere obedience to orders or performance of a duty in which the employee or official has no choice in performing. Discretionary acts are afforded immunity; ministerial acts are not. The duties of public park and recreation officials and employees are ministerial in nature; hence they have no immunity from lawsuits. Other important factors in the flood of recreation-related litigation are the adoption of the comparative negligence standard, the contingent fee system for attorneys, and the liberalized practice of paying off insurance claims. These and other elements will be discussed later in this book.

The increasing litigious nature of users, participants, spectators, and citizens is also rooted in changing societal values and economics.[15] Today's lawsuits are a reflection that individuals are losing a sense of community feeling and are moving from a "we" to a "me" attitude. Users have increasingly taken the approach that if an injury occurs it is the fault of the sponsor and staff, never the fault of the user.

Concomitant with precipitating changes in our legal system and social values are the economic factors in litigation. Not all plaintiffs are avaricious in suing an agency or individual, nor do all subscribe to the attitude that financial times are tough and "I will get money from whatever source I can." It is true that spurious claims and lawsuits are filed for a host of maladies allegedly arising from injuries, but there is rarely a windfall element in the quadriplegic, paraplegic, and gross disfigurement in million-dollar settlements. Some problems exist in our legal and medical systems to foster inflationary and excessive damage awards. The contingent fee system allows a plaintiff to hire an attorney on a commission basis. The fee ties the attorney's compensation to the size of the damages award sought (and the loquaciousness of counsel). Contingent fees may encourage exaggerated claims and questionable lawsuits. Awarding damages based on the amount of pain and suffering also increases costs. The assessment of pain and suffering awards are often based on the amount of medical costs encumbered by the plaintiff. This prompts claimants to resort to the most expensive medical practices even when they may be unnecessary. Another economic factor that encourages the filing of claims is the settlement practices of insurance companies. Often it is cheaper for the company to pay off a small claim than to contest it, particularly when the contesting costs are greater than the amount sought by the plaintiff. This reasonable business judgment may actually increase the number of spurious claims, as agencies are slowly forced to charge higher premiums.

These litigation trends will continue unless changes are made in our legal, economic, and social systems, which is unlikely. What can the park, recreation, and sports manager do to prevent litigation? The answer is very little to stop lawsuits but a great deal to minimize legal liability. The following observations are offered to allow the professional to deal with litigation:

1. Lawsuits are part of normal business operations, and the professional cannot prevent them. Professionals must learn to accept litigation as a normal part of business and not personalize every lawsuit as an attack.
2. Injuries cannot be eliminated from recreation and sports activities. Participants are likely to seek damages for their injuries if they believe them to be the result of unreasonable risks of harm.
3. Professionals and other employees are likely to be sued along with the organization. Insurance should be considered for all employees.
4. Although many claims and lawsuits are spurious and without merit, the majority have arguable questions of fact and law.
5. The mere filing of a lawsuit is not to be equated with legal liability.
6. Professionals must begin to manage all forms of legal liability and risk and not be intimidated by the law. Administrators must be educated to manage legal risk.

Concern for the legal education of administrators and managers is recent and has never been more important. The sooner the mystique of law and liability is debunked and understood by the professional, the quicker risk management will be incorporated into public and private recreation, sports, and leisure enterprises. This book was written toward that goal.

DISCUSSION QUESTIONS

1.   Critics have described the trend in recreation and sports litigation as out of control and in need of change. What are some of the changes in the law that account for the increases in recreation and sports litigation?

2.   Concomitant with changes in the law are social and economic factors that have contributed to the increase in litigation. What are some of these economic and social factors?

3.   What are some steps that the park, recreation, and sports manager can take to minimize legal liability?

4.   How has the abolition of the doctrine of governmental immunity increased the liability of public park, recreation, and sports agencies?

NOTES

[1]*Bryan-College Station Eagle,* Sept. 20, 1981, p. 7A.

[2]*Houston Chronicle,* May 28, 1981, p. 11.

[3]*Lewis* v *Great Southwest Corporation* 473 S.W.2d 228 (TX 1971).

[4]"Why Is Everyone Suing?" *U.S. News and World Report,* Dec. 4, 1978.

[5]*Journal of Insurance,* Sept./Oct., 1978, p. 24.

[6]*New York Times,* Oct. 20, 1977, p. B3.

[7]*Davis* v *City of New York,* 270 N.Y.S.2d 265 (NY 1966).

[8]*Toone* v *Adams,* 137 S.E.2d 132 (NC 1964).

[9]*Everett* v *Bucky Warren, Inc.,* 380 N.E.2d 653 (MA 1978).

[10]*Smith* v *United States,* 383 F.Supp 1976 (WY 1974).

[11]JETHRO LIEBERMAN, *The Litigious Society* (New York: Basic Books Inc., 1981) p. 18.

[12]"Professional Liability." Staff Background Paper to California's Citizens Commission on Tort Reform (Los Angeles, 1979) p. 100.

[13]*Monell* v *Department of Social Services,* 436 U.S. 658 (1978).

[14]DAVID LA BREC, *Civil Rights Liabilities of Municipalities and their Officers and Employees Under 42 U.S.C., Section 1983* (Austin: Institute on Public Law 1981), p. D-4.

[15]BETTY VAN DER SMISSEN, "Where Is Legal Liability Heading?" *Parks and Recreation,* May 1980, p. 50.

two

the judicial system

An exposure to law and the legal system can be a bewildering experience. A person reviewing a law case or consulting with an attorney is often confused about the mechanics of our legal system. Recreation and sports educators, administrators, managers, and students must have a rudimentary understanding of the legal system before they can comprehend the portions of the law that directly affect recreation and sports. This chapter, therefore, outlines the sources of law, organizations of court systems (a step-by-step process when a case reaches the courts), and a brief description of legal research and case briefing. This introduction to the legal system provides a road map for the reader's understanding of legal risks associated with recreation and sports programs.

All business and services are governed by some form of laws. The term incorporates a variety of rules and regulations governing society. From the time Moses brought ten basic statements of law down from the mountain, scholars, writers, academicians, philosophers, lawyers, social scientists, and others have devoted impressive amounts of time and prose analyzing law. There writers have postulated various definitions of law, and while many agree to the purpose and attributes of law, there is no general agreement about a true definition of law. Consider for example the following observations about the nature of law.

We have been told by Plato that law is a form of social control, an instrument of the good life, the way to the discovery of reality, the true reality of the social structure; by Aristotle that it is a rule of conduct, a contract, an ideal reason, it is the agreement of reason and nature, the distinction between the just and the unjust, a command or prohibition; by Aquinas that it is an ordinance of reason for the common good, made by him who has care of the community, and promulgated (thereby); by Bacon that certainty is the prime necessity of law; by Hobbes that law is the command of the sovereign; by Spinoza that it is a plan of life; by Leibniz that its character is determined by the structure of society; by Locke that it is a norm established by the commonwealth; by Hume that it is a body of precepts; by Kant that it is a harmonizing of wills by means of universal rules in the interests of freedom; by Fichte that it is a relation between human beings; by Hegel that it is an unfolding or realizing of the idea of right.[1]

Recognizing that definitions flow from the aim or function of the definer, it is easy to understand the lack of a universal definition of law. Sources of law are more important than definitions to recreation and sports educators, administrators, and managers. Public and private recreation enterprises are regulated not only by federal and state statutes but also by municipal ordinances and state agency rules.

SOURCES OF LAW

The sources of law in the United States are derived from federal and state constitutions, enactments of legislative bodies, and from the decisions of the federal and state courts. Thus we have fifty-one separate lawmaking governmental entities—the federal government and the fifty states. In addition to legislative and judicial sources, a new source of law has evolved in recent years—the administrative agency.

Federal and state constitutions, statutes, executive orders, and city ordinances form the basis for statutory law. Congress and state legislatures have wide-ranging authority to enact laws dealing with a variety of subject matter. Their powers are limited only by the federal constitution and their respective state constitutions. In theory at least, the federal government is a sovereign of limited powers; limited to those express powers given to Congress in the Constitution and those necessarily "implied" from the express powers by authority of the necessary and proper clause. For example, Congress has authority under Article I, Section 8 of the Constitution to (1) lay and collect taxes, (2) regulate commerce, (3) create courts inferior to the Supreme Court, (4) declare war, (5) make rules for government and regulation of its land, (6) provide for the general welfare, and (7) make all laws necessary and proper for executing the foregoing powers.

The Tenth Amendment provides that all powers not specifically enumerated in the Constitution are reserved to the states. Hence the states have residual authority, including the power to regulate resources and human activity within their jurisdictions for the promotion of health, safety, and welfare. This regulatory authority is frequently termed police power. The power of a state to regulate activity by legislative enactment must conform to a due process and equal protection requirement. Due process can incorporate either a procedural or substantive requirement. Procedural due process requires that in any exercise of police powers the aggrieved person be given *notice* and *hearing* before rights can be denied. Substantive due process requires that the activity regulated by statute bear a reasonable relationship to health, safety, and welfare.

Administrative agencies, part of the executive branch of government, engage to some extent in functions that are legislative and judicial. Agencies act in a legislative capacity when they issue rules and regulations to implement the authority granted them by statutes. Agency rules and regulations promulgated to implement legislation have the force and effect of law. Agencies can also act in a judicial capacity. For example, when an agency believes that a person has violated one of its rules, it may conduct a quasijudicial hearing on the matter before undertaking action. This hearing, held before an administrative law judge, is conducted in a similar manner to a trial. After the hearing, the agency may take action against the person.

Court decisions form the basis for the common law. In addition to court law, the judiciary is responsible for interpreting and construing constitutional provisions and statutes. Interpretation of a statute is a process of ascertaining legislative intent of the act by a reading of specific language and by a review of legislative history. Construction of a statute is the process of determining the legal effect of a statute.

THE COURTS

In our system of jurisprudence, courts are the forum for resolving conflicts involving legal rights of individuals, corporations, and the government. This section describes the types of courts and their organization.

Courts are frequently classified by the types of cases they are empowered to decide. A criminal court is one that hears cases that are offenses against society. Civil courts adjudicate issues involving private rights, duties and obligations. In most states, the same court handles both types of cases. A court is given certain authority called jurisdiction either by constitution or statute to adjudicate certain types of cases.

While court systems vary depending on the state, all have two types of courts, trial courts and appellate courts. The procedures and responsibilities of trial and appellate courts differ substantially.

Trial Courts

When parties cannot settle disputes amicably and resort to the judicial system, their initial contact will be with a trial court. The basic responsibility of trial courts is to decide disputed questions of fact. In fulfilling this responsibility trial courts make detailed findings of fact based on the evidence presented and apply rules of law to these facts in arriving at judgments. Trial courts can be divided into limited jurisdiction courts and general trial courts.

Limited jurisdiction courts are restricted to adjudicating selected types of cases or to disputes involving specific amounts of money. Common examples are municipal, probate, traffic, family law, and justice of the peace courts. Most deal with minor matters such as ordinance violations or motor vehicle violations. Park rule violations often fall within the jurisdiction of these courts.

General trial courts handle all the cases not specifically assigned to limited jurisdiction courts. Most recreation cases are adjudicated in general trial courts. Cases involving contracts, negligence, and criminal law originate in these courts. All states have courts of general jurisdiction. In Michigan these courts are called Circuit Courts, while in New York they are called the Supreme Court.

Appellate Courts

All states have courts which review cases decided by trial courts. A person aggrieved by a trial court decision may appeal as a matter of right or as a matter of privilege to an appeals court. These courts do not generally conduct evidentiary trials but review questions of law. In most states there is an intermediate court between a general trial court and the Supreme Court. Texas, for example, has fourteen intermediate state appellate courts, organized on a geographical basis, to consider appeals from trial courts in that state.

The dual system of federal and state government has resulted in fifty-one separate court systems—fifty state court systems and one federal system. Although there are variations in the state and federal system each has courts of limited jurisdiction, general trial courts, and appellate courts.

Federal Courts

Article III, Section 1 of the United States Constitution provides that, "the judicial power of the United States shall be vested in one Supreme Court, and in such inferior courts as the Congress may from time to time ordain and establish." Congress has the constitutional authority to struc-

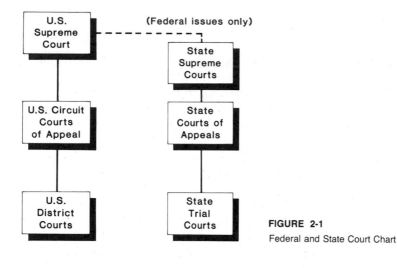

FIGURE 2-1
Federal and State Court Chart

ture and limit the jurisdiction of the federal courts. Two major categories of dispute relevant to recreation and sports provide federal jurisdiction. The disputes must involve

1. Federal questions arising under the Constitution, acts of Congress, treaties, disputes between states and disputes in which the United States is a party; or
2. Diversity of citizenship where the plaintiff and the defendant are citizens of different states and the amount in controversy is over $10,000.

Jurisdiction is further complicated because federal courts do not have exclusive jurisdiction over cases that fit into these two categories. Federal courts have exclusive jurisdiction only in controversies involving treaties, admiralty and ambassadors, and concurrent jurisdiction with state courts on other federal matters of diversity of citizenship actions.

General trial courts in the federal system are called district courts and are organized on a geographical basis within each state. Each state has at least one U.S. District Court while the more populous states have several districts. Michigan, for example, has two districts, while California and Texas have four districts. Congress has also created limited jurisdiction trial courts such as the U.S. Court of Customs, Court of Claims, and U.S. Tax Court. These tribunals are limited to deciding cases involving a particular subject.

There are two tiers of federal appellate courts. The first tier is the US Circuit Courts of Appeal, covering all regions of the United States. Each Circuit Court has jurisdiction over the U.S. District Courts within their geographical boundaries. The United States Supreme Court is the second tier and is the court of last resort in the federal judiciary. Appeals can be taken from the federal Circuit Courts of Appeal and State Supreme Courts to the United States Supreme Court. The Supreme Court has discretion to select the cases it will hear. Not all appeals will be given a full hearing, in fact only a small number, 100 out of 4,000 appeals annually, receive a full hearing.

State Courts

Although there are some variations all the states have the three basic types of courts—limited jurisdiction, general trial, and appellate. The more populated states have a two tiered appellate system similar to the federal system, while the less populated states have only one appellate level. Most states have a unified appellate system; criminal and civil appeals are taken to the same appellate court. Texas, an exception to this rule, has two supreme courts. The Texas Supreme Court is the court of last resort for civil matters, while the Texas Court of Criminal Appeals is the supreme court for criminal appeals. If a case is instituted in a state court system it will normally remain in the system through the court of last resort. Thus on matters of state law, state supreme courts are the courts of last resort.

TRIAL COURT PROCEDURES

Since the recreation and sports administrator is often directly involved in trial court proceedings, this section provides a general explanation of the procedures from the time the litigant decides to sue until final court judgment is rendered. Although the procedures may vary slightly from state to state, the anatomy of a lawsuit can be divided into a pretrial and trial phase as outlined in Fig. 2.2.

Pretrial Phase

This portion of a lawsuit has three separate and distinct phases—the pleadings, discovery, and pretrial conference. Each may overlap to some extent but usually they are separate.[2]

Pleadings A lawsuit is started by the plaintiff filing with a court of competent jurisdiction a complaint and requesting the court to issue a summons notifying the defendant that a complaint is on file. A complaint is a document formally outlining to the defendant the basis of the claim. It contains the plaintiff's allegation of facts constituting the cause of action and includes a request for judicial relief.

The defendant responds to the complaint by filing an answer with the court. The answer contains a denial of the plaintiff's allegations and lists one or more defenses to the claim.

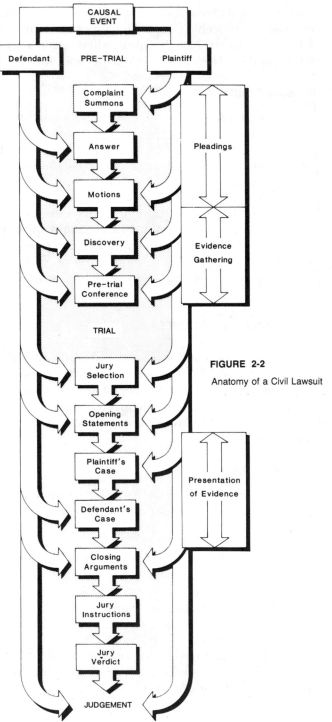

FIGURE 2-2

Anatomy of a Civil Lawsuit

Discovery At one time there was a feeling in the legal profession that a lawsuit should be a battle of wits with each side guarding its case jealously and making the adversary's trial preparations as difficult and onerous as possible. Often the parties did not know until the day of trial what witnesses the other party would call to testify. In order to minimize the element of surprise, to improve and speed up the trial, and to encourage settlements before trial, all states today provide for and encourage the parties to learn as much as possible about the adversary's case prior to trial. There are five major devices for discovery of facts before trial, (1) depositions, (2) interrogatories, (3) inspections of documents, (4) physical and mental examinations, and (5) requests for admissions.

A deposition is the testimony of witnesses under oath made at a hearing held out of court. Ordinarily, each party will request permission to take a deposition from the other party and their key witnesses. A hearing is arranged at the office of one party's attorney. A court reporter records the questions and answers and prepares a written transcript for the parties to sign. Depositions allow litigants to discover what testimony to expect at the trial, to obtain testimony while it is fresh in the mind of a witness, to impeach (discredit) a person's testimony at the trial by showing that the testimony varies from the deposition, and to memorialize testimony where there is danger that it may be unavailable at the trial.

Interrogatories are written questions addressed by one party to the other. Such questions help gather information that can be used as a basis for further questions at a deposition hearing or at the trial. The questions asked must be pertinent to the issue involved in the case.

Either party to a case may secure a court order pertaining the inspection of documents or tangible things in the possession or control of another. For example, in a case where the plaintiff alleges personal injury the defendant may wish to inspect medical or hospital records pertaining to the injury. When the physical or mental condition of a party is in controversy, the court is empowered to issue an order requiring physical and mental examinations by a physician. In many lawsuits both parties will request an examination by physicians. Often, the doctors' opinions as to a party's condition are at odds with one another and the judge or jury must then weigh the credibility of each physician.

Pretrial conference Many states require a pretrial meeting of the judge and attorneys. The conference serves two purposes. One is to shorten the trial time by narrowing the issues, and placing a limitation on the number of witnesses and exhibits. The second purpose of the pretrial conference is to encourage an out-of-court settlement. If no settlement is reached at the end of the conference the judge sets a date for the trial.

Trial Phase

If the dispute cannot be settled an evidentary trial is held. At the trial a jury will be selected (if the parties request a jury), evidence presented, a verdict returned, and a judgment entered.

Jury selection   Selection of jurors is the responsibility of the parties in the lawsuit. Attorneys, and sometimes the judge, question jurors to determine their impartiality. Where questioning reveals a problem, the juror can be removed from the panel by a challenge for cause, e.g., a potential juror can be "challenged for cause" if it can be shown that the juror knows one of the parties. When both sides are satisfied with the composition of the jury, the jurors are sworn in and the parties are ready to proceed.

Presentation of evidence   Under the usual order of proceeding, the plaintiff, who has the burden of proof, will introduce the evidence to prove the facts alleged in the complaint. At this stage the plaintiff will bring forward all the witnesses and other documents to establish the facts. Each witness of the plaintiff will be questioned by the plaintiff's attorney, upon direct examination, then cross-examined by opposing counsel. Upon completion of the plaintiff's case, the defendant proceeds.

The defendant usually presents evidence supporting any affirmative defenses outlined in the pleadings. When the defendant has completed the presentation of proof the defense rests. At this stage, the plaintiff is entitled to rebut any of the defendant's evidence and the defendant is then entitled to a rejoinder of the plaintiff's rebuttal. When both parties have announced that they have closed, the trial proceeds with the closing arguments and the court's instruction to the jury.

Jury charge and judgment   Prior to jury deliberations the judge will charge the jury by stating the rules of law they must apply in reaching their decision. For example the judge will tell the jury, "[I]f you find that the defendant failed to act as an ordinary, reasonable man and that this failure was the proximate cause of the injury to the plaintiff, then this is negligence for which the defendant is liable in damages, but if you find that the plaintiff's action contributed in part to his injury this will relieve the defendant from liability." Upon receiving the instructions the jury considers the case and returns its verdict. After the verdict is rendered, a party not satisfied with it may request a judgment notwithstanding the verdict (N.O.V.), a new trial, or a relief from judgment. If the judge does not grant a motion for any of these three requests a final judgment is entered by the judge.

Either party may appeal the decision to an appellate court if dissatisfied with the judgment. When the appellate court hears the case they do not retry it but review the record of the trial court to determine if the judge improperly admitted evidence, failed to follow proper procedure, or improperly applied a rule of law. After a review of the record, the appellate court announces its findings through a written decision. The decision upholds, reverses, or modifies the lower court judgment and outlines the court's reasoning in disposing of the case.

FINDING AND BRIEFING COURT CASES

Legal research involves a search for sources of law. In order to determine the law on a particular question, it may be necessary to examine federal and state constitutions, statutes, and court decisions. Although federal and state statutes and administrative regulations are important to recreation and sports agencies and professionals, most of the law regarding tort liability will be found in the court cases. While it is unreasonable to expect the recreation and sports professional to undertake complicated legal research, they should be able to find, study, understand, and apply the principles outlined in court cases.

When a case is taken to federal or state appellate courts, the courts dispose of the case through a written opinion. The opinion, or decision, is published in a court reporter following a nomenclature referred to as a case citation. A case citation includes the names of the parties, the court issuing the decision, the name of the court reporter, and the volume and page number where the case is located in the reporter. For example, a Texas Court of Appeals case involving an injury at the Six Flags over Texas Amusement Park is cited as: *Lewis* v *Great Southwest Corp.*, 473 S.W.2d 228 (TX 1971). This case is printed in volume 473 of the *Southwestern Reporter*, 2nd edition, p. 228. Usually the plaintiff's (Lewis) and the defendant's (Great Southwest Corp.) names remain in that order when the cases are appealed, however, in some states the names are reversed and the defendant on appeal becomes the plaintiff in error.

Over three million judicial opinions are published in the United States and an additional 30,000 cases are added to this list each year. Appellate court decisions are published in various court reporters in the order of their decision date and are not categorized by subject matter. For the sake of simplicity, it is convenient to list separately the case reporters.

Federal court decisions   All the written opinions of the United States Supreme Court and the Courts of Appeals are published, while only selected opinions of the United States District Courts and other courts of limited jurisdiction are published. Decisions of the Supreme Court are printed in three different reporters published by different companies. Supreme court cases are printed in (1) United States Reports (U.S. Government publication), cited "U.S.," (2) United States Supreme Court Reports (Lawyers Cooperative Pub. Co.), cited "L.Ed.2nd," and (3) Supreme Court Reporter (West Publishing Co.), cited "S.Ct."

The opinions of the Circuit Courts of Appeals are printed in the *Federal Reporter* cited "F.2d," a publication of the West Publishing Company. Cases of the District Courts are printed in the *Federal Supplement,* cited "F. Supp," also a publication of the West Publishing Company.

State court decisions   Private companies also publish decisions of the various state courts. About one-third of the states no longer publish their state court decisions but rely on the National Reporter. This Reporter, published by the West Publishing Company, aggregates court decisions from several states into one volume. All of the states are included within one of these regional reporters. The division of state court reporters on a geographical basis is shown in Fig. 2.3.

Case law, the study of factual patterns and court holding, is a way to study law as a preventative tool for management. Under court doctrines the results of a previous court case will guide the courts in deciding future cases with similar factual patterns. The study of the case law in this book should help the reader develop lateral thinking to prevent similar occurrences in their recreation and sports programs. The reader should also be cautioned that seldom is only one point of law involved in a case. In this book, procedural and other points of law have been edited from cases so that only the relevant rules remain.

In studying a case the reader should look for these important components

1. The citation describing date and place where the case was decided and where it can be found.
2. The type of action involved in the trial. Is it assault and battery, negligence, strict liability, or a contract action?
3. An identification of the parties involved.
4. The facts of the case upon which the court relied in reaching its decision.
5. The rule of law involved in the dispute and the rationale used by the court in reaching its decision.
6. The court decision at the trial and appellate levels.
7. The implications of the case for the manager.

If the reader can answer these points after reading the case this will help develop the lateral thinking necessary to avoid becoming a case in the law books.

As an aid to the reader in briefing the cases the following case brief is offered by the author. It covers a case presented in Chapter 9.

SAMPLE BRIEF
Lewis v Great Southwest Corp.
473 SW2d 228
(Texas CA 1971)

Action

Civil Action alleging strict liability for keeping dangerous animals.

Facts

The defendant is the owner/operator of a petting zoo containing goats, sheep, and pigs. Patrons enter the pens and are encouraged to touch, pet, and feed the animals. An attendant is usually on duty, to collect trash and prevent mistreatment of the animals. All of the goats in the zoo, except two females, were not older than six months of age. The male goats had been castrated.

On July 21, 1966, a fifty-seven year old woman, accompanied by her grandson, purchased a ticket and entered the petting zoo. Without warning or provocation one of the goats butted Mrs. Lewis knocking her to the ground and injuring her. Prior to the incident there had been no harassment of the animals and nothing had occurred which would be calculated to cause excitement to the animals. The goat on its own volition butted the plaintiff.

Plaintiff brought this action alleging that the defendant, as keepers of dangerous animals, are strictly liable for any injuries caused by the animals. The trial court granted judgment for the defendant and plaintiff—appellant brings this appeal.

Issue(s)

Are domestic goats within the classification of dangerous animals so that an owner will be strictly liable for any injuries caused by them?

Held

No! Judgment of trial court affirmed.

Reason

As a general rule of law, an owner of wild animals (*farae naturae*) that have vicious or dangerous propensities are strictly liable for injury caused by the animals. Animals of a wild nature are such that they must be tamed, trained, or kept in confinement to prevent escape. Domesticated animals are those which are naturally tame through long associatons with man and no longer possess an inclination to escape nor have dangerous propensities.

In this case, the goat alleged to have caused the injury is a domestic animal without the wild characteristics of *farae naturae.* Domestic goats are not vicious by nature. Male goats, billys, may be more aggressive than females and have been known to butt. A castrated goat is no longer a billy and there were no billy goats present in the petting zoo because they were castrated at birth.

There are cases of liability involving domestic animals at rodeos, however, these animals (horses and bulls) are tormented, frightened and infuriated and forced to act as dangerous animals. There is no evidence that the goats in the petting zoo were aggressive or antagonized prior to the incident. From the standpoint of public policy, the benefit of maintaining a touch of farm life in an urban area far outweighs the risk that a lively animal might by unprovoked accident do injury to a bystander.

Rule

Absent a showing of known dangerous propensities, an owner of domestic animals will not be held strictly liable for injuries caused by the animal.

SUMMARY

While a portion of the laws affecting parks, recreation, and sports programs can be found in federal, state, and local legislative enactments, the law of liability is derived from court precedent. Prior judicial decisions are used as a basis for resolving subsequent liability issues unless the prior cases are specifically overruled. Judicial decisions in one state are often used by other states in resolving disputes.

Although court systems vary all state judicial systems include trial courts and appellate courts. Trial courts make detailed findings of fact and apply rules of law to these facts in resolving disputes. Appellate courts determine whether the trial courts applied the correct rule of law in resolving the dispute. Thus appellate courts establish the rules of law regarding liability for user injuries.

Many people involved in parks, recreation, or sports professions are discovering that anyone can file a lawsuit against anybody for just about any type of injury, but liability must be proven before a recovery is made. Establishment of liability comes in most instances at the trial or in the structure settlements before a full trial. Since park, recreation, and sports professionals are intimately involved in the factual phase of litigaton it is important that they understand the process and what to do if involved in a lawsuit.

All federal and state courts are guided by very technical rules, called

Showing the States included in each Reporter group

The National Reporter System also includes the Supreme Court Reporter, the Federal Reporter, the Federal Supplement, Federal Rules Decisions, West's Bankruptcy Reporter, the New York Supplement, West's California Reporter, West's Illinois Decisions, and West's Military Justice Reporter.

Adapted from *West's Law Finder,* West Publishing Company.

FIGURE 2-3 National Reporter System Map

rules of civil procedure, that must be followed in resolving the recreation and sports injury lawsuit. Among other things these rules outline how a lawsuit is filed, the notice that must be given to the parties, procedures for responding to allegations made by the plaintiff, and a prescribed method and time for a discovery period. The purpose of this discovery period is for all parties to ascertain matters of a factual nature, such as how the injury occurred, who are the witnesses to the accident, what are the actions and procedures of the parties, and others. Discovery is accomplished through the verbal questioning of the parties and witnesses at depositions or by reviewing records and documents. Once discovery has been completed, the attorneys must decide how best to resolve the lawsuit. If there is not a material dispute over the facts and the law is clear, the lawsuit will probably be settled before trial. In those instances where there is a material dispute over the facts or the law a trial is usually the next step.

A trial generally begins with the selection of the jury. The jury's main task is to make findings of fact based on the evidence presented. After the jury is selected, the attorneys use their opening statement to tell the jury what they will attempt to prove or disprove. This is followed by the plaintiff's and defendant's presentation of their cases. After all the evidence is presented, if the judge does not dispose of the case through a directed verdict, the attorneys present their closing arguments and the case goes to the jury. The judge instructs the jury on the law to be applied to the facts and the jury retires to reach a verdict and report it back to the judge. The court then translates the verdict into a final judgment disposing of the case.

Either party may then appeal the judgment to an appellate court for a review of the record regarding errors of law or abuse of discretion. Appellate decisions are reported and become binding as the law on future disputes.

Since administrators' involvement is most direct during the factual phase of litigation and not the appellate the following advice is offered to administrators to protect their interests. Obviously the best means to reduce accident generating litigation is to use the safest facilities and equipment, conduct programs as carefully as possible and disclose as much program information as possible to users, but when accidents do occur what can the administrator or professional do? The first thing is to call your attorney and insurance carrier to seek their advice or a prompt investigation. Be sure to keep accurate records of factual events, witnesses, and accident reports. Do not make admissions of guilt or discuss specifics of the accident without the advice of counsel. Document your operating, maintenance, and scheduling procedures as well as safety rules and regulations. All of the factual information possible should be documented since it may be used at the trial, anywhere from one to five years after the accident.

DISCUSSION QUESTIONS

1.   What is the role of appellate courts in American jurisprudence?
2.   Since federal courts are courts of limited jurisdiction, what types of cases can they adjudicate involving recreation and sports?
3.   What are the major devices for discovery of facts before trial and how are recreation and sports professionals involved in this phase of litigation?

4. In studying an appellate court case what information should the recreation and sports professional seek?
5. Why is case law important to the recreation and sports field?

NOTES

[1]RATE HOWEL AND OTHERS, *Business Law* (Hinsdale: IL: The Dryden Press, 1978), p. 5.
[2]The pretrial phase was adapted from RALPH HUEBER AND OTHERS, *Contemporary Business Law* (New York: McGraw-Hill Book Co., 1980), p. 33.

three

framework for public parks, recreation, and sports

The efficacy of the public park and recreation agency and the school recreation and sports program is controlled, in part, by the legal framework under which it operates. Legal authorization is required before a public agency can acquire, develop, construct, and maintain recreation and sports facilities and offer a program of activities. This authorization is applicable to not only federal, state, and local park and recreation agencies but also to the public school recreation and sports program. The exercise of power without legal authority is unlawful; hence the concept of authorization. The legal framework is provided by constitutions, statutes, administrative rules, and court decisions. These sources are not all of equal authority and when they come into conflict an understanding of their relative weight and interaction becomes crucial. This chapter will examine the interaction of this legal authority in setting the parameters for the public system.

FEDERAL FRAMEWORK

The primary authority for federal involvement in park and recreation services is derived from the United States Constitution. Congress, under the property, general welfare, and commerce clauses of the Constitution, has established a number of federal agencies to provide recreation services and manage resources. As a shareholder in the public recreation system the federal government is the biggest landholder, managing over 730 million acres of land for *inter alia* outdoor recreation.[1] The federal role has evolved over the years expanding into areas beyond land management until today federal recreation functions are of three basic types, (1) ownership and operation of recreation areas, (2) research, regulatory, and advisory services, and (3) financial aid to state and local governments.

Property Clause

Article IV of the U.S. Constitution provides that "the Congress shall have power to dispose of and make all rules and regulations respecting the Territory or other Property belonging to the United States." Pursuant to this constitutional authority, Congress has passed a number of statutes, often referred to as organic acts, creating federal land managing agencies. Established in 1916, the National Park Service is mandated by its enabling act to "promote and regulate the use of federal areas known as national parks, monuments and reservations." Its purpose is "to conserve the scenery, the natural and historical objects, and the wildlife of the parks and to manage the parks in such manner that leaves them unimpaired for enjoyment of future generations."[2] Congress has also created other recreation land managing agencies including the Bureau of Land Management, the Fish and Wildlife Service, the Forest Service, the Bureau of Reclamation, and the Tennessee Valley Authority. In addition to mandating land management, the organic acts may allow these agencies to conduct research and provide technical assistance to other public and private agencies.

General Welfare Clause

Congress under Article I, §8, Cl. 1 has "the power to . . . provide for the common defense and the general welfare of the United States." The term general welfare has been broadly applied by the courts. The breadth of the courts' definition of the public welfare is illustrated in *Berman* v *Parker,* 348 U.S. 26 (1954) where the court stated

> The concept of public welfare is broad and inclusive . . . the values it represents are spiritual as well as physical, aesthetic as well as monetary.

In 1936, the Supreme Court affirmed that Congress may establish and fund grant-in-aid programs under the General Welfare Clause.[3] The latitude of Congress to determine whether the nation's welfare will be served by a particular grant program was expanded in *Helvering* v *Davis* when Justice Cardozo writing for the majority stated

Nor is the concept of general welfare static . . . What is critical or urgent changes with the times . . . When money is spent to promote the general welfare, the concept of welfare . . . is shaped by Congress not the States.[4]

Federal grants-in-aid programs have generated a body of federal grant law focusing not only on the rights and obligations of the grantor and grantee but also on their obligations beyond the grant. This includes all the rules and regulations attached as "strings" to the grant.[5]

Commerce Clause

In conjunction with the *necessary and proper* clause, Congress has developed extensive regulatory programs affecting parks and recreation. Article I, §8, Cl. 13 provides "the Congress shall have power . . .to regulate commerce with foreign nations, and among the several states . . . ." Exam-

FIGURE 3-1 Federal Framework

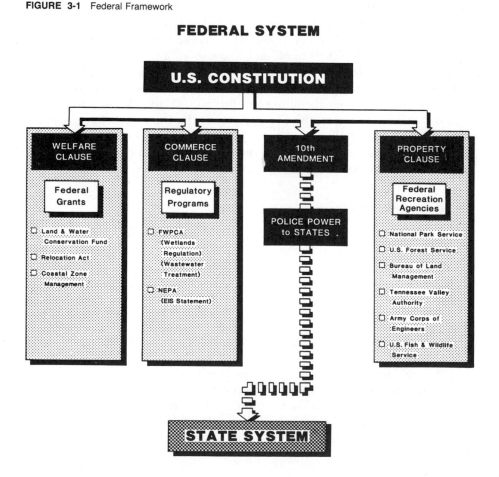

FEDERAL SYSTEM

ples of programs impacting on recreation include the wetlands regulations of the Corps of Engineers and wastewater regulations of the Environmental Protection Agency. Under Section 404 of the Clean Water Act of 1972, the Corps of Engineers is responsible for issuing permits for activities that involve placement of dredged or fill material in wetlands. Public recreation agencies with wetlands in park areas are subject to regulation under this act and must obtain the requisite federal permits prior to altering wetlands. Similarly, public park and recreation agencies are subject to federal and state water discharge regulations for public wastewater facilities as are other parties discharging wastes into the nation's waters.

STATE FRAMEWORK

The residual powers granted to the states by the Tenth Amendment of the U.S. Constitution includes the plenary authority to regulate resources and human activity. This authority is commonly referred to as police power. Police power regulations are enacted for the protection and promotion of the health, safety, and welfare of citizens. Zoning ordinances, subdivision regulations, building codes, and mandatory parkland dedication ordinances are examples of police powers. It is in the judicial arena that the limits of police powers, such as zoning and recreation programs, are determined. See Fig. 3.1.

Police Power

Recognition by state courts that recreation is a legitimate exercise of the police power evolved during the nineteenth and twentieth centuries. For example, in 1875, just thirty-seven years after statehood, the Michigan Supreme Court upheld the authority of cities and townships to acquire and develop public parks.[6] In the twentieth century, recognition was universal. As one court has said

> It is a proper function of government to provide places in such a community where commercialism, unpleasant noises and scenes are eliminated. Experience has shown that public parks have not only contributed to public welfare, generally, but have specifically and directly restored and improved the public health. It is generally well known that the natural beauty, quiet and opportunities for exercise and amusement to be found in the public parks, away from business and the noise and bustle of industry and trade, have been the tonic to better health and inspiration to better living. Certainly these things are not only worth while but are important . . . As was said by this court in *Furlong* v *South Park Comm'rs.*, 320 Ill. 507, 151 N.E. 510, 511: Park purposes are not confined to a tract of land with trees, grass and seats, but mean a tract of land ornamented and improved as a place of resort for the public. The construction and maintenance of a building for museums, art galleries, botanical and zoological gardens, and many other purposes, for the public benefit, are recognized as legitimate purposes.[7]

Since police power resides in the states, the necessary authorization for providing state and local recreation services is derived from state constitutions or legislation. States exercise their plenary powers in developing a recreation system by

1. Acquiring and developing state parks and recreation facilities,
2. Providing technical and financial assistance to local governments,
3. Delegating to local governments, through permissive enabling legislation, the authority to provide recreation services, and
4. Enacting public health, safety and welfare regulations.

Each state, through appropriate legislation, determines the state and local government role in a recreation delivery system. Highly urbanized states such as Michigan, New York, Pennsylvania, California, and Texas have extensive programs in each area, while the less populated states may undertake limited roles in recreation. See Fig. 3.2.

FIGURE 3-2 State Framework

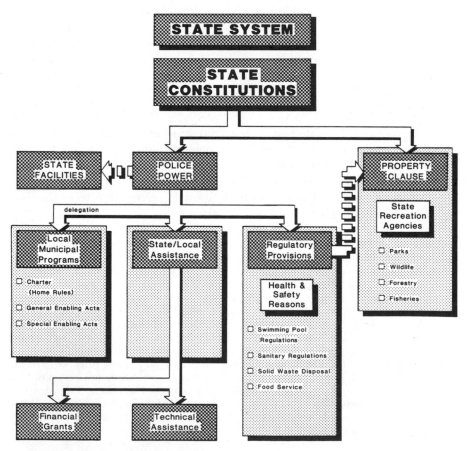

State Recreation Programs

Throughout the U.S. about forty-two million acres of state owned lands are available for recreation. Although this acreage total is less than ten percent of federal recreation holdings, the proximity of state parks to population centers generates greater visitations. State organizational structures for providing recreation services are as diverse as the states themselves. Some states have small, loosely organized commissions to acquire and manage recreation resources, while others have large, professionally staffed agencies. Each has its own unique organizational history dictated by the cultural, historical, political, and natural features of that state. These features have created different attitudes and techniqes for acquiring, developing, operating, and financing recreation resources as manifested in state constitutions and statutes.

State recreation agencies   Historically, these agencies evolved from or became an integral part of state game, fish, forestry, or natural resource departments. Most park and recreation agencies were minor functions in these departments until the 1950s. Beginning in this period and continuing through the 1970s, state park and recreation organizations experienced phenomenal growth in parks, personnel, capital expenditures, and operating budgets. Two organizational trends that emerged in states' recreation programs are centralization of functions into one department and decentralization of agencies into specialized functions. States favoring centralization combined game, fish, forestry, parks, and natural resource functions into natural resource or conservation departments. Michigan followed this approach, and further consolidated environmental protection programs such as solid waste management, water pollution, air pollution, and toxic substance control into the same agency. States adopting a decentralized approach either placed park and recreation agencies in game, fish, forestry, or tourist development departments or established separate state park and recreation departments.

State assistance to local government   During the state government expansion period that swept the country in the 1960s and 1970s many states instituted technical and financial assistance programs benefiting municipal and county park and recreation agencies. Technical and educational consultant services to local government is provided by departments of natural resources, parks, or community affairs in California, Georgia, Michigan, Maryland, Pennsylvania, Virginia, and South Carolina. In other states these programs are provided through the cooperative extension services of the land grant universities.

Through the power of the purse federal and state governments have a significant impact on the local park and recreation agency. Nearly all states provide some form of financial assistance to local agencies using state or federal "pass thru" funds. The federal Land and Water Conservation

Fund is an example of a program through which states may provide federal funds to local governments for land acquisition and facility development. These state grant programs are not self-implementing and they require authorizing legislation. In addition to the basic enabling statute a plethora of other statutes and regulations may affect these grants. It behooves the park and recreation director to become familiar with the law of federal and state grants.

LOCAL ENABLING ACTS

Provision of recreation services, as an exercise of police power, is inherent in the sovereign government and may only be exercised by local government if properly delegated. Local governments, a generic term, refers to municipal corporations, school districts, and special purpose districts. Municipal corporations are defined as

> . . . bodies politic, created under the authority of the state into corporations, invested by the legislature to assist in the administration of the state. . . .[8]

Although frequently referred to as a municipal corporation, a county is an agent of the state, functioning to discharge the duties of the state. Municipalities are wholly creatures of the state from which all their powers are derived. The power to create or abolish a municipal corporation, to enlarge or reduce its geographical boundaries, or to expand or contract its powers, is a power of the state legislature. In the absence of constitutional restrictions, the power is unlimited. This subordination was aptly described and upheld by the United States Supreme Court in *Hunter* v *Pittsburg*, 207 U.S. 161, 177–79 (1907).

> . . . This court has many times had occasion to consider and decide the nature of municipal corporations, their rights and duties, and the rights of their citizens and creditors. Municipal corporations are political subdivisions of the State, created as convenient agencies for exercising such of the governmental powers of the State as may be entrusted to them. For the purpose of executing these powers properly and efficiently they usually are given the power to acquire, hold, and manage personal and real property. The number, nature and duration of the powers conferred upon these corporations and the territory over which they shall be exercised rests in the absolute discretion of the State . . . . The State, therefore, at its pleasure may modify or withdraw all such powers, may take without compensation such property, hold it itself, or vest it in other agencies, expand or contract the territorial area, unite the whole or a part of it with another municipality, repeal the charter and destroy the corporation. . . . Although the inhabitants and property owners may by such changes suffer inconvenience, and their property may be lessened in value by the burden of increased taxation, or for any other reason, they have no right by contract or otherwise in the unaltered or continued existence of the corporation or its powers, and there is nothing in the Federal Constitution which protects them from the injurious consequences.

Courts have universally recognized the power of the legislature to create, abolish, or modify legislation affecting powers and duties of municipal corporations. While the majority of cases concern education agencies and other municipal services, this plenary power directly applies to parks and recreation services.[9]

Park and Recreation Legislation

Legislation delineating the powers, duties, and organizational structure of the local park and recreation system is provided through home rule, general enabling, or special district statutes. A municipal corporation is usually free to select the organizational structure for a park and recreation agency, subject to any statutory constraints.

Home rule   Municipalities are allowed under home rule to exercise the full power of local self-government, including parks and recreation, which are strictly of municipal concern and not in conflict with the constitution or general laws of a state.[10] Home rule requires approval of a charter by residents of a geographical area. A charter is a document specifying the corporate structure and powers and duties of a governing unit. Most states provide for home rule with constitutional authorization and statutory implementations. Texas follows this pattern by providing in the Constitution of 1876, Article II, §5, the basic authority for home rule.

> Cities having more than 5000 inhabitants may by a majority vote of qualified voters of said city . . . adopt a charter . . . .

Implementation of home rule in Texas is by statute. Article 1175 of Vernon's Annotated Texas Statutes provides

> Cities adopting . . . the charter shall have full power of local self-government, and among other powers . . . the following are hereby enumerated for greater clarity.
>   To have the power to appropriate private property for public purposes whenever the governing authority shall deem it necessary to take private property . . . for . . . parks . . . playgrounds . . .

General enabling acts   Local governments without home rule authority derive power to provide park and recreation services through general enabling legislation. All states have enacted some type of general enabling legislation for parks and recreation with no two states having identical legislation. Therefore the park and recreation professional should carefully review and understand the nuances of their enabling authority. For example, Texas' enabling legislation imposed a land standard on some cities requiring that there should not be more than two city parks for each 2,000 residents.[11]

Special districts   A park district is a special district created by enabling legislation. It is independent and autonomous from a city and county even though its boundaries may be conterminous with them. Special districts embody five characteristics that distinguish them from park and recreation agencies of a city or country, (1) a resident population and a defined area, (2) a governing body, (3) a separate legal identity, (4) the power to provide one or more public services, and (5) a degree of autonomy with power to raise at least a part of its own revenue. State enabling legislation for special districts takes one of two forms. General application authorizes districts on a statewide basis. Local application creates a single district. California, Illinois, Oregon, and North Dakota have general application legislation, while Michigan with legislation creating the Huron Clinton Metropolitan Authority is a local application state. Illinois has 345 park districts, North Dakota 275, California 118, and Oregan 17.[12]

Local Actions

Pursuant to state law, local governments may establish a recreation system by adoption of a charter or charter amendments, special elections, ordinance enactment, or a resolution. The stability of a recreation system, measured by the degree of difficulty in repealing prior local actions, is a direct reflection of the local enactment creating the system. The methods of enacting local legislation cited above are in the order of their degree of changeability, with charter provisions most difficult to change and a resolution the easiest.

City charters vary in detailing the powers and procedures for the local recreation system. Most charters authorize the establishment of a park and recreation commission and supplement the general authorization with ordinance provisions. Park and recreation systems created by city charters are the most difficult to modify because to change any provision requires a city election. In some states enabling legislation requires voter approval as a condition before establishing a recreation system. In Ohio and Michigan, when petitioned by five percent of the qualified voters and fifty taxpayers, the city council or township board must submit the question of establishment of a park and recreation commission to the voters at the next general election. Failure to conform to these statutory prescriptions will invalidate local action. Most park district legislation also requires voter affirmation to establish the special district.

Municipalities are authorized to enact local legislation called ordinances. An ordinance has the effect and force of law. Ordinance enactments follow a precise legislative process, including a public hearing(s) process. Butler, in his text on administration of community recreation programs, suggests that an ordinance normally gives the recreation department greater stability than a resolution, since once it passes, it cannot be replaced except after a public hearing.[13] The ordinance, however, must conform to the charter and to state enabling acts. See Fig. 3.3.

FEDERAL SYSTEM

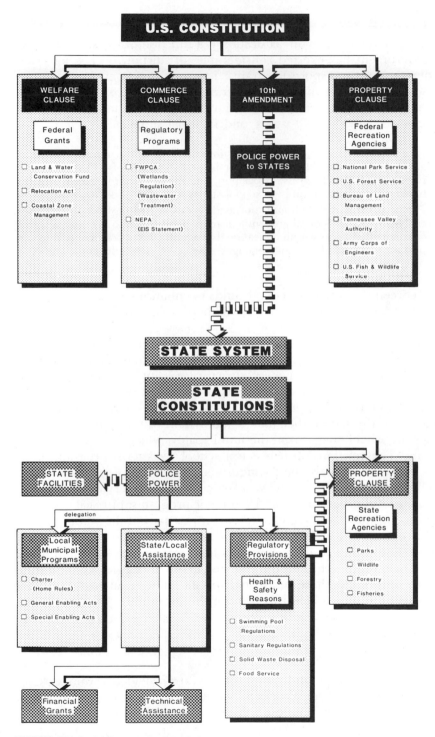

FIGURE 3-3 Legal Framework—Total System

School Recreation and Sports Programs

Despite the expression "education is a function of the state" the federal government has exerted considerable jurisdiction over schools and school recreation and sports programs. This federal influence on state and local school recreation and sports programs has come through decisions of the United States Supreme Court regarding civil liberties, congressional enactments relative to civil rights, and financial support.

1. Civil liberties.   Constitutional protections and civil rights statutes protect the abridgment of civil liberties whether in or out of schools. The panoply of freedoms of speech, press, association, and immunity from racial- and sex-based discrimination apply to school sports and recreation programs.
2. Financial support.   Although not as direct as regulating the protection of civil liberties, the federal government may spend funds to promote a variety of curriculum areas within educational programs. Funds can be used to support the teaching of foreign languages, science, physical education, and other programs.

Between the carrot of federal funds to enhance school revenues and the stick of federal enforcement of civil liberties the federal influence over schools is substantial.

Among the fifty states the organization and administration pattern of public schools and their recreation and sports programs vary considerably in detail but not in terms of general structure. Except in Hawaii, the operation of the schools of the state is delegated to local boards of education through a pattern of state legislation. Thus the local board of education is an agency of the state rather than a subdivision of the state. This distinguishes the school board from the municipality, which is a subdivision of the state. The relationship between a school recreation program and a sports program must also be distinguished. When the program is part of the school curriculum, or even extracurricular but still serving the student, it is a state level program. Typically, athletic programs, physical education programs, or intramural recreation activities are part of the school's educational program and are subject to state regulation. When the recreation program is a service to the community and not a direct extension of the educational program the board is engaged in the discharge of a local function. In this case, there must be specific state enabling legislation authorizing the school board to provide the program.

SUMMARY

Public park, recreation, and sports services are provided within a clearly defined framework of constitutional, statutory, and charter provisions. No authority exists to carry on these services except as the power is granted by specific enactments. Within the legal framework the several levels of government—federal, state, county, municipal, and school district conduct their described functions. The United States Constitution is the cornerstone of the public system. All aspects of park, recreation, and sports enterprises must conform to the Constitution even if they are contrary to state law. Where no constitutional prohibition exists, the state is presumed to have jurisdiction.

The federal framework in parks and recreation emanates from the "property," "general welfare," and "commerce" clauses of the Constitution. Federal regulatory authority stems from the civil liberties provision of the Constitution and civil rights legislation. In a variety of cases the United States Supreme Court has upheld all rights guaranteed by the Constitution and federal statutes regardless of the services involved.

States have the plenary legislative power to authorize and regulate state, local, and school park, recreation, and sports programs. Under the police power state agencies may be established to acquire, develop, and operate park and recreation facilities. The pattern of organizational structure is varied but all states provide some level of park and recreation services.

Authorization to provide park, recreation, and sports services may be delegated to municipalities and local schools. This power must be found in constitutional and statutory enactment and these units of government have no authority beyond that extended by these documents. Administrators should ascertain their legal authorization before undertaking new services.

School sponsored recreation and sports programs that are part of the school curriculum are generally held to be state endorsed functions, whereas municipal services are local in nature and are discretionary to the unit of government. When school recreation and sports programs are mandated in the state school code the local school district must strictly adhere to its provisions.

DISCUSSION QUESTIONS

1. Under what authority is the federal government authorized to provide park and recreation services?

2. Do municipalities and schools have the inherent authority to provide recreation and sports services?

3. In what areas is the federal government involved in school sports and recreation programs?

4. Review the legislation in your state that authorizes municipalities and schools to provide recreation and sports activities. Does this legislation provide for:

   a. The leasing of land or facilities to user groups or organizations?

    b.   The charging of user fees for participation in recreation and sports activities?

    c.   Cooperative programming between cities and schools?

NOTES

[1]U.S. Department of the Interior, *The Third Nationwide Outdoor Recreation Plan—An Assessment, 1979* (Washington, D.C.: Government Printing Office, 1979), p. 55.

[2]39 Stat. 535, 16 U.S.C. 1.

[3]*United States v Butler,* 297 U.S. 1 (1936).

[4]*Helvering v Davis,* 301 U.S. 619, 640–641 (1937).

[5]See RICHARD CAPPALLI, *Rights and Remedies Under Federal Grants* (Washington D.C: Bureau of National Affairs, 1979), for an exhaustive review of federal grant law.

[6]*Bissell v Burrell,* 21 Mich. 25 (MI 1875).

[7]*Chicago Park Dist. v Canfield,* 19 N.E.2d 376 (IL 1938).

[8] 56 Am Jur 2d, Mun. Corps §4.

[9]*Kosmicki v Kowalski,* 171 N.W.2d 172 (NE 1969). (2) *Dobrovolny v Reinhart,* 173 N.W.2d 837 (IA 1970); *Cohen v State,* 52 Misc.2d 324, 275 N.Y.S.2d 719 (NY 1966). (3) *Lanza v Wagner,* 183 N.E. d 670 (NY 1962). (4) *Sturgis v Allegan County,* 72 N.W.2d 56 (MI 1955). (5) *San Antonio Ind. School Dist. v Rodgriguez,* 411 U.S. 1 (1973); *In re Advisory Opinion,* 211 N.W.2d 28 (MI 1973). (6) *Child Welfare Society of Flint v Kennedy School Dist.,* 189 N.E.2d 81 (OH 1962).

[10]*People v Sell,* 17 N.W.2d 193 (MI).

[11]V.A.T.S. Art. 6080.

[12]ROBERT TOALSON, "Special Districts," *Park and Recreation Magazine,* July 1980, p. 29.

[13]GEORGE BUTLER, *Introduction to Community Recreation* (New York: McGraw-Hill Book Co., 1959), p. 453.

four

liability in parks, recreation, and sports

Park, recreation, sports, and leisure services are affected by many areas of the law. As outlined in Chapter 3, constitutions and statutes dictate the framework for these services but represent only a small body of law. Perhaps no other area of law touches the field more than the broad topic of legal liability. No attempt is made to provide encyclopedic discussion of all the forms of liability for that is beyond the scope of this book. An introduction will be provided to many topical areas with a substantial discussion given to negligence, nuisance, intentional torts, and strict liability, for under these legal theories the bulk of recreation and sports cases are filed.

Legal liability is a generic term referring to responsibilities and duties between persons and is enforceable by the courts. A person seeking legal redress must establish a basis for a claim—the person must show that he or she has suffered a legal wrong. In our judicial system, legal wrongs are classified as civil or criminal acts and are distinguished by the interests affected and the legal remedies available. A wrongful act may result in both criminal and civil liability since they are not mutually exclusive and different interests are protected by each. The actions may be brought concurrently or successively. It is the prevailing view that a decision for or against the defendant in one is not conclusive as to the other.[1] Since a crime is an act against society, the court punishes a defendant by imposing a prison

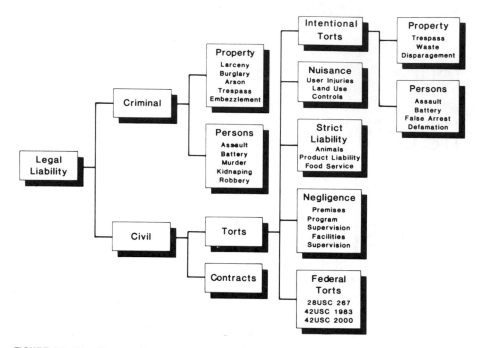

FIGURE 4-1   Classification of Legal Liability

sentence, a monetary fine, or both. A civil action involves a dispute between persons involving a breach of an agreement or breach of a legal duty. It may include a degree of punishment through an award of punitive damages but it does not involve a jail sentence. Fig. 4.1 graphically illustrates the variety of legal wrongs that involve park, recreation, sports, and leisure services.

CRIMINAL LIABILITY

A crime is an offense committed by an individual against the public at large, even though there may be an individual victim. The government, representing the public and the victim, seeks redress for the crime through the appropriate criminal proceeding. A criminal proceeding is not concerned with compensating the victim but with protecting the public interest by punishing the offender.

A crime is generally defined as an act committed or omitted in violation of a public law and made punishable by it. Crimes can be defined with reference to the severity of the offense, to moral turpitude, to procedure, to infamy, or to the social harm caused. Historically, the common law provided the starting point for most definitions of crimes. Today, most states have incorporated these common law definitions into penal statutes.

State statutes generally classify crimes as felonies or misdemeanors. Felonies are the most reprehensible offenses and carry the stiffest punishment. Felonies generally include first and second degree murder, felony murder, rape, burglary, larceny, and sodomy. Imprisonment is generally in a state penitentiary. Misdemeanors, a class of offenses with mild jail sentences or fines, typically include disorderly conduct, fish and game law violations, most traffic offenses, and municipal ordinance violations.

States have the authority to define crimes, establish criminal justice procedures, and proscribe punishment for crimes. This authority is not exclusive to the states, however, as Congress has the constitutional power to define offenses and provide punishment. Thus we have a dual federal and state criminal justice system. A wrongful act may constitute an offense against both. Federal crimes generally relate to the function of the federal government or involve acts against federal officials or institutions. Robbing a federally insured bank, counterfeiting, kidnapping, and transportation across state lines, federal income tax evasion, and murdering the president are examples. Federal crimes are only those defined by federal statutes and if an act is not defined it is not a federal offense.

CIVIL LIABILITY

Civil litigation permeates the recreation and sports industry now more than ever before. Clearly, there is a trend in American society to rely on the courts more than ever to solve a variety of problems. As one park and recreation educator has noted, "Lawsuits have become a way of life with Americans and the park and recreation field is certainly a prime target."[2] This reflects a recognition on the part of many professionals that legal liability may become a codeterminant of recreation services along with economic, societal values, and politics.

Civil liability is based on a breach of a legal duty or a breach of contract. It is concerned with defining conduct, rights, and obligations between individuals. Historically, civil liability evolved from common law origins and still is guided by these principles. Civil liability is split into *tort* and *contract* liability. Some areas overlap, such as product liability, but most are clearly separated.

Contracts

The performance of promises is a foundation of contract law. Liability is imposed on the parties to agreements to assure that the promises they make will be enforced. Since recreation and sports enterprises and professionals are involved in a variety of contracts, it is essential that contract principles be understood.

Contracts are formed when parties agree to perform certain promises for valuable consideration. They can be broken down into three parts, (1) offer, (2) acceptance, and (3) consideration. An offer is a proposal made by one person to another indicating what the offeror will give in return for a specific promise. If the person to whom the offer is made indicates a consent to be bound by the terms of the offer this constitutes acceptance. To change an agreement into a contract requires consideration. In contract law, consideration is a detriment to the promisee or a benefit to the promissor, bargained for and given in exchange for a promise. The law requires consideration to have legal value usually expressed as money. While the law does not equate consideration to money most contracts express consideration in dollar values. Two other elements are necessary to form an enforceable contract, capacity and legality. Capacity refers to the legal status given to the parties which qualifies them as competent. For example, a minor child is presumed to lack the capacity to sign an enforceable contract. Thus the contract is not valid to bind the minor child to its terms. Legality means the contract subject matter fulfills a goal subject to legal attainment. When a contract involves the conveyance of a product or service whose sale is illegal, the contract cannot be enforced against a person who breaches the contract.

The following hypothetical example illustrates the formation of a contractual arrangement. Curtis Lee, a city parks director, pursuant to authorization from the city council, advertised for bids on five playground slides. After reviewing all of the bids, Curtis Lee selected the low bid of $5,000 from the Scott Alan Playground Company. Curtis Lee notified the company that their bid was accepted and he forwarded for the company's signature a standard playground purchase form prepared by the city attorney. Scott Alan signed the form for the company and Curtis Lee signed it as a representative of the city. The agreement provided that "the Scott Alan Playground Company, for a price of $5,000, would provide and install five Slippery Slides in Tuni Park within thirty days from the date specified herein according to the specifications of the city." In contract terms, the scenario includes an offer by the playground company in their bid to install the specified playground equipment at the bid price. The city, in selecting the low bid and furnishing the agreement form to be signed by the company, accepted the offer. Consideration for the contract was $5,000. Both parties had a contractual capacity to enter into such an agreement for a legal purpose. They assented to the contract in a form required by law by signing the written purchase agreement.

Most contracts have a definite starting and ending date. When a contract is completed, it is said to be discharged. A discharge is the termination of contract obligations. If a party to an agreement breaches the contract before it is discharged the nonbreaching party may seek the following remedies: (1) damages, (2) specific performance of the contract, (3) rescission and restitution, and (4) reformation. A contract breach is the failure to perform the specific terms in the contract. This nonperformance gives rise to the following remedies.

Damages   Monetary damages are designed to compensate an injured party for a loss of the bargain. In a contract for a sale of goods the usual measure of damages is an amount equal to the difference between the contract and the market price. In contracts involving land, the measure of damages depends on the breaching party and the stage at which the breach occurs.

Specific performance   This remedy requires that the breaching party perform the act as promised in the contract. Essentially the court compels the performance of the contract. Because this remedy is extraordinary, it is available only in cases when monetary damages will not compensate the injured party. Courts uniformly refuse to grant this remedy in cases involving contract disputes for the sale of goods and personal service contracts. Specific performance is generally granted in a contract for the sale of land or in a contract for sale of unique goods such as paintings, rare books, or artifacts. The remedy of damages is inadequate in these instances because land and certain art and artifacts are considered unique and not readily replacable.

Rescission and restitution   This remedy is basically an action to cancel a contract and to restore the parties to the status occupied prior to contract. The cancellation of the contract may be mutual, where both parties agree to undo the contract, or unilateral, where only one party cancels. The remedy is generally available where fraud, mistake, and duress are present in the transaction or when the other party fails to perform. Notice must be given by the rescinding party to the breaching party that the contract is cancelled. Restitution refers to restoring the parties to their original positions. If there was an exchange of goods or property, those original items must be returned or restitution made in money. Many states allow consumers to unilaterally rescind contracts made in the home by door-to-door salespersons within a specified period of time.

Restoration   As the term indicates, this remedy allows the parties to rewrite a contract to conform to their true intentions. It is available where the parties have made a mutual mistake or where through oversight they have failed to cover all the contract terms. A typical example involves a land transaction where the grantor agrees to sell a tract of land to a purchaser but makes a mistake about the tract to be sold. Under this remedy, a court could modify the contract to conform to the true intent of the parties.

It is difficult to imagine the operation of a recreation enterprise without transactions involving some type of contract. While policy, political,

managerial, budgetary, and philosophical considerations provide motivation for many contracts, certain legal principles and rules must be followed.
Although managerial considerations may not include legal concerns, the
prudent administrator should consider the following basic points:

1. Authorization—Check with legal counsel to ascertain statutory and municipal
    charter or ordinance authorization for the contract contemplated.

2. Contract Terms—Prior to entering into contract negotiations, the administra-
    tor should compile a list of nonnegotiable and negotiable contract require-
    ments. These requirements along with compensation, contract time periods,
    and contract parties should be clearly identified. Contracts that are ambigu-
    ous and lack detail are invitations to a breach and litigation. The administra-
    tor should be guided by the rule that the contract must be of sufficient detail
    to guarantee the level of service contemplated within a reasonable time pe-
    riod and for adequate consideration. Unrealistic terms and criteria lead to
    problems. Incorporate all terms into the written document.

3. Bidding—Public agencies generally are required to seek bids on certain types
    of contracts or on contracts above certain dollar values. This procedure is
    governed by state statute as well as local procedures and ordinances. A pru-
    dent administrator should determine bid requirements and specifications
    prior to negotiating any contract. Frequently, nonprofit recreation agencies,
    as a matter of corporate policy, seek bids on selected purchases. These proce-
    dures are not as elaborate as the public bid process.

4. Contract Review—An administrator should develop policies and procedures
    for reviewing contracts with a legal counsel. The key to successful contract
    reviews is establishing and adhering to policy and procedure.

Contract law is a very complex area of law, and the advice of legal
counsel should be part of contract considerations. Attorneys should not
make management and budget-related decisions on contracts but should
assist the administrator in preparing a contract document that is
unambiguous and meets the goals sought by the parties.

Torts

Tort law is the progeny of the common law. Today, when most other
areas of law have been codified in state statutes, tort law remains within the
purview of the courts. Derived from Latin and French the word tort means
"twisted" and "wrongs." It is a generic word describing a number of individual causes of action. Recognizing the difficulty in drafting a simple, all-
inclusive definition, a noted legal scholar classifies a tort as, "a civil wrong,
other than a breach of contract, for which the court will provide a remedy
in the form of an action for damages."[3] The law of torts functions to determine if a particular action is wrongful and then to provide the victim with a
compensatory remedy. Beyond the notion that tort law involves wrongs
and compensation, all torts include three key elements, breach of legal
duty, causation, and injury.

Breach of legal duty   Existence of a legal duty and failure to conform to that duty are implicit in this element of tort law. The concept of legal duty recognizes that individuals are free to act in any manner so long as their actions do not infringe on the interests of others. A duty matures into a legal duty when the law gives recognition and effect to the obligation. Changing societal standards give rise to new legal duties, and courts, as societal barometers, establish a legal duty "when, in general, reasonable men would recognize it and agree that it exists."[4] In the last thirty years the emergence of *strict liability for product defects* is an example of a new tort created by the courts. It was developed as a matter of social policy to transfer the cost of an injury to manufacturers of products because they had the ability to pay and could reflect this payment in the price of their product. The second requirement is a failure to conform to the duty. This failure or breach may be an intentional act, a careless act, or a careful but dangerous act that results in injury. The character of the breach will determine if the act constituted an intentional tort or negligence.

Causation   There must be a reasonable connection between the breach of duty and the injury. There can be no action for a tort without this causal connection. The issue is not whether there is a connection between the act and injury but whether it is so closely related as to impose liability. On a continuum of responsibility, proximate or legal cause marks the point of legal responsibility. It is a question of law as established by social policy. As noted by Prosser, "The fatal trespass done by Eve was cause for all our woe, but any attempt to impose liability upon such a basis would result in infinite liability for all wrongful acts."[5]

Injury   Since tort law is concerned with compensation resulting from a wrongful act it follows that there must be some type of injury. Monetary compensation often is granted as recompense for the injury. Tort law provides a remedy for a variety of protected interests and acts affecting those interests. Acts causing personal injury, mental distress, or loss of social standing are compensable under tort law.

PERSONS SUBJECT TO LIABILITY

Legal risk is a bittersweet dilemma for the manager of recreation and sports enterprises. It encourages responsible and professional conduct which protects the user and at the same time has a chilling effect on the provision of new services. Targets of legal risks include the array of institutions, sponsors, and employees in the parks, recreation, sports, and leisure fields. Certainly no exceptions are made for federal, state, and local governmental agencies, private recreation enterprises, and officials and employees of program sponsors. This section outlines the liability of each of these parties.

When representing a client the plaintiff's attorney follows the pragmatic maxim of sue all possible persons directly or remotely connected with injury. This joinder of all defendants is based in part on court procedural rules, but more importantly on the *deep pocket doctrine*. It is a hollow victory for the plaintiff to win a substantial monetary award from a defendant who is unable to pay. Therefore the targets of lawsuits are the collectible parties and public treasuries. In recreation and sports litigation these targets include (1) the program sponsor, (2) board members, (3) administrators or supervisors, (4) the employee whose conduct is the direct or proximate cause of the injury, and (5) the independent contractor. See Fig. 4.2.

Program Sponsor

Sponsor liability for participant injury is often determined by the public or private nature of the enterprise. If the sponsor is a federal, state, municipal, or school agency, liability is often dictated by the doctrine of governmental immunity. Where the sponsor is a person, private partnership, or corporation, the doctrine of *respondeat superior* is often an issue. This doctrine provides that the enterprise is liable for the conduct of their employees. The following discussion is based on the governmental vs private categorization of the recreation and sports sponsor.

The doctrine of sovereign immunity as a defense to negligence is rap-

FIGURE 4-2 Parties Subject to Legal Liability

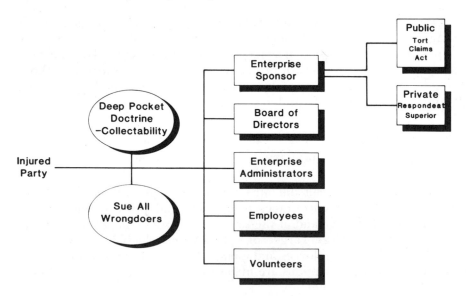

idly disappearing from the vocabulary of public officials. By 1980 thirty-seven states had modified or rejected the doctrine. Only five states (Georgia, Maryland, Mississippi, South Carolina, and South Dakota) retain anything resembling total immunity for all acts of government.[6]

Federal park and recreation agencies In 1946 Congress enacted the Federal Tort Claims Act which permitted, for the first time, the filing of lawsuits against the federal government and its administrative agencies.[7] The statute allows an injured person to file a claim for injury or property loss with the agency prior to instituting a lawsuit. Pertinent provisions of the statute provide

§2672 ADJUSTMENT OF CLAIMS

The head of each Federal agency. . . . may consider, ascertain, adjust, determine, compromise and settle any claim for money damages against the United States for injury or loss of property or personal injury or death caused by the negligent or wrongful act or omission of any employee of the agency while acting within the scope of his employment, under circumstances where the United States, if a private person, would be liable to the claimant in accordance with the law of the place where the accident occurred.

§2674 LIABILITY OF UNITED STATES

The United States shall be liable, respecting the provisions of the act relating to tort claims, in the same manner and the same extent as a private individual under like circumstances but shall not be liable for . . . punitive damages.

In interpreting this Act, the courts have ruled that tort liability is determined by the law of the state in which the tort occurred. For example, in a case filed against the National Park Service by a visitor to Yellowstone National Park for injuries sustained when he fell into one of the thermal pools in the park, the court applied the tort law of Wyoming.[8] In finding no liability for the National Park Service, the court concluded that the United States is not an insurer of the safety of visitors in Yellowstone and it would not be reasonable to erect boardwalks, guardrails, fences, and signs around every natural thermal feature in the park, particularly when the danger is apparent and obvious.

The Act applies the doctrine of *respondeat superior* to the United States by holding the government liable for the negligent acts and omissions of governmental employees acting within the line of duty. The provisions of the Act do not apply to

Claim(s) arising out of assault, battery, false arrests, malicious prosecution, libel, slander, misrepresentation, deceit, or interference with contract rights.[9]

Thus an employee committing any of these intentional torts may be individually liable, but this does not expose the United States to liability.

State and municipal agencies   In considering the tort liability of states, municipalities, and school districts the doctrine of governmental immunity must be discussed since this issue is frequently involved in recreation and sports injury cases. In its application the doctrine provides that a state and its instrumentalities shall not be subject to suit or liability unless the state gives its consent. The doctrine has been subject to widespread criticism and is on the decline in most jurisdictions.

Judicial dissatisfaction with the harshness and inequity of governmental immunity led to the creation of exceptions to the doctrine or to its outright abolition. Reacting to the judicial abrogation of the doctrine many state legislatures adopted "tort claim statutes." Today, most states deal with the immunity issue through these statutes.

State tort claim statutes can roughly be divided into three general categories, statutes recognizing governmental immunity but with exceptions based on governmental/proprietary or ministerial/discretionary distinctions, e.g., Colorado, Tennessee; statutes imposing liability but only for specific conduct, e.g., Iowa, Oregon, Utah, Texas; and statutes imposing liability on the basis that purchase of insurance by the municipality constitutes a waiver of immunity. Other provisions frequently incorporated into these statutes include authorization to purchase insurance, indemnification of employees if they are sued, notice of claim requirements, and monetary limitations for damages. By establishing monetary limits for recovery against public agencies, the legislatures recognized the liability but placed a ceiling on damage claims. In Texas, for example, the statute allows citizens to sue park and recreation agencies but limits recovery to $100,000 per person and $300,000 for any occurrence.[10]

The immunity and liability status of public agencies for the tortious conduct of its officers, administrators, and employees is not static but is constantly evolving through judicial and legislative actions. There is a clear trend to allow citizens injured in park and recreation services to recover money damages from the managing agency for the torts of its employees. (See Appendix for a listing of the status of the states.)

School districts   Originally the status of school districts' tort liability rested primarily in the common law doctrine of governmental immunity. The principal reason for applying the doctrine to school districts is the fact that they are agencies of the state and perform a governmental function. When the doctrine was applied to school districts recreation and sports programs the doctrine was rife with exceptions that limited its effect. The widespread criticism of the doctrine also enveloped school districts and its protection is on the wane. With the erosion of the doctrine it is necessary to consult state court cases and statutes to determine the current status of the doctrine in each state.

Private sponsors Immunity from liability is not a protection afforded to the private person or corporation. The doctrine of *respondeat superior* applies to the private recreation enterprise, hence the corporation or business may be liable for the tortious conduct of its officers, trustees, or employees. This doctrine normally does not apply when the sponsor is a government agency.

Board of Directors

The common law doctrine of official immunity is related to the concept of governmental immunity in terminology and history. Under this doctrine an elected or appointed official is not liable in damages for tortious conduct when acting within the scope of discretionary authority. Many state tort claim statutes include provisions codifying this common law immunity. In those states, members of municipal, county, and state park and recreation commissions are immune from liability for actions undertaken as a board if those actions are within the legal scope of the commission's authorization. Acts of individual board members or the board as a whole, if beyond the statutory or legal scope of duties, are *ultra vires* actions for which board members are individually liable.[11] Board members may also be liable when they breach statutory duties. One example is a violation of a state open meetings law. Legislatures in every state have passed some type of statute requiring the meetings of governmental bodies to be open to the public. Open meetings statutes generally require that notice of the time and location of the meeting be given to the public prior to the meeting. Another element generally included in these statutes requires that the agenda items and board actions be discussed in a public forum. Unless the statute specifically authorizes discussion of a subject in a closed session, such as personnel matters or attorney-client communications, the action must be taken in the public forum. Violations of open meetings notice and agenda requirements may subject individual board members to criminal and civil penalties when these remedies are provided for by statutes.

Administrators

The doctrine of *respondeat superior* does not apply to administrators and supervisors since they are considered employees of the enterprise. Thus, in the absence of a statute imposing liability, such officials are not liable for the tortious conduct of subordinates when liability is based soley on supervisory responsibility. There are two exceptions, however, when liability may be imposed on administrative and supervisory officials. First, if the supervisor directly participates in, ratifies, or condones the tortious conduct of a subordinate then the supervisor may be liable. Second, a supervisor may be subject to liability for negligence in hiring, training, retaining, or supervising a subordinate employee whose tortious conduct injures a third party. For example, a supervisor may be liable for improperly training an employee in the handling of recreation equipment which results in injury to a third person.

Individuals—Staff, Teachers, and Coaches

Employees of public park and recreation agencies and teachers and coaches are not covered by the doctrine of governmental immunity and may be individually liable for injuries caused by their tortious conduct as are their counterparts in the private sector. To protect public employees most states have passed indemnification statutes, allowing the agency to pay tort damage judgments assessed against their employees. Thus, a state or local parks and recreation agency may pay the damage award or injury claim assessed against a recreation leader or maintenance employee.

Indemnification of employees generally is not mandatory but is discretionary to the agency. Prior to an agency becoming responsible for indemnifying an employee two conditions must be met. First, the employee must be acting within the scope of responsibility when the tort was committed, and second, the tort must not be the result of a willful, wanton, or intentional act. For example, if a recreation center supervisor, after removing a belligerent teenager from the center, subsequently gets into a fight with the youth in the parking lot, the agency would be precluded from indemnifying the employee for damages from this assault and battery—an intentional tort. Although the agency may cover the employee's attorney's fees, court costs, and damage judgment, punitive damages may not be paid by the agency. Statutes do not allow for indemnification against the employee in criminal proceedings.

One method used to protect the employee is through employer purchased liability insurance. Through enabling legislation most states authorize agencies to purchase employee liability insurance. The legislation generally is permissive and not mandatory, so the employee would be well advised to inquire about this coverage.

Independent Contractors

An independent contractor is one hired to provide a service or undertake a piece of work without restrictions imposed by the hiring party as to the means to be used, quality control, the employment of labor, training of staff, provision of supplies and materials to produce certain results required by the contract.[12] Generally, an enterprise is not liable for the tortious conduct of its independent contractors. There are exceptions to this rule of nonliability. The most noteworthy to the recreation enterprise is when it retains significant control for the contractor's work or when the agency retains supervision and control over the contractor's employees.[13] Mere supervision or inspections to assure quality control or conformance with contract requirements or audits of records to verify contract payments is not sufficient to render an agency liable.

Private Enterprises

The doctrine of governmental immunity and official's immunity does not protect the private recreation enterprise or its employees. Owners of private recreation enterprises are liable for their employee's negligent acts which cause injury to their customers. State landowner liability statutes which lower the standard of care that owners of outdoor recreation areas owe to users, are generally not applicable to the commercial recreation enterprise. Forty-six states have enacted legislation reducing the standard of care required of landowners who permit their property to be used by the public for recreation purposes. When the landowner charges a person to enter on the land or to use a facility, the lower standard of care authorized in most state statutes does not apply.[14] Thus, a profit-motivated recreation operator owes a duty to paying customers to use reasonable care for their protection, to inspect the premises to discover hidden defects and hazards, and to warn the customers. The owner, however, is not the absolute guarantor of the customers' safety.

Volunteers

Most recreation and sports programs rely on voluntary labor in their programs. Volunteers serve as instructors, supervisors, trainers, and administrators. A question that frequently arises concerns the liability of volunteers and the program sponsor for negligent acts of the volunteer. Both are issues that must be addressed by any agency using voluntary leadership.

As a general rule, volunteers are personally liable for their own acts of negligence. The sovereign and official immunity doctrines that protect the public agency and official do not shelter the volunteer working in a public agency from liability. Volunteers are expected to use reasonable care in fulfilling their assigned duties. The case of *O'Brien v Township High School District,* 392 N.E.Ed 615 (IL 1969), is a reminder that volunteers' work should be closely supervised. In this case a volunteer athletic trainer caused further damage while attempting to treat a knee injury. The court held that when medical treatment is undertaken by a volunteer for the school it must be competently rendered.

A related issue in volunteer negligence lawsuits is the liability of the sponsor or enterprise for the negligence of the volunteer. In these cases the plaintiff seeks to impute the negligence of the volunteer to the sponsor.

This is often called vicarious liability or the doctrine of *respondeat superior.* Literally it means let the employer be liable for the negligence of the employee when it is committed in the course of employment. Since the recreation and sports sponsor is responsible for directing and supervising the volunteer's efforts, the volunteer is classified as an employee. The sponsor is only liable for those acts committed within the "scope of employment" of the volunteer. When the volunteer's negligence arises from a factual pattern that was beyond the responsibilities of the position the sponsor is not liable. However, the volunteer may retain personal liability.

SUMMARY

Park, recreation, and sports enterprises and agencies, administrators and employees are subject to various forms of liability. Although some actions may lead to criminal liability, a major concern is civil liability for user injuries. Civil liability arises from a breach of a contract or from a breach of a legal duty of care. These two categories are referred to as contract liability and tort liability.

The subject of contracts is one of the largest in the field of law. In the course of providing park, recreation, and sports services the sponsoring agencies enter into contracts for such things as employment of staff, purchase of supplies, equipment, and materials, leasing of land and facilities and construction of facilities. When public agencies contract they have only that authority as granted by state legislation. Therefore administrators should ascertain the extent of contract authority and understand contract principals before entering into such arrangements.

Four elements are essential to all contracts: legal capacity of the parties to enter into contracts, lawful contract subject matter, mutual assent of the contracting parties, and consideration. Once a binding contract is formed and a party breaches the contract by failing to perform the specific terms in the contract an action for damages, specific performance, rescission, or restitution arises. In most contract actions the relief sought is damages.

Tort law is the second category of liability concern for parks, recreation, and sports enterprises and agencies. In general a tort is a wrong committed against the person or property of another and may range from a direct personal injury (assault, battery, slander, negligence) to damage to property (nuisance or trespass). A civil action for a tort is brought by an injured party to obtain compensation from the wrongdoer for the injury suffered. In determining whether a given act constitutes a tort the following elements must be shown

1. Breach of a legal duty requiring a person to conform to a standard to prevent injury.
2. A causal connection between the breach of the duty and the injury, and
3. An actual injury or damage to the person or property.

Unless these elements can be proven the defendant will not be liable for the injuries.

In most tort cases the plaintiff names as many people and enterprises as possible as defendants. This is based on court procedural rules and a desire to recover from a collectible party. The fact that a person is named in a lawsuit does not mean that they are liable but only that they may have been involved in the accident. Targets of park, recreation, and sports injury lawsuits include the sponsoring agency, the agency's board of directors, administrators, staff and employees, and agency volunteers. The tort liability of each of these parties depends on the common law, state statutes, and judicial rulings.

Tort liability of public park, recreation, and sports agencies is contingent on the application of the doctrine of governmental immunity. Under the common law, the state and its agencies were immune from tort liability. Public agencies still rely on the doctrine but this protection is on the wane as the federal government and most states have enacted legislation making these agencies liable for the torts of its officers, agents, and employees. The trend is to treat the public park, recreation, and sports agency on the same basis as the private provider of these services.

As a general rule, elected and appointed officers, trustees, and commissioners of public and private recreation and sports agencies are not personally liable for loss or injury resulting from an act which is within the scope of their policy making authority. Nor are they liable for injuries which result from the negligent acts of employees unless they participated in the acts. They are liable for injuries caused by acts which are outside the scope of their policy-making authority. If they act without authority, they are liable for their actions.

Administrators, supervisors, coaches, teachers, and other agency employees are liable under the general principles of tort law for their own acts which cause injury. Employees do not enjoy the protection of governmental immunity which is only applicable to public agencies. Employees have been sued for a variety of reasons, with the majority of cases involving supervision, instruction, first aid, transportation, and equipment and facility maintenance.

Most agencies rely on volunteers to conduct some of their programs. As a general rule, volunteers are personally liable for their negligent acts. When acting within the scope of their voluntary responsibilities these individuals may also subject the agency to liability for their negligence.

DISCUSSION QUESTIONS

1. What conditions must be met to establish an enforceable contract to purchase recreation and sports equipment?

2. What recourse does a recreation and sports agency have when an equipment vendor fails to fulfill a contract?

3.   What are the various types of tort liability and how are they applicable in recreation and sports? Give examples of each.

4.   How does the doctrine of *respondeat superior* apply to the recreation and sports agency?

5.   Under what circumstances are volunteers liable if they are working for municipal park and recreation departments?

6.   Does the doctrine of governmental immunity protect the park and recreation employee, teacher, or coach from liability? Why?

NOTES

[1]ROLLIN PERKINS, *Perkins on Criminal Law, 2nd ed.* (Mineola, N.Y.: Foundation Press, 1969), p. 9.

[2]BETTY VAN DER SMISSEN, "Where is Legal Liability Heading?" *Parks and Recreation,* May 1980, p. 50.

[3]WILLIAM PROSSER, *Law of Torts, 4th ed.* (St. Paul: West Publishing Co., 1971), p. 2.

[4]PROSSER, p. 327.

[5]PROSSER, p. 236.

[6]KENNETH DAVIS, *Administrative Law Treatise,* Supplement (Rochester: Lawyers Co-Operative Publishing Co., 1980), sec. 25., p. 203.

[7]28 U.S.C.A. §2671–2680.

[8]*Smith* v *U.S.,* 383 F. Supp. 1076, affirmed 546F.2d.872 (1972).

[9]28 U.S.C.A. §2680(h).

[10]V.A.T.S. 6252–19(3).

[11]*Holderson* v *Devils Lake,* 246 N.W. 641 (1933).

[12]41 Am.Jur.2d §1, citing a long list of cases.

[13]*Davis* v *Kansas City,* 464 P.2d 154 (MO 1970); *Smullen* v *New York,* 268 N.E.2d 763 (NY 1971).

[14]*Kesner* v *Trenton,* 216 S.E.2d 880 (NJ 1975).

five

negligence law

Most recreation and sports injury cases arise in the area of negligence. No person, employee, or sponsor is safe from a negligence lawsuit. While lawsuits cannot be prevented they can be minimized when employees understand negligence principles and practice good management. This chapter analyzes the elements of negligence through cases and rhetoric allowing managers to minimize accidents and injuries and reduce the probability of negligence.

Negligence means one thing to the layman and quite another to the lawyer and judge. Pragmatically, negligence means monetary compensation to the injured park user. To the recreation and sports administrator it means an added financial burden in the payment of claims, out of court settlements, and costs associated with lawsuits and court awards. To the legal profession it means a failure to perform a legal duty thereby causing an injury.

ELEMENTS OF NEGLIGENCE

Unlike an intentional tort, negligence does not involve a mental state but is concerned with a type of conduct. If the person's conduct creates unreasonable risks of harm this may constitute negligence, even though the ac-

tor's state of mind was one of concern for the safety of others. In such instances, legal fault and moral blame diverge. Negligence is conduct which
falls below the standard of care established by law for the protection of others against unreasonable risks of harm.[1] Under this definition, a person
may recover damages only when there is actionable negligence consisting
of

1. A duty or obligation, recognized by law, requiring the actor to conform to a
    certain standard of conduct for the protection of others against unreasonable
    risks.
2. A failure . . . to conform to the standard required. . . .
3. A reasonably close causal connection between the conduct and the resulting
    injury. . . .
4. Actual loss and damages resulting to the interests of another.[2]

These elements apply to actions against all tortfeasors—including municipal, state, and county park and recreation departments, schools, and commercial recreation ventures.

In negligence cases, proof of these elements involves questions of fact
and law. It is often stated that the court decides questions of law and the
jury questions of fact. Thus the court decides if a recreation and sports enterprise has a legal obligation to inspect athletic equipment. The jury must
decide, based on the facts, whether the enterprise adhered to the standard
of conduct required to protect users against harm.

LEGAL DUTY

To meet the first test of actionable negligence, a legal duty must exist between the person causing an injury and the person injured. This duty requires a person to conform to a standard of conduct to prevent unreasonable risks of harm. Therefore the legal duty must incorporate both risk and
conduct. Risk is the recognition of danger and conduct is the action required to prevent it from becoming unreasonable. A legal duty can be
illustrated by comparing it with a duty not recognized by law—a moral
duty. As a rule, the law imposes no general duty to rescue or assist a person
in peril. Moral and humanitarian feelings may move a person to act but the
law imposes no obligation to act as a good Samaritan. While danger invites
rescue, the law does not impose it. This proposition is cited in 65 C.J.S.
Negligence §63(106) at p. 858

> One who sees another in peril, for which he is in no way responsible and
> which is completely disconnected from any agency . . . with whose control he
> is concerned, is not under any legal obligation to attempt rescue or assist such
> person, and he need not exercise care to protect such persons against the haz-
> ards of the perilous situation.

However, the law recognizes that if one attempts rescue, the attempt must be undertaken with due care. For example, if a person with lifeguard training observes another in peril of drowning, there is no legal duty to rescue. However, if the person voluntarily attempts to save the swimmer's life the rescuer must use reasonable care not to injure others or to create further peril for the person in distress.

Distinguishing between legal and moral duties and determining the existence of a legal duty is an issue of law for the court and not for the jury.[3] A court determines this issue by examining the factors giving rise to a duty. A relationship sufficient to constitute a legal duty may arise by statute, municipal ordinance, administrative rule, contract, business transaction, voluntary assumption, business invitation, or judicial decision. As noted by Prosser, "there has been little analysis of the problem of duty for the courts can generally find a duty in one of these sources."[4]

Satisfaction of the legal duty requires a level of conduct to prevent unreasonable risks of harm. Conduct and risk are inseparable in the concept of legal duty. Risk involves a recognition and knowledge of danger by the actor coupled with a reasonable belief that harm may follow.[5] Risk of harm triggers and controls the level of conduct expected from the actor. As risk increases, based on probability and gravity of injury, so does the burden of taking precautions and as risk decreases the burden decreases. A person is not expected to be a guarantor of safety against any and all harm but only to protect against that harm which is unreasonable.

Courts have universally agreed that a determination of negligent conduct is made by comparing the actor's actions against the conduct of a hypothetical ordinary, reasonable, and prudent person under like or similar circumstance. The most succinct statement of the character of this hypothetical, ordinary, reasonable, and prudent person is offered by A.P. Herbert.

> He is an ideal, a standard, the embodiment of all those qualities which we demand of a good citizen. . . . He is one who invariably looks where he is going, and is careful to examine the immediate foreground before he executes a leap or a bound; who neither stargazes, nor is lost in meditation when approaching trapdoors or the margin of a dock; . . . who never mounts a moving omnibus and does not alight from any car while the train is in motion . . . and will inform himself of the history and habits of a dog before administering a caress; . . . who never drives his ball until those in front of him have definitely vacated the putting green which is his own objective; who never from one year's end to another makes an excessive demand upon his wife, his neighbors, his servants, his ox, or his ass; . . . who never swears, gambles, or loses his temper; who uses nothing except in moderation, and even while he flogs his child is meditating only on the golden mean. . . . In all that mass of authorities which bears upon his branch of the law there is no single mention of a reasonable woman.[6]

The reasonable person is a hypothetical individual having the same physical characteristics as the actual defendant, the normal mental capacity for that age, at least as much information and experience as is common to the community, and such superior skill or knowledge as the person actually has or claims to have. Fundamentally, the attributes of the reasonable person are matters of common sense for a jury of laymen to determine. Thus, it is common practice to give the jury merely a short definition of negligence and the reasonable person test, leaving it to the jury to apply its common experiences to the evidence. The jury may be aided in its deliberation by expert testimony as to the customary conduct of others in the class or community. The chief function of experts in negligence cases is to establish the standard of care against which the actor's conduct is compared. In recreation cases, the testimony of professionals such as physical educators, landscape architects, engineers, and planners is often used to help establish a standard of conduct.

Physical characteristics   The reasonable person is given all the physical characteristics of the defendant. If the defendant is blind, the question is not did the defendant act as a reasonable person with sight, but rather were the actions those of a reasonable and prudent blind person.

Mental capacity   The measure of mental capacity is the skill and knowledge of the average person in the community or in a particular class. This means that the manager must act not only as an ordinary and reasonable person in exercising duties, but also as an ordinary and reasonable recreation manager. The standard of care required is that of the best professional practice.

Minor children are one important exception to this objective standard of capacity. Children cannot be held to the same standard as adults. A child is compared to children of like age, intelligence, and experience.[7] Young children are frequently considered incapable of negligence because they cannot appreciate dangers and are unable to weigh cause and effect. The courts have created certain presumptions to serve as guides in evaluating this mental capacity. Generally, a child below the age of seven is presumed to be incapable of negligence; between seven and fourteen the child is presumed to be incapable but may be shown to be capable; and over fourteen the child is presumed to be capable. This is significant in the doctrine of attractive nuisance and the defense of contributory negligence.

Skill and knowledge   Similarly, the reasonable person has at least the information, experience, skill, and knowledge of the average prudent person in the community. One who undertakes an activity or occupation is ordinarily charged with the knowledge common to those who regularly engage in it. Thus, a lifeguard must understand lifesaving; a golf instructor, the mechanics of golf; a forester, the practices of silvaculture; and an aerobics instructor, the principles of exercise physiology and dance.

The question of legal duty is an issue of law for the courts. Whether the defendant conformed to the conduct of a reasonable and prudent man is a jury question. The jury must also create the ordinary and reasonable man and assign all the physical and mental attributes to this fictitious person before judging whether the defendant's actions conformed to the standard.

As a rule, when a recreation and sports enterprise invites the public to use facilities or participate in programs a legal duty of care arises. The following cases illustrate some of the legal duties of recreation enterprises and participants. In *Miller* the issue is the duty to warn of hidden dangers; in *Dibortolo* the duty to provide the correct instruction, and in *Nabozny* the duty to adhere to the rules of the game. This is by no means a complete list of all obligations but provides a sample of the range of duties owed by sponsors to participants and participants to each other.

MILLER v UNITED STATES
U.S. Court of Appeals—Seventh Circuit
597 F.2d 614 1979

Bauer, Circuit Judge

In this civil action arising under the Federal Tort Claims Act, the district court awards Richard P. Miller one million dollars for injuries he sustained in a diving accident at the Crab Orchard National Wildlife Refuge in southern Illinois. The United States appeals from the lower court's judgment on the issue of liability. We affirm the decision for the reasons noted below.

As a first step, we must briefly outline the relevant facts. The Crab Orchard National Wildlife Refuge is owned by the United States and is administered by the Department of the Interior. Within the refuge is a 7,000 acre lake, approximately two-thirds of which is open to the public for water-related activities such as boating, fishing, swimming, and water skiing.

The accident in question occurred at a boat dock on the far west end of the lake. The dock area is served by a paved road from one of the major thoroughfares around the lake. It also includes a paved ramp that runs into the lake so that boats may be launched off trailers, a restroom facility, a mowed grassy area, a wooden pier that extends fifty feet into the water, and two paved parking areas. On the road that enters the dock, there is a sign that reads "Boat Launching." The area is not authorized for swimming or diving, but, at the time of the accident, there were no signs to that effect. The pier is not equipped with a swimmer's ladder or raft.

On May 23, 1972, twenty year old Richard P. Miller arrived at the dock with a group of friends who had been searching for a place to go swimming. A swimmer and diver for most of his life, Miller had never been to the dock area before the day of the accident. Upon arrival, he removed his tank top and sandals, and walked on the pier to a point that was approximately ten feet from its end. The lake bottom at this point was not visible due to the murky water. Miller saw one man in the water toward the end of the pier who appeared to be treading water. In addition, he saw two or three people in the water along the left side of the pier about twenty feet from shore. After someone shouted that the water was "fine," Miller dove into the lake from the left side of the pier. The water depth, however, was only about three feet, and he apparently struck his head on the lake bottom. Miller is now a quadriplegic.

The central question thus becomes whether the United States breached a duty of care to the appellee. In our view there is credible evidence to support the district court's finding that the government was negligent in failing to post "no swimming" or "no diving" signs at the west end boat dock. On this point, the following facts are significant: (1) the boat dock was an improved area with restrooms, a wooden pier, and two paved parking areas, (2) the pier extended fifty feet into the lake, (3) the water was shallow but murky, (4) the appellant was aware of the water depth, (5) the appellant knew that individuals had previously used the boat dock area for swimming and wading, (6) the appellant's own safety plan recommended that "warning signs giving notice that swimming is permitted only at designated beaches should be erected at all unsupervised locations where visitors are likely to swim." Under these circumstances, we cannot say the district court erred in concluding that the United States "did not act with reasonable care when it failed to post any warnings or take any precautionary measures with respect to swimming and diving at the west end boat dock."

The district court also rejected the United States' claim that Miller was contributorily negligent as a matter of law. The court reasoned as follows:

"Plaintiff approached an imporved area by way of a paved access road. There was a parking lot. There were wash room facilities. There was a path to the pier. The boat launch was separate and not visible from the pier. The pier extended out into the water fifty feet. The water near the shore was clear and the plaintiff observed that the bottom was sandy and sloped. People were in the water about a third of the way out with water at various points on their bodies. There was a man off the end of the pier in the water to his shoulders who appeared to be treading water. There were people at the end of the pier of whom plaintiff inquired about the water who responded to him that it was 'fine.' One of the plaintiff's friends had assured him that the spot was 'perfect' for swimming. The evidence shows that her opinion was based on her own experience there when the water was at least four to four and one-half feet deep. Most significantly, there were no warnings of any kind. Plaintiff's dive was not a deep one. The risk was a hidden one of which the plaintiff had no comprehension or awareness. On these facts, we are not persuaded that Miller was contributorily negligent as a matter of law.

Affirmed

DIBORTOLO v METROPOLITAN SCHOOL DISTRICT OF WASHINGTON
Court of Appeal of Indiana
440 N.E.2d 507 1982

Sullivan, Judge

Plaintiff, Mary Ann Dibortolo, brought a negligence suit against defendant, Metropolitan School District of Washington Township, for injuries which she sustained during a physical education class taught by the school's physical education teacher. At the conclusion of the plaintiff's case the trial court entered judgment on the evidence. Plaintiff appeals.

On March 15, 1977, Mary Ann Dibortolo was eleven years of age and a sixth grade student at John Strange Elementary School. On that day, she broke a permanent front tooth during a regularly-scheduled physical education class taught by the school's instructor, Mrs. Dorothy Merriman. Approximately half the class of about twenty-five to thirty students including the plaintiff were required to perform an exercise known as the vertical jump.

According to plaintiff's expert witness, Joanne Gassert, the safe and proper way to perform this exercise is to first stand with the body parallel and the shoulders perpendicular to the wall, and with an arm upraised, to crouch momentarily, then to jump and reach the highest possible point on the wall. Throughout her twenty-four years' experience as a physical education teacher, she has never permitted her students to run toward the wall in performing the vertical jump. It was her opinion that to instruct students to run or to even take a "leap step" toward the wall is to subject them to unreasonable risk of harm. Mrs. Gassert believed that to allow such activity is to transform this relatively safe exercise into an "inherently dangerous" one.

Mrs. Dorothy Merriman, a physical education teacher since 1955, testified that she did not consult any textbooks in preparation for this exercise; however, she considered "safety aspects." According to Mrs. Merriman, she demonstrated the exercise to the students before allowing them to perform it. She had not used a floor mat placed perpendicularly to the wall, and she had not instructed the students to run toward the wall. She admitted, however, that they were taking two or three "quick steps" in the direction of the wall.

In conflict with her testimony was that of the plaintiff and three other witnesses. They performed the exercises ahead of the plaintiff and saw the plaintiff's mouth hit the concrete wall. They further testified that the plaintiff did not fall or stumble at any point before the impact. It was adduced that the plaintiff and these three students had never performed the vertical jump before that day, and that Mrs. Merriman neither demonstrated the exercise nor warned the class about any dangers associated with the exercise. The plaintiff introduced evidence which showed that Mrs. Merriman explicitly instructed her pupils to run toward the wall to improve their performance. The record reveals that the majority of the students first stood about six to eight feet away and then ran toward the wall before executing the vertical jump. In addition, there was testimony that the students were running on a mat placed in a position perpendicular to the wall.

There are three questions of law regarding these elements which the court must decide before it may submit the case to the jury. The initial question is whether the law imposes a duty upon the defendant to conform his conduct to a certain standard for the plaintiff's benefit.

In this case, the relationship between the parties is one of pupil and defendant's school personnel. The relationship of school pupils and school authorities invokes the well-recognized duty in tort law that persons entrusted with children, or others whose characteristics make it likely that they may do somewhat unreasonable things, have a responsibility recognized by the common law to supervise their charges. Thus, our Supreme Court has imposed a duty upon school authorities to exercise reasonable care and supervision for the safety of the children under their tutelage. Whether or not the trial court determined that such a duty existed here is not clearly discernible from the record. However, the prevailing authority compels the conclusion that Mrs. Merriman had a duty to conform her conduct as a physical education teacher to a certain standard, not only for the plaintiff's, but also for the other pupil's benefit.

The second question within the trial court's purview concerns the applicable standard of care. Although our Supreme Court noted that schools are not intended to be insurers of the safety of their pupils, nor are schools strictly liable for any injuries that may occur to pupils, the Court nonetheless held that the appropriate standard is whether a defendant exercised his duty with the level of care that an ordinary prudent person would under the same or similar circumstances.

We turn next to the third question of law, which asks whether the evidence introduced by the plaintiff was sufficient to permit the jury to find that the plaintiff has established the elements of the cause of action.

The plaintiff produced evidence which indicated that Mrs. Merriman did not demonstrate the exercise before she allowed the students to perform it. The plaintiff also introduced evidence that the students, including the plaintiff, were expressly instructed to run toward the wall if they wished to attain a higher score. Expert testimony was offered to show that the proper method for performing this exercise is to stand parallel to the wall, and that to permit, much less instruct, students to run toward the wall is to subject them to an unreasonable risk of injury. The jury may have given weight to this expert testimony and reached a rational inference that the teacher's conduct exposed the students to an unreasonable risk. The fact that Mrs. Merriman denied having instructed the students to run during this exercise only demonstrates that the evidence was at least in a state of conflict such that reasonable minds might draw differing conclusions. To enter judgment on the evidence in the face of such conflicting evidence was improper.

In this case, the evidence that Mrs. Merriman did not demonstrate the exercise, that she specifically directed the students to run during a structured physical education activity such as the vertical jump, when juxtaposed with the expert testimony that such an instruction is not only erroneous, but is actually unsafe, would have entitled a jury to reasonably infer that the teacher's conduct exposed the students to an unreasonable risk.

Furthermore, there was sufficient evidence from which the jury could have justifiably concluded that Mrs. Merriman's instructions were the proximate cause of plaintiff's injury. A proximate cause of plaintiff's injury is one which sets in motion the chain of circumstances leading to the injury. An essential element of proximate cause is considered to be the foreseeability of an injury. The negligence will be deemed to have been the proximate cause of the injury where the injury was one which, under the circumstances, should have been reasonably foreseen. The record indicates that the plaintiff did not fall or stumble as she approached the wall. Nor was there evidence that an intervening event occurred, such as another pupil tripping or obstructing the plaintiff's path. Thus, the jury may well have found that the injury which the plaintiff incurred in colliding with the wall was a direct and foreseeable consequence with the teacher's instruction.

We find that there was sufficient evidence of probative value to support the plaintiff's claim, or conflicting evidence such as to lead reasonable minds to reach differing conclusions. Thus, we deem the trial court's entry of judgment on the evidence against the plaintiff to be erroneous, and we therefore reverse that judgment and remand for further proceedings.

Reversed

NABOZNY v BARNHILL
Appellate Court of Illinois
334 N.E. 2d 258 1975

Adesko, Justice

Plaintiff, Julian Claudio Nabozny, a minor, by Edward J. Nabozny, his father, commenced this action to recover damages for personal injuries allegedly caused by the negligence of the defendant, David Barnhill. Trial was before a jury. At the close of plaintiff's case on motion of defendant, the trial court directed a verdict in favor of the defendant. Plaintiff appeals from the order granting the motion.

A soccer match began between two amateur teams at Duke Child's Field in Winnetka, Illinois. Plaintiff was playing the position of goalkeeper for the Hansa team. Defendant was playing the position of forward for the Winnetka team. Members of both teams were of high school age. Approximately twenty minutes after play had begun, a Winnetka player kicked the ball over the midfield line. Two players, Jim Gallos (for Hansa) and the defendant (for Winnetka) chased the free ball. Gallos reached the ball first. Since he was closely pursued by the defendant, Gallos passed the ball to the plaintiff, the Hansa goalkeeper. Gallos then turned away and prepared to receive a pass from the plaintiff. The plaintiff, in the meantime, went down on his left knee, received the pass, and pulled the ball to his chest. The defendant did not turn away when Gallos did, but continued to run in the direction of the plaintiff and kicked the left side of plaintiff's head causing plaintiff severe injuries.

All of the occurrence witnesses agreed that the defendant had time to avoid contact with plaintiff and that the plaintiff remained at all times within the "penalty area," a rectangular area between the eighteenth yard line and the goal. Four witnesses testified that they saw plaintiff in a crouched position on his left knee inside the penalty zone. Plaintiff testified that he actually had possession of the ball when he was struck by defendant. One witness, Marie Shekem, stated that plaintiff had the ball when he was kicked. All other occurrence witnesses stated that they thought plaintiff was in possession of the ball.

Plaintiff called three expert witnesses. Julius Roth, coach of the Hansa team, testified that the game in question was being played under "F.I.F.A." rules. The three experts agreed that those rules prohibited all players from making contact with the goalkeeper when he is in possession of the ball in the penalty area. Possession is defined in the Chicago area as referring to the goalkeeper having his hands on the ball. Under "F.I.F.A." rules, any contact with a goalkeeper in possession in the penalty area is an infraction of the rules, even if such contact is unintentional. The goalkeeper is the only member of the team who is allowed to touch a ball in play so long as he remains in the penalty area. The only legal contact permitted in soccer is shoulder to shoulder contact between players going for a ball within playing distance. The three experts agreed that the contact in question in this case should not have occurred. Additionally, goalkeeper head injuries are extremely rare in soccer. As a result of being struck, plaintiff suffered permanent damage to his skull and brain.

The initial question presented by this appeal is whether, under the facts in evidence, such a relationship existed between the parties that the court will impose a legal duty upon one for the benefit of the other. "(M)ore simply, whether the interest of the plaintiff which has suffered invasion was entitled to legal protection at the hands of the defendant."

There is a dearth of case law involving organized athletic competition wherein one of the participants is charged with negligence. There are no such Illinois cases. A number of other jurisdictions prohibit recovery generally for reasons of public policy. We can find no American cases dealing with the game of soccer.

This court believes that the law should not place unreasonable burdens on the free and vigorous participation in sports by youth. However, we also believe that organized, athletic competition does not exist in a vacuum. Rather, some of the restraints of civilization must accompany every athlete onto the playing field. One of the educational benefits of organized athletic competition to our youth is the development of discipline and self control.

Individual sports are advanced and competition enhanced by a comprehensive set of rules. Some rules secure the better playing of the game as a test of skill. Other rules are primarily designed to protect participants from serious injury.

For these reasons, this court believes that when athletes are engaged in an athletic competition, all teams involved are trained and coached by knowledgeable personnel, a recognized set of rules governs the conduct of the competition, and a safety rule is contained therein which is primarily designed to protect players from serious injury, a player is then charged with a legal duty to every other player on the field to refrain from conduct proscribed by a safety rule. A reckless disregard for the safety of other players cannot be excused. To engage is such conduct is to create an intolerable and unreasonable risk of serious injury to other participants. We have carefully drawn the rule announced herein in order to control a new field of personal injury litigation. Under the facts presented in the case at bar, we find such a duty clearly arose. Plaintiff was entitled to legal protection at the hands of the defendant. The defendant contends he is immune from tort action for any injury to another player that happens during the course of a game, to which theory we do not subscribe.

It is our opinion that a player is liable for injury in a tort action if his conduct is such that it is either deliberate, willful, or with a reckless disregard for the safety of the other player so as to cause injury to that player, the same being a question of fact to be decided by a jury.

Defendant also asserts that plaintiff was contributorily negligent as a matter of law, and, therefore, the trial court's direction of a verdict in defendant's favor was correct. We do not agree. The evidence presented tended to show that plaintiff was in the exercise of ordinary care for his own safety. While playing his position, he remained in the penalty area and took possession of the ball in a proper manner. Plaintiff had no reason to know of the danger created by defendant. Without this knowledge, it cannot be said that plaintiff unreasonably exposed himself to such danger or failed to discover or appreciate the risk. The facts in evidence revealed that the play in question was of a kind commonly executed in this sport. Frank Longo, one of plaintiff's expert witnesses, testified that once the goalkeeper gets possession of the ball in the penalty area, "the instinct should be there (in an opposing player pursuing the ball) through training and knowledge of the rules to avoid contact (with the goalkeeper)." All of plaintiff's expert witnesses agreed that a player charging an opposition goaltender under circumstances similar to those which existed during the play in question should be able to avoid all contact. Furthermore, it is a violation of the rules for a player to simply kick at the ball when a goalkeeper has possession in the penalty area even if no contact is made with the goalkeeper.

Reversed and Remanded

Failure to Perform

A second element in the negligence formula is conduct that fails to conform to the legal duty of care. This negligent conduct may arise out of active misconduct or passive inaction. The distinction is important in some states. Active misconduct is classified as *misfeasance* and passive inaction as *nonfeasance*. Misfeasance refers to incorrect or improper performance of a required duty. For example, a coach who inflicts excessive physical punishment as a teaching technique may be committing an act of misfeasance. Nonfeasance is considered the omission to perform a lawful duty. To establish liability for an act of nonfeasance there must be a duty to take positive action. In recreation and sports cases this positive action ranges from removing users from positions of peril (rescuing the drowning swimmer) to furnishing appropriate first aid. Affirmative duties of care fall upon owners and managers of recreation and sports facilities.

Proximate Cause

Negligence requires that there be some causal connection between the defendant's conduct and the damages to the plaintiff. Often referred to as proximate or legal cause, the law requires the nexus to be reasonable. Legal cause does not mean that the breach of duty was the sole cause of injury but only that it was a substantial factor. Every event has many contributing causes, albeit some are very remote. The law places the responsibility for the act on the defendant if the conduct was a substantial factor in causing the plaintiff's injury. Ultimately the question before the court is whether the conduct has been so significant and important a cause that the defendant should be legally responsible.

Perhaps no other field of law has called forth more disagreement, nor have the legions of writers and the attempts to clarify the subject produced any agreement on the proper approach. In most recreation and sports litigation, the causal connection is not difficult to prove, although there are some bizarre factual patterns.

SOARES v LAKEVILLE BASEBALL CAMP, INC.
Supreme Judicial Court of Massachusetts
343 N.E.2d 840 1976

Rescript, Justice

In this action by a minor, represented by his father, to recover for personal injuries, and by the father for expenses incurred for medical care, a judge of the Superior Court directed a verdict for the defendant at the close of the plaintiff's case. We affirm the judgment for the defendant entered thereon.

Then aged fourteen, the boy was a camper at a summer camp owned and operated by the defendant. The boy had been hazed by his bunk mates on the day of the accident and on previous occasions during his three-week stay. On leaving the bunk room after some teasing or horseplay, he fell, putting his arm through a glass panel in the upper part of a door between the bunk room proper and a vestibule which led to an outer screen door. Applying the test "whether there was any evidence viewed in the light most favorable to the plaintiff that would support (his) cause of action," we think the motion was properly granted. Even assuming that the hazing was excessive and should have been moderated by counselors exercising due care, Restatement (Second) of Torts 320, comment d (1965), there is no showing of causal connection between the hazing and the accident, as might have been demonstrable if there was an indication that the boy had been goaded into heedless flight. Nor was there evidence to support a hypothesis that the fall was due to a dangerously slippery condition of the floor for which the defendant could be held responsible in negligence. A suggestion that the presence of the glass panel itself created an unreasonable risk of injury was also unsupported in the proof.

Affirmed

Injury

The fourth requirement for actionable negligence is resulting injury. The phrase *injuria absque damna,* meaning injury without damages, is often used to explain the rule that a wrong without injury is not actionable. Hence there can be no negligence without an injury. Although injury and damages are used interchangeably, there is a material distinction between them. Injury is the invasion of a legal right, damages are the monetary loss resulting from the injury. In negligence actions, the plaintiff's basic remedy is monetary damages. The two types of damages recoverable in negligence actions are compensatory damages and consequential damages. Unlike intentional torts where nominal or punitive damages may be assessed, a plaintiff must prove injury and monetary loss in order to be awarded compensatory damages. Failure to prove damages results in a directed verdict for the defendant.

The objective of compensatory damages is restoration of a party to the same financial position occupied prior to the commission of the tort. Compensatory damages may be categorized as general or special. General damages are awarded for losses that are the natural and usual consequence of the injury, typically including noneconomic losses such as pain and suffering. Special damages refer to those awarded for injuries arising from special circumstances and are directly traceable to the defendant's breach of duty. These damages generally include economic losses such as medical expenses or lost wages.

When a plaintiff proves compensable injury, recovery may be had for all past, present, and future physical and mental consequences of the injury.[9] Determination of the monetary value for these compensatable injuries is a question of fact. Thus, it is within the province of the jury to assess in dollars and cents the amount of damages. With the exception of pain and suffering, the plaintiff must offer proof of the monetary value of all damages.

When one person is injured, other members of that person's family may also be vicariously harmed. Such indirect injury or consequential harm to a third person may give rise to a separate cause of action for their damages. Under most state statutes, the beneficiaries of a decedent may seek damages for not only the decedent's pain and suffering, medical expenses, and loss of earnings but also compensation for future earnings. At common law, the husband was entitled to damages for loss of domestic services, society, companionship, affection, and marital relations when his wife was injured. The wife had no corresponding right for the services of her husband. Today, the loss of a marital relation, called loss of consortium, is actionable by either spouse. Injuries to unemancipated minors may provide parents a cause of action to recover for loss of a child's earnings, medical expenses and, in some jurisdictions, a child's society, companionship, and affection.

Degrees of Negligence

The idea that negligence can be classifed as slight, ordinary, or gross has been condemned by legal writers and rejected by nearly all courts but not by state legislatures. There are statutes in many states listing gross negligence as a basis for a civil action. Typically, automobile guest-passenger and state recreational liability statutes incorporate gross negligence as a basis for recovery. Thus, the courts are forced to deal with the concepts in actions instituted under these statutes. To the extent that degrees of negligence are recognized, the distinctions most commonly are:

Slight negligence   The failure to exercise great care or an absence of that degree of care and vigilance which persons of extraordinary prudence and foresight are accustomed to use.[10]

Gross negligence   A failure to use even slight care or the omission to use ordinary care and diligence to avoid a discovered or apparent danger.

Willful, wanton, and reckless   An intentional act of an unreasonable character in total disregard of a human safety so obvious that one must be taken to be aware of it and to make it highly probable that harm would follow.[11]

Degrees of negligence are significant in those states incorporating the concepts in state recreational liability statutes. Only Alaska, Mississippi, Rhode Island, and Utah have not enacted landowner liability statutory provisions regarding recreation use of private lands.

NEGLIGENCE DEFENSES

Obviously, the best defense is the absence of negligence. Conforming to professional standards of conduct, building, and safety codes and accepted standards of maintenance and programming help establish the conduct of the reasonable and prudent person. Beyond the absence of negligence, the law recognizes a number of defenses to bar legal liability. Contributory negligence, assumption of risk, and governmental immunity are the defenses most frequently raised in park, recreation, and sports injury cases. Depending on the parties, the facts and relevant statutes, the following are generally recognized as defenses to negligence:

1. Contributory negligence,
2. Comparative negligence,
3. Assumption of risk,
4. Governmental immunity,
5. Statutes of limitations,
6. Notice of claim,
7. Failure of proof, and
8. Waiver/release.

These are affirmative defenses which the defendant must allege and prove. If alleged and established by the defendant, some defenses will result in a dismissal of the case even before trial, while others involve factual questions for the jury. For example, the statute of limitations defense requires a plaintiff to file a lawsuit within the prescribed time period or the lawsuit will be dismissed, so it is an issue to be resolved by the court prior to the trial. Assumption of risk is a question of fact to be resolved by a jury after presentation of evidence at trial. Both are legitimate defenses to bar liability but are applied at different times in the judicial proceedings.

Contributory Negligence

Contributory negligence is conduct on the part of the plaintiff contributing as a legal cause of the harm he has suffered, which falls below the standard to which he is required to conform for his own protection.[12]

As an affirmative defense, contributory negligence is similar to ordinary negligence, requiring proof of the same elements, except that negligence refers to a duty and harm to others while contributory negligence is conduct which creates an unreasonable risk of harm to the plaintiff. The defendant must allege and prove the contributory fault of the plaintiff as a cause of the injury. When plaintiff's conduct is a legally contributing cause of the injury, recovery will be denied even though the defendant's negligence was also a cause.

Children   The standard of conduct is different for children than for adults. The standard of conduct for a child is that of a reasonable and prudent child of the same age, intelligence, and experience. Most courts have adopted special rules for dealing with issues of a child's contributory negligence. The following presumptions are frequently applied:

1. A child under seven years of age is conclusively adjudged to be incapable of negligence;
2. A child between seven and fourteen years of age is rebuttably presumed to be incapable of negligence;
3. A child over fourteen years of age is presumed capable of negligence.

Parents   In recreation and sports injury cases the issue of the parents' contributory negligence in failing to properly supervise a young child often arises. Most states follow the rule that the contributory negligence of the parents or guardian cannot be imputed to the child. Thus if a lawsuit is filed on behalf of the child, the contributory negligence of the parents cannot bar the child from recovery. However, if the parents file suit to recover for the child's injury they may be precluded from recovering. The Restatement (Second) of Torts § 496 bars a parent, but not the child, for recovery for a child's injury if

1. The child is too young to exercise self-protection,
2. The child's incapacity is a contributing factor in harm, and
3. The parent has failed to exercise reasonable care to prevent the child from placing itself in a situation in which lack of self-protective capacity may reasonably be expected to result in harm to the child.

Several cases are included throughout this book where contributory negligence of either a parent or a child was an issue.

Comparative Negligence

In its application, contributory negligence is an all or nothing doctrine totally disregarding apportionment of fault. Thus if a defendant is 90 percent at fault and the plaintiff 10 percent, the plaintiff could not recover. Dissatisfaction with the all or nothing contributory negligence rule has been expressed by judges and legal commentators. As a result, judges have been reluctant to rule that a plaintiff's conduct is negligent as a matter of law to avoid the all or nothing result and juries are inclined to find no contributory negligence. In response to this criticism, legislatures in many states have adopted *comparative negligence* statutes. In 1968, only seven states had comparative negligence statutes of general application; today most states have adopted this approach.

There are two basic variations of comparative negligence. Under the minority view, a plaintiff may recover no matter how great the fault in comparison to that of the defendant. For instance if a plaintiff's contributing fault was 75 percent and the defendant's 25 percent, the plaintiff could still recover 25 percent of the damages. The majority view is a 50 percent rule allowing no recovery when the plaintiff's contributory negligence is as great or greater than 51 percent. The jury allocates fault in percentages when assessing damages. The following case illustrates the comparative negligence rule.

VIVEIROS v STATE OF HAWAII
Supreme Court of Hawaii
513 P.2d 487 1973

Richardson, Chief Justice

This appeal arises out of a civil action brought by plaintiffs-appellants against the State of Hawaii under HRS ch. 662 commonly known as the State Tort Liability Act. Trial by the court without a jury was held in the first circuit on March 23, 1972. The trial judge found that the State of Hawaii was negligent in failing to provide supervision at a program sponsored by Kailua High School during regular school hours. Pursuant to HRS 663-31, the trial judge determined that defendant was seventy-five percent negligent and that plaintiff, Jo Ann Viveiros, was twenty-five percent negligent for "failing to leave the scene prior to her being injured." The present appeal is from the trial judge's findings on general damages and comparative negligence.

The facts reveal that on December 3, 1970, at about 9:30 A.M., a school sponsored "light show" created by students began in a lecture hall at Kailua High School. At this time, an educational assistant acting as a supervisor represented the only staff member present in the auditorium. Soon after the show started, this supervisor departed to observe a fifteen to twenty minute coffee break. Though the show was to be supervised by three or four teachers, due to a mix-up, the hall was left in the hands of the students who were producing the light show.

At approximately 9:30 A.M. plaintiff Jo Ann Viveiros, age fifteen, along with two friends paid the twenty-five cent admission fee and entered the darkened hall to observe the performance. They could not find seating, so they stood in the aisle. Although the audience was quiet at the time plaintiff entered, a few minutes later a small group in a corner of the hall became "noisy." A student in charge of the production told the group to keep quiet or "the teachers would come in." Plaintiff was standing about thirty-five feet away from this group and did not feel any concern for her safety, although at this point she knew that no teachers were present.

Shortly after the announcement, plaintiff and two other students were struck by metal objects apparently thrown by the rowdy group. Plaintiff suffered permanent damage to her left eye. Glasses will not correct her vision, because of the severe injury to the macula area of the inner eye. She does have normal vision with both eyes open, although her damaged eye will not improve beyond 20-200. She has suffered severe impairment to her depth perception within three feet, though her peripheral vision appears normal.

We subscribe to the rule that a child is only required to use that degree of care appropriate to his age, experience, and mental capacity. We must reverse the finding by the trial judge that plaintiff was twenty-five percent negligent if we find that she conformed to the above standard by remaining in the auditorium after she discovered that the event was unsupervised.

At the time the isolated group of students became boisterous, Jo Ann was standing approximately thirty-five feet in front of them. The record reveals that the group was merely vocal. There is no mention made in the record of threats being shouted or evidence that objects were being thrown during the concert. Apparently none of Jo Ann's peers felt endangered, because no one was shown to have left the program once the group became boisterous. Jo Ann did not fear for her safety possibly because she harbored the reasonable belief that she was in no imminent physical danger.

Since Jo Ann could not reasonably anticipate that she was in danger, we must find that the trial judge erred in finding her twenty-five percent negligent. In our view, plaintiff conducted herself as a reasonable person would have under the same conditions.

Reversed and Remanded

Assumption of Risk

A second doctrine which has significant application to park, recreation, and sports injuries, is assumption of risk. This doctrine provides that a party who voluntarily assumes a risk of harm arising from another's conduct cannot recover if harm results. Only those risks created by the negligent conduct of the defendant are included in this doctrine.

The two forms of assumption of risk are expressed assumption and implied assumption. In an express assumption of risk, the plaintiff agrees in advance to waive defendant's obligations. Express assumption of risk is outlined in the Restatement (Second) of Torts §496 (b) (1965) as

> A plaintiff who by contract or otherwise expressly agrees to accept a risk of harm arising from defendant's negligence or reckless conduct cannot recover for such harm, unless the agreement is invalid as contrary to public policy.

This principle finds expression in the form of liability releases, disclaimers, or waivers. The agreement must be knowingly and voluntarily made and is usually governed by contract law principles. Courts have refused to enforce such agreements where the parties are not equal in bargaining power, where there is an overriding public policy prohibiting such releases, or where the risks are created by willful and wanton misconduct or intentional torts.

A second form of assumption of risk may be implied or inferred from the plaintiff's conduct. Three criteria must be satisfied to established implied assumptions of risks: (1) manifest consent to risk, (2) voluntary acceptance, and (3) full knowledge and appreciation of risks and dangers. Failure to meet each requirement will negate any implied assumption. Implied assumption of risk is epitomized by Restatement (Second) of Tort § 496 (c) 1965:

> A plaintiff who fully understands a risk of harm to himself or his things caused by the defendant's conduct or by the condition of the defendant's land or chattels, and who nevertheless voluntarily chooses to enter or remain, or to permit his things to enter or to remain within the area of that risk, under the circumstances that manifest his willingness to accept it, is not entitled to recover for harm within that risk.

Recreation and sports injuries cases involving implied assumption of risk usually arise under two separate circumstances. The first is when a participant or spectator voluntarily enters into a program with knowledge and acceptance of a known risk inherent in that activity. The clearest example of this occurred in the case of *Murphy* v *Steeplehouse Amusement Company, Inc.,* 250 N.Y. 479, 166 N.E. 173 (NY 1924). A young man was thrown from his feet and fractured a knee cap when he voluntarily went on an amusement ride known as the "Flopper," a moving belt upon which participants stood or sat. The belt ran upward on an inclined plane between padded walls which caused the tumbling of bodies. In denying recovery, Justice Cordoza eloquently outlined the assumption of risk rule for recovery in recreation and sports injuries cases.

> One who takes part in such a sport accepts the dangers that inhere in it so far as they are obvious and necessary, just as a fencer accepts the risk of a thrust by his antagonist or a spectator at a ballgame the chance of contact with the ball. The plaintiff was not seeking a retreat for meditation. Visitors were tumbling about the belt to the merriment of onlookers when he made his choice to join them. He took the chances of a like fate, with whatever damage his body might ensue from such a fall. The timorous may stay at home.
>
> A different case would be here if the dangers inherent in the sport were obscure or unobserved, or so serious as to justify the belief that precautions of some kind must have been taken to avert them. Nothing happened to the plaintiff except what common experience tells us may happen at any time as the consequence of a sudden fall. Many a skater or a horseman can rehearse a tale of equal woe. A different case there would also be if accidents had been so many as to show that the game in its inherent nature was too dangerous to be continued without change. . . Some quota of accidents was to be looked for in so great a mass.

Participants in recreation and sports activities assume all of the *known* and *inherent* risks in those activities so long as they are conducted according to recognized practices and the injury is not the result of an intentional or willful act. Risks not the ordinary and inherent part of an activity are not assumed by the participant or spectator. Thus in *Lee* v *National League Baseball Club,* 89 N.W.2d 811 (IL 1958), the court affirmed a judgment against a baseball club in favor of a sixty-nine year old patron who was trampled by other fans chasing a foul ball that landed two rows in front of her seat. Stating that there was an implied assumption of risk by a spectator who is hurt by batted or thrown balls at a game, the court pointed out that one who sits in an unscreened seat cannot recover from the owner if struck by a batted or thrown ball because it is a matter of common knowledge of the game. The court concluded that it was not common knowledge that spectators at baseball games who scramble for foul balls are likely to forcibly knock other patrons out of their seats with such force as to injure them. This situation is very different from one in which a spectator who buys a ticket for a seat in an unscreened section is struck by a batted ball.

A second set of circumstances giving rise to implied assumption of risk occurs when one is explicitly aware of a risk or danger caused by the potential negligence of another and yet voluntarily proceeds to encounter it. In *Rich* v *Lubbock*, 544 S.W.2d 958 (TX 1976) the plaintiff was injured when he fell to the ground and struck his shoulder on a concrete ring surrounding a water sprinkler while playing softball in a city park. Since the plaintiff had played softball in this park several times and admitted to knowing the concrete rings protected the sprinkler heads the court concluded that he voluntarily assumed the risk. A spectator or participant will not assume the risk that the owner or operator of a facility will fail to meet its duty. It is only upon discovery of the failure to meet the duty that assumption of risk may arise.

To reiterate the points of implied assumption of risk: A person only assumes those risks that are ordinary and inherent in the activity or that are discovered when not readily apparent and the individual voluntarily proceeds to encounter the risks. Risks created by intentional or willful acts, from acts outside the normal practice of the activity, by lack of skill or improper conduct of other participants or spectators, or arising from unseen third parties are not assumed by the plaintiff.

The doctrine does not enjoy universal acceptance in all jurisdictions. There appears to be a trend to abolish it as a defense, particularly in those states which have adopted comparative negligence statutes.[13] The following case examples involve aspects of *knowledge of risks*, and risks *normal* and *inherent* to the activity.

CHASE v SHASTA LAKE
UNION SCHOOL DISTRICT
California Court of Appeals
66 Cal. Rptr. 517 1968

Friedman, Associate Justice

With the consent of the school authorities an adult, evening softball league used the ball field of an elementary school. Plaintiff, playing the left field position, was pursuing a fly ball when he ran into a nearby concrete incinerator, suffering severe skull injuries. His damage action against the school district went to trial before the court sitting without a jury. The court found the school district negligent in knowingly maintaining a dangerous condition; absolved plaintiff of contributory negligence; concluded that he had assumed the risk and rendered a defense judgment, from which plaintiff appeals.

The softball field was small, the bases being forty-five feet apart as compared to sixty feet on a standard softball diamond. The boundaries of the outfield were not marked. The incinerator, a towerlike structure about ten feet tall and three feet square, stood in a grassy area in the outer reaches of center field, beyond the range of most hit balls but within range of an occasional hard hit ball. It was built of concrete, its verticle edges bound by angle irons, and stood on a concrete base about six inches high and five feet square. The edge of the base protruded two feet beyond the incinerator on each side. Although a nearby septic tank was protected by a fence, the incinerator was unfenced. Photographs demonstrate that the incinerator and its concrete base were visible from all parts of the playing area. The structure was so located that persons approaching the field would pass nearby.

The softball league had been organized by the school principal. It used the elementary school field with the consent of the district superintendent. The superintendent, the principal, teacher, and fathers of students participated in the ball games. Plaintiff had played in four games at that field before the day of his injury. His usual position was shortstop, but he had moved out to the left field position shortly before the accident. Running to his left to catch a fly ball hit over center field, he collided with the incinerator. Retrograde amnesia occurred, depriving him of memory of the accident and of his participation in the ball games preceding the accident.

Since the school district is a public entity, its liability for dangerous conditions on its property does not vary with the victim's status as an invitee or licensee. Contributory negligence and assumption of the risk are available defenses in suits involving dangerous conditions on public property. There is no inconsistency between the finding absolving plaintiff of contributory negligence and the conclusion that he had assumed the risk of injury. Assumption of the risk rests upon the victim's consent, requiring actual knowledge of danger; but contributory negligence may rest upon constructive knowledge, that is, that a reasonable man should have or could have discovered the danger by the exercise of ordinary care. Where the victim momentarily forgot a known danger, the trier of fact may find that he acted reasonably and was not contributorily negligent. In a memorandum opinion the trial judge explained the finding against contributory negligence by declaring application of the "momentary inattention" rule.

On appeal plaintiff assails the finding of the trial court which forms the basis for the conclusion that he had assumed the risk. The finding recites, "That the plaintiff did in fact see the hazard and appreciate the risk, even though he has no present recollection of doing so, or he reasonably should have seen the hazard and reasonably should have appreciated the risk."

The evidence here is close. The risks assumed by a participant in a game are usually limited to its natural and ordinary risks; if a danger, such as a defect in the premises, occurs outside the range of those inherent in the game, he assumes that danger only if he knows of it. In part, but only in part, the player's assumption of the risk depends upon the obtrusiveness of the defect; in part, upon his personal recognition of the danger it poses. To warrant the assumption defense, the evidence must show not only that the victim had general knowledge of a danger, but that he appreciated the specific risk confronting him.

In this case the incinerator was not an intrinsically dangerous defect. The specific risk was that a fast-running outfielder, intent on the ball, might blindly collide with it. Ascertainment of plaintiff's awareness of that specific risk was complicated by his retrograde amnesia. Proof of his awareness did not demand direct evidence, but could be inferred from circumstantial evidence, such as his experience and opportunity to observe.

At bat, running the bases or playing infield, an experienced ball player might be fastened with knowledge of the normal risks of the sport; might be held to anticipate spurts of intense physical striving, temporarily obliterating consciousness of all concerns except the game itself; might be familiar with the particular field and aware of the obtrusive concrete incinerator in the outer reaches of center field; yet, having no occasion to play in the incinerator's vicinity, he might form no specific awareness of the risk posed to a player who did. Plaintiff's usual position was shortstop and he had moved to the left field position at some unspecified time preceding the accident. Although both the district superintendent and the school principal had been participants in the softball game, no one had warned the players of the specific hazard the incinerator posed to the outfielders. Indeed, the district superintendent, playing center field, testified that prior to the accident he himself was aware of the incinerator but had not considered it a hazard. In short, the inference that plaintiff did not recognize and did not voluntarily assume the specific risk of colliding with the incinerator might be as appealing to a fact finder as the opposite inference.

Reversed

CASSADY v CITY OF BILLINGS
Supreme Court of Montana
340 P.2d 509 1959

Castles, Justice

This is an appeal from a judgment of nonsuit. The matter was submitted to the trial court on an agreed statement of facts which constituted the appellant's testimony, and it was stipulated that the appellant would corroborate the testimony with other evidence.

The facts are these: The appellant was thirty-six years old, married, and had three children. She lived in Billings since 1945 and had used the City of Billings Municipal Park ice skating rink, maintained, conducted, and operated by the respondent City without charge for skating, since 1945 each skating season until 1956. On January 8, 1956, appellant, accompanied by her family, went to the rink between 11:30 A.M. and noon on a bright clear day. She had her skates on when she arrived. They were figure skates with the front end on the blade curled up and notched like saw teeth. She entered the rink at one corner.

Before she started to skate, she observed the ice and it appeared rough. As soon as she started to skate, she knew the ice was rough, and it had pits in it, consisting of small depressions with a little ridge around the edge. As she and her husband skated over the ice, they noticed the roughness and pits, and skated to the far end to see if the entire rink was rough; it was. She testified that when they found the entire surface rough they figured they might as well skate all over it. They went around the rink about three times, and between five and ten minutes after starting, and while she and her husband had their four year old child suspended between them, she fell, suffering the injuries complained of.

There were no holes in the ice, it was simply a situation where the entire surface of the ice had frozen in the pitted manner; a condition the appellant observed and tested. The appellant was not exactly sure what caused her fall but thinks that her skate must have hit one of the pits. She did not know whether the saw teeth on the front of her skate caught in the ice or not; it simply stopped. At the time she had the weight of her four year old child suspended between herself and her husband, in addition to her own weight.

All of these facts are the appellant's own story. The district court granted the motion for nonsuit, relating in a memorandum that the appellant, as a matter of law under such circumstances, assumed the risk of falling on the ice, and was guilty of contributory negligence.

As to the latter charge, we recognize that there is a distinction between the two defenses and in a given case the distinction might be important. But, in the instant case it appears to us that both defenses are apparent as a matter of law. Skating on observed and tested rough ice with sawteeth edge skates certainly is a risk, and then attempting to carry, suspended between two skaters, a four year old child would be contributory negligence under the circumstances. We can see no reason to attempt to distinguish on the record before us, between the two defenses.

It is well-established in Montana that a landowner is obligated toward an invitee to either use ordinary care to have the premises reasonably safe, or to warn the invitee "of any hidden or lurking danger therein." He is not an insurer against all accidents and injuries to such persons while there.

There was no hidden or lurking danger under the circumstances herein requiring a warning. The plaintiff saw and tested the ice. The condition was open, visible, and obvious. In the face of this knowledge, beside skating, she saw fit to carry a four year old child suspended between herself and her husband. We fail to see where the respondent breached any legal duty owed the plaintiff. On this ground alone, the district court was correct in granting the nonsuit.

In addition, although this disposes of the appeal, clearly the defense of contributory negligence appears as a matter of law. The plaintiff knew or in the exercise of reasonable care for her own safety, should have known of the danger in skating on the ice as she did. It was the condition of the ice or the failure to warn of its condition that was charged as the negligent act which was alleged as the proximate cause of the injury.

We have read the many cases cited by counsel for appellants from the jurisdictions involving skating rinks. Of all the cases read, we note that the only cases which have imposed liabiity are cases where there was a hidden, lurking, structural defect, or where the defendant permitted rowdy, rambunctious, dangerous use by patrons or employees which were the proximate cause of the injuries. We have been unable to find any case, nor was one cited, which allowed recovery in the circumstances herein set forth.

Affirmed

SUNDAY v STRATTON CORPORATION
Supreme Court of Vermont
390 A.2d 398 1978

Larrow, Justice

On February 10, 1974, plaintiff, then just under twenty-one, was injured while skiing as a paying patron on the premises of the defendant's ski resort in Stratton, Vermont. His injuries resulted in permanent quadriplegia. In the instant suit, he alleges in substance that defendant negligently maintained its ski trails and failed to give notice of hidden dangers. Trial by jury, demanded by both parties, resulted in a plaintiff's verdict for $1,500,000 and judgment for that amount plus costs. The verdict was based upon a finding that defendant's negligence was 100 percent the cause of the plaintiff's injuries.

Defendant moved for a directed verdict at the end of plaintiff's case and renewed the motion at the close of all the evidence. In substance the motion was based upon its claim that recovery was precluded by the doctrine of assumption of risk asserted to have survived adoption of the comparative negligence statute and to operate as an absolute bar in the instant case.

Viewing the evidence in the light most favorable to plaintiff, he was a novice skier, skiing on a novice trail owned and maintained by the defendant. While traversing the trail at a speed equal to a fast walk, his ski became entangled in a small bush, or a clump of brush, about eight feet by twenty feet, some three to four feet in from the side limits of the travelled portion of the trail. The brush was concealed by loose snow. Unseen by him before the accident, it was seen shortly after by himself and his skiing companion.

A novice is a beginner, the lowest classification of skier, and novice trails are designed to be easy and are more carefully maintained to compensate for the lesser skills of the users. At Stratton the trail here in question (the Interstate) is the best maintained of the many trails on the mountain. Defendant uses highly sophisticated equipment and machines for this purpose. Witness after witness, employed by and testifying for the defendant, described the procedures employed, all aimed at establishing, not that the clump of brush was an inherent danger of the sport as defendant now asserts, but that it simply was not there, as the plaintiff testified. Each witness testified that no such growth had ever been observed on the Interstate.

In laying out the trail, every effort was made to achieve a "perfect surface for skiing." After cutting the trees, elaborate machines moved everything, stumps and brush included, from the trail to achieve a "complete new surface," like a "fairway, absolutely flat." The surface was then raked and fertilized and all stones over three inches were removed by hand labor. Seeding was then done with a "carpetlike" grass cover to kill other growth. Any other growth was cut by hand or mower, even tall grass, because such growth is considered a danger to the novice skier. As a last step the slope was scaled "as smooth as it can be." Single shoots, as they may occur, were regularly checked and cut, and regular rolling was carried out. The Interstate, in particular, was maintained with the best base of all trails, because it was regularly used as a road by all the company equipment, which is radio controlled. Trail cutting went to within one foot of the tree line, and the packed area was about sixteen feet wide where the plaintiff was injured. One expert witness called by the defendant testified that any brush or shrub in the skiable portion of the Interstate should have been eliminated.

At the time of the accident some fifty-two ski patrolmen were on duty, plus a trail crew charged with checking for hazards. At least seventeen pieces of heavy equipment were available for use, plus other transportation. Prior to 1974, Stratton had widely advertised its worldwide reputation for trail maintenance, "meticulous grooming" and "top quality cover."

The foregoing facts are emphasized because defendant argues that, in some manner, this case is controlled by *Wright v Mt. Mansfield Lift, Inc.,* 96 F. Supp. 786 (VT 1951). In that case the Federal District Court held that a tree stump, from cutting, covered by snow on an intermediate trail, was a part of the inherent risk of the sport of skiing, assumed by the plaintiff and therefore barring her recovery. The accident in Wright occurred in 1949.

Of course, Wright is not a binding decision on this Court. Nor do we regard it as completely significant that since its rendition it has been cited in our decisions only twice, neither time with anything like general adoption. The simple fact of the matter is that the general rule which it lays down has wide acceptance, even by the plaintiff here. But its application to particular facts is not as simple. The general principle of Wright is that a person who takes part in any sport accepts as a matter of law the dangers that inhere therein insofar as they are obvious and necessary. We are not called upon here to pass upon what dangers are inherent in an intermediate trail, as in Wright, but we could not subscribe to the theory that a stump created by the defendant in a novice trail would be such a danger. We cannot agree that such a stump would be, in the language of Wright, a "mutation of nature." Nor do we subscribe to the theory that the brush here in question is such an inherent danger, given defendant's unchallenged testimony, the basis for its whole defense, that its modern methods of care have made such a growth, within the travelled trail, impossible. Arguing to the jury its excellent grooming practices, so perfected as to render plaintiff's claim of brush in the trail impossible, may indeed present an issue as to its alleged negligence, but it does not sustain the burden of proving an assumption of the risk by the plaintiff. It is clear from the evidence that the passage of time has greatly changed the nature of the ski industry.

There is concerted effort to attract skiers and to provide novice trails suitable for their use. This is the state of the evidence in the case tried below; none of it was calculated to show the brush to be a danger inherent in the use of a novice slope as laid out and maintained by the defendant. Like many other fields, the "art" has changed vastly. Defendant admits as much by conceding in its brief that "the stump that injured the plaintiff in Wright may well be the basis for negligence today in view of improved grooming techniques." And, unlike 1949, the maintenance here is performed by the defendant itself, rather than by the communal efforts of individuals, corporations, innkeepers, and the like.

While skiers fall, as a matter of common knowledge, that does not make every fall a danger inherent in the sport. If the fall is due to no breach of duty on the part of the defendant, its risk is assumed in the primary sense, and there can be no recovery. But where the evidence indicates existence or assumption of duty and its breach, that risk is not one "assumed" by the plaintiff. What he then "assumed" is not the risk of injury, but the use of reasonable care on the part of the defendant. The motion for directed verdict was correctly denied.

Affirmed

MALTZ v BOARD OF EDUCATION
OF NEW YORK CITY
Supreme Court
114 N.Y.S.2d 856 1952

Norton, Justice

The plaintiff was injured on February 10th, 1945, while participating in a game of basketball in a gymnasium operated and controlled by the defendant at Seth Low Junior High School in this County, and this action is brought by the then infant plaintiff for damages sustained by reason of such injuries. His father also joins in this action and seeks recovery for loss of services and medical expenses.

There is no evidence that there was anything in disrepair or any defective condition of this basketball court. The court was used as a recreation community center. The plaintiff was not a student in this school and the activity in which he was participating at the time of the happening of the accident was not part of a school curriculum. He had permission to engage in basketball tournaments with other clubs. The backboard to which the "basket" was attached protruded only two feet from a brick wall in the gymnasium in which there was a door almost directly behind the backboard and basket and two feet therefrom. At the time of the happening of the accident the plaintiff was nineteen years of age and had played basketball on this court many times during a period of three or four years, during which time the basketball court was in the same condition as it was on the night of the accident. On the night in question, while running along the court at considerable speed and going up for a shot at the basket, his momentum carried him beyond the basket, causing him to hit against the jamb of the open doorway in the wall of the gymnasium two feet in the rear of the backboard and basket, with the result that he suffered the injuries claimed. Plaintiff testified that on other occasions in the past when he was going for this particular basket at this end of the court he landed in the same direction as at the time of the accident; sometimes he would go right through the door without hitting anything. In the course of a game he had come in contact with the wall before. He further testified that he did not have to go to this gymnasium if he did not want to.

It is the contention of the defendant that in the circumstances disclosed by the evidence in this case the plaintiff assumed the risks of danger inherent in the playing of a game of basketball on this court under the conditions existing at the time of the happening of the accident and for some time prior thereto, and that he knew of the conditions existing and also had a knowledge and appreciation of the danger produced by such condition.

"Assumption of risk . . . consists in the actual doing of the deed with foresight of the consequences. The essential requisite to invocation of the application of the doctrine of assumption of risks embraces not only a knowledge of the physical defect but includes also an appreciation of the danger produced by the physical condition. "(A person) may have known that there was a defect, but it does not follow that he knew the danger. It is not 'the obviousness of the physical situation or condition' which makes out a defense; it is 'the obviousness of the dangers which the physical condition or situation produces.' "

The plaintiff was no infant. He was a boy nineteen years of age, who had played basketball on this court many times prior to the accident. The risk of the court and the door being open and the wall being near the end of the basketball court were risks that were obvious and necessary to the sport as played on this particular court. His prior experience made him aware of the very hazards and dangers of which he now complains. He was not only aware of these dangers but had experienced them before, and he voluntarily assumed them. He not only knew of the existing conditions but had or should have had an appreciation of the danger produced by the physical conditions existing.

I therefore find as a fact that the plaintiff assumed the risks of engaging in the basketball game herein under the conditions existing which were known to him, and that he had or should have had knowledge and an apprehension of the danger involved. I direct judgment in favor of the defendant dismissing the complaint.

Judgment for Defendant

Governmental Immunity

"The king can do no wrong." This medieval law evolved in American jurisprudence as the doctrine of governmental immunity. The doctrine operates as a bar to state and local government liability for the negligent acts or omissions of its employees while engaged in the performance of governmental functions. Historians generally trace the genesis of the doctrine to *Russell v Men of Devon*, 100 Eng. Rep. 359 (1788). In this English case, a citizen of the town sued the Men of Devon, seeking compensation for the injury of his horse which fell through the village bridge. The court denied recovery on three grounds: the lack of a corporate fund, the absence of legislative intent to impose liability, and the need to avoid a trend for lawsuits and the inconvenience and cost to the public. American courts adopted this English precedent, rationalizing that states were sovereigns and could not be sued without their consent. This protective arm was extended to encircle not only the state but also counties, cities, school districts, and special purpose districts. The logic of the doctrine has been exceeded by a judicial history of dissatisfaction.

Initially all units of government enjoyed absolute immunity; however, courts began fabricating exceptions to the doctrine. In *Bailey* v *Mayor of New York*, 15 N.Y. 674 (NY 1842), the court created a governmental-proprietary classification, distinguishing a municipality's public (governmental) function from its private (proprietary) function. Activities classified as governmental retained the immunity protection but those labeled proprietary were no longer cloaked with immunity. Although there is no universal rule, police, fire, and education are generally accepted as governmental in nature while the proprietary functions are those that could be provided by the private sector, e.g., gas, electric, water, and garbage service. For a few years, it was a relatively simple task to ascertain which activities of a municipality were governmental and which were proprietary. As the services and complexity of local government increased, the dividing line between these two distinctions became fuzzy. The U.S. Supreme Court recognized this in *Trenton* v *State of New Jersey*, 262 U.S. 182 (1922).

> The basis of distinction is difficult to state, and there is no established rule for the determination of what belongs to one or the other class. It originated with the courts. Generally it is applied to escape difficulties, in order that injustice may not result from the recognition of technical defenses. . . .

Because Massachusetts was the first to hold that parks and recreation services were governmental, this view is sometimes called the Massachusetts rule. States adhering to the view that parks and recreation are a proprietary function are sometimes said to hold the New York view.[14] It would seem to be a simple task to determine in a state whether an activity such as parks and recreation is proprietary or governmental. This has not been the case. For example, in Texas the cases illustrate the difficulty the courts have in following this governmental-proprietary dichotomy. Maintaining a public park has been held at different times to be both a governmental and a proprietary function. Maintaining a public park was held to be governmental in *Vanderford* v *Houston*, 286 S.W. 568 (TX 1926) and held to be proprietary in *Waco* v *Branch*, 5 S.W.2d 498 (TX 1928).

In some states monetary consideration and profit motive is a significant factor in classifying the service. When a user fee is charged for a park and recreation service, there is a tendency to find the service to be proprietary. However, the imposition of a user fee does not make this automatic. A user fee that provides a profit creates a stronger tendency for finding the service to be proprietary and a profit coupled with an agency's profit policy creates a near certainty that service is proprietary.

To bury governmental immunity is a notable achievement, but to keep it interred is quite another problem. It has not been unusual for courts to abolish the doctrine, only to have the legislature revive it. When the California Supreme Court abolished governmental immunity the legislature enacted a two year moratorium on its effect, calling for a study of the immunity issue. The study resulted in a state tort claims statute.

Despite this judicial vs. legislative sparring over the doctrine of governmental immunity, the positive judicial prodding has resulted in legislative action to clarify the problem in many states. Changes have taken two directions

1. General immunity statutes, but with exceptions designated, for premises and road defects, negligent operation of motor vehicles and governmental-proprietary or discretionary-ministerial tests, or
2. General liability statutes, but with exceptions specified for discretionary duties.

The statutes usually authorize units of government to purchase liability insurance, provide for indemnification of employees and allow notice of claim conditions to be attached in municipal charters. In addition, many states place monetary limits on the amount of money parties could recover from governmental entities. Schools have been singled out for individual treatment in many states with general immunity given for education functions.

While the preceding presents a generalization, one must be careful to examine statutes and court decisions to determine the applicable rules in each jurisdiction. (See Appendix for the status of the states on immunity.) Generally, total reliance on governmental immunity by public park and recreation agencies would be ill advised.

Statute of Limitations

At common law, the time period fixed for the commencement of tort suits was limited by the duration of the life of either party. By legislation, the common law has been modified and definite time limitations have been placed on the commencement of legal actions. These time limits are found in statutes of limitations. A statute of limitations has been defined as "the action of the state in determining that after a lapse of a specified time a claim shall not be enforceable in judicial proceedings."[16] Statutes of limitations are justified as a pragmatic way to spare the courts from litigating stale claims, to suppress the assertion of fraudulent claims and to compel the settlement of claims within a reasonable period while the evidence remains fresh in the memory of witnesses.

Limitation periods vary for contract and tort actions. In most states a two year time period is listed for negligence actions. A number of states also place reduced time periods for certain activities, such as a one year statute of limitations for skiing. Vermont is a state that has imposed this condition.[17]

Notice of Claim

Many state statutes and municipal ordinances require that a person file a notice of claim within a certain number of days after the injury. These notice of claim periods range from thirty to 120 days. This practice is justified on the basis that it allows the agency time to investigate and settle meritorious claims without the expense of litigation. In the absence of a statutory provision, notice of the accident need not be given the agency before suit is brought to recover damages. Notice of claim provisions generally require that the notice must be in writing and be filed with certain city officials within a specified time from date of the injury. The notice must state the place, time, and date of the injury, the character and circumstances of the injury and that the injured person claims damages from the unit of government.[18]

There is a split of authority on whether the failure to give this notice precludes recovery. It has often been stated that such notice requirements should be liberally construed, but the majority rule seems to favor strict construction against the governmental unit and liberal construction if favor of the citizen. The bulk of litigation however involves the sufficiency of notice and exceptions to strict compliance. If compliance with the requirement is temporarily impossible because the claimant is mentally or physically incapacitated or is a minor, failure to comply cannot serve as a defense to the public agency. These notice provisions are applicable only to units of government and do not apply to the private sector.

Failure of Proof

Legal liability for negligence requires more than establishing a failure to conform to a standard of conduct. As described in this legal chapter, liability for negligence requires the existence of a legal duty, that reasonable care was not followed in the performance of the duty and that the failure to use reasonable care was the cause of the injury. Since the plaintiff has the burden of proof, any failure on the part of the plaintiff to allege and prove every element in the cause of action jeopardizes a victory. In this sense a failure of proof is a defense to the party sued and can be raised at the pleadings stage or at the trial. If the plaintiff does not meet the burden of proof, the lawsuit will be dismissed.

Liability Release

It is a common practice of park, recreation, and sports enterprises to require that participants agree in writing to assume all risks and release the agency from liability. In common parlance, these releases are often called waivers, liability permission slips, or consent forms. In legal terminology, a release is a voluntary relinquishment of a claim, right or privilege by a person to someone against whom it might be enforced.[19] It is a voluntary action to forego a claim or an action for damages.

Liability releases have been reviewed by many courts with varying results for the sponsors and participant. The difficulty created by the use of such agreements is between the contract law tenant of freedom of parties to contract and the negligence law principle that "one is responsible for negligent acts which cause injury to others." Further complicating matters of principles of law concerning duties and responsibilities of public recreation agencies. Generally, courts will uphold agreements exempting a person or agency from liability for negligence if it is clear from the language of the contract that the parties' intent was to shift the risk of loss.[20] Public park and recreation and school sports programs are an exception to this rule. Releases used by public agencies are invalid when

1. Contrary to public policy,
2. Ambiguities in the agreement make it difficult to determine extent of rights waived, and
3. Minors or their parents sign the release.

Due to the one-sided nature of liability release courts carefully scrutinize them.

Public policy   This exception is frequently cited by the courts when invalidating a release. It is difficult to precisely define public policy. As stated by one court

> the public policy of a state is to be found in its constitution and its statutes, and when cases arise concerning matters upon which they are silent then its judicial decisions.[21]

Since few states have constitutional or statutory mandates concerning recreation agencies, one must look to court cases for guidance. A determining factor in the public policy exception is the sponsorship of the program. The majority of courts hold that agencies providing public services cannot contract away their liability to their clients. *Gore* v *TriCounty Raceway, Inc.,* 407 F.Supp. 489 (AL 1974). On the other hand, private enterprises can enter into such contracts and these will generally be sustained by courts. This rule is illustrated in *Owen* v *Vic Tanney's Enterprises,* 199 N.E.2d 280 (IL 1964), cited later. In a similar case, involving a fall on a slippery pool deck in a Vic Tanney gym, the court also upheld the release on similar grounds.[22] After that case, New York state enacted a statute declaring void as against public policy releases in contracts and tickets of admission for any "pool, gym, place of amusement, or recreation."[23]

Language ambiguity   A release found not to violate public policy is subject to invalidation if it contains ambiguous language or does not extend coverage to the actual accident. An illustration is *Rosen v LTV Recreational Development, Inc.,* 569 F.2d 1117 (1978), where a skier was injured when he collided with a metal pole set in concrete near a ski run. The skier had purchased a season ski pass at the resort which included a specific waiver, reading in part

> I understand that skiing is a hazardous sport and that hazardous obstructions, some marked and some unmarked, exist in any ski area. I accept the existence of such dangers and that injuries may result from the numerous falls and collisions which are common in the sport of skiing, including the chance of injury resulting from the negligence and carelessness on the part of fellow skiers.

In deciding that the ski pass waiver was ambiguous the court ruled that the waiver was so one-sided that doubts arose as to its representation as a voluntary and uncoerced agreement. The court, determined that the exculpatory language did not waive injuries resulting from the negligence of the ski resort but only from the negligence of fellow skiers. Mere acknowledgment of the existence of such hazards and even acceptance of such dangers does not constitute a waiver of negligence exonerating the ski resort from negligence.

Minors and releases   A release signed by a minor child or by a parent on behalf of the child provides another basis for court invalidation. In the Massachusetts case of *Del Santo, Jr. v Bristol County Stadium, Inc.,* 273 F.2d 605 (MA 1960) the court held that a minor can disaffirm a contract or release as long as it is done during his or her minority or within a reasonable time after reaching majority. The court stated that "any acts or words showing unequivocally a repudiation of the contract are sufficient to avoid it." A further problem exists when a parent or guardian signs a waiver on behalf of a child. It is generally accepted that a parent can surrender his or her future tort claim, however, they may not surrender the independent claim of a minor child.[24]

Given their tenuous status, liability releases still have certain values. If carefully drafted and used in conjunction with risk management programs liability releases can

1. Discourage an injured party from filing a lawsuit, and
2. Enhance the defense of assumption of risk by increasing participant awareness of program risks, rigors, and hazards.

Many people have the mistaken belief after signing a release that they cannot sue the agency because they have given up this right. This belief can further be reinforced if the release has all the appearances of a legal document.

A second and equally important reason for use of release is the enhancement of other possible legal defenses, such as *assumption of risk*. Releases that inform the participant of known program risks preclude the participant from claiming lack of knowledge about program hazards. For example, if a release lists some of the hazards of overnight backpacking including freezing temperatures and the participant fails to heed the warning thereby suffering frostbite, the agency may claim that the participant was informed of the risk and assumed it.

OWENS v VIC TANNEY'S ENTERPRISES
Illinois Appellate Court
199 N.E.2d 280 1964

Murphy, Justice

This is a personal injury action in which plaintiff, a member of defendant's gymnasium, sues to recover for injuries received while on defendant's premises. The answer relied on an exculpatory clause in the membership contract. A $2,000 verdict and judgment for plaintiff resulted. Defendant appeals from the denial of its motion and for a judgment notwithstanding the verdict.

The facts are not in dispute. At the time of the occurrence, the defendant corporation was engaged in the business of providing gymnastic facilities for its members. On February 11, 1961, plaintiff used the facilities offered under the membership contract and slipped and fell as she left the defendant's swimming pool, suffering an injury to her right wrist. At the trial, plaintiff testified, "The floor was wet . . . some kind of stone floor, what they have in any shower room floor. . . It just didn't have the roughness to it as the rest of the floor had." An employee of defendant testified that the "smooth spot" had been there for a period of time, and she "reported it to the management. . . The management did nothing about it."

The determinative question is whether, under such circumstances, the exculpatory clause is a complete defense. It reads as follows:

"Member, in attending said gymnasiums and using the facilities and equipment therein, does so at his own risk. Tanney shall not be liable for any damages arising from personal injuries sustained by Member in, on or about the premises of any of the said gymnasiums. Member assumes full responsibility for any injuries or damages which may occur to Member in, on or about the premises of said gymnasiums and he does hereby fully and forever release and discharge Tanney and all associated gymnasiums, their owners, employees and agents from any and all claims, demands, damages, rights of action, or causes of action, present or future, whether the same be known, anticipated or unanticipated, resulting from or arising out of the Member's use or intended use of the said gymnasium or the facilities and equipment thereof."

In Illinois, clauses that exculpate the landlord from the consequences of his negligence were sustained in residential as well as commercial leases in the absence of a statute voiding them. We believe the pronouncements in those cases, made in sustaining exculpatory clauses, apply here. Although the Illinois legislature enacted a statute that such clauses in leases "shall be deemed to be void as against public policy and wholly unenforceable," we are not persuaded, as plaintiff argues, that the legislature intended to extend the provisions of the Act to any other type of contract. If exculpatory clauses in contracts for gymnastics and reducing activities were intended to be "deemed to be void as against public policy," the legislature would have so provided.

Plaintiff's principal contention is that an exculpatory clause will be strictly construed against the party whom it favors, and other terms of the instrument may be considered in weighing the parties' intent with regard to the clause. We agree with this statement. The rule of construction to be applied here is that "an agreement protecting one from the consequences of his own negligence must be in clear and explicit language or expressed in unequivocal terms." We find no merit in plaintiff's contention that the clause refers only to injuries arising from the use of the facilities which are not, in themselves, necessarily defective, or that it is not applicable where a portion of the building is defective. The mishap occurred in the shower room adjacent to the swimming pool, which we believe is within the provisions of the clause relating to "on or about the premises of said gymnasium" and "resulting from or arising out of the Member's use of intended use of the said gymnasium or the facilities and equipment thereof."

The New York case of *Ciofalo* v *Vic Tanney Gyms, Inc.,* 177 N.E.2d 925 (NY 1961), is factually similar. The plaintiff fell at or near the edge of the swimming pool on defendant's premises and claimed that the fall was due to excessive slipperiness and lack of sufficient personnel. Defendant set forth the contract as an affirmative defense. The trial court granted a summary judgment for defendant and, in affirming the Court of Appeals, said:

"The wording of the contract in the instant case expresses as clearly as language can the intention of the parties to completely insulate the defendant from liability for injuries sustained by plaintiff by reason of defendant's own negligence, and, in the face of the allegation of the complaint charging merely ordinary negligence, such agreement is valid.

"Here there is no special legal relationship and no overriding public interest which demand that this contract provision, voluntarily entered into by competent parties, should be rendered ineffectual. Defendant, a private corporation, was under no obligation or legal duty to accept plaintiff as a 'member' or patron. Having consented to do so, it had the right to insist upon such terms as it deemed appropriate. Plaintiff, on the other hand, was not required to assent to unacceptable terms, or to give up a valuable legal right. . . ."

We believe the foregoing pronouncements in *Ciofalo v Vic Tanney Gyms, Inc.,* apply here. The scarcity of facilities for gymnastic and reducing activities hardly creates such a disparity of bargaining power that plaintiff is forced to accept such terms without alternatives. If the public interest is involved, it is for the legislature to make such pronouncements. Absent appropriate legislative action, we must hold that the instant exculpatory clause barred plaintiff's suit, and the court erred in not directing a verdict for the defendant and in denying defendant's motion for a judgment notwithstanding the verdict.

Reversed

SUMMARY

The concept of negligence is deeply ingrained in tort liability. Allegations of negligence form the basis for most user injury lawsuits against park, recreation, and sports agencies, professionals, and staff. The key to the negligence liability is the failure of the agency or staff to protect the user from unreasonable risks of harm. To recover compensation for an injury the plaintiff must prove the four elements of negligence.

1. A legal obligation (duty) requiring conduct so as to protect users against unreasonable risks.
2. A failure to conform to the legal duty.
3. A causal connection between the failure to conform to the legal duty and the injury.
4. Actual loss or damage as a result of the injury.

If the plaintiff fails to prove each of these four elements the defendant will not be liable for injuries sustained. While the burden of proof rests with plaintiff the existence of negligence and the amount of compensable damage arising therefrom are questions to be decided by the courts.

In view of the potential exposure of park, recreation, and sports agencies, professionals, and staff to tort liability, it is important that they are aware of some of the elements involved in the cases to help minimize negligence lawsuits. It must be recognized that the law relating to negligence is complicated, consequently only the key elements have been discussed.

A legal duty of care to users arises when the park, recreation, and sport agency invites participation in their programs. To meet this legal duty the agency and its employees must use that degree of care which a reasonable and prudent person, charged with like duties would exercise under the circumstances to prevent unreasonable risks of harm. While the standard of care is rigid it may be elastic in its application depending upon the user and the facts and circumstances in each case. For example, the standard of care which is adequate in dealing with adults generally will not be adequate when dealing with young children. The law recognizes that children do not possess the same degree of foresight, caution, knowledge, and mental maturity as adults and that children may not be judged according to the standard of care required for adults.

In judging whether agencies used the degree of care required, the inquiry often focuses on "what a reasonable person" would have done under the circumstances. The actions of this hypothetical reasonable person are established by the testimony of experts in the field. This is illustrated by *Nabozny* v *Barnhill,* whereby the experts testified on the standard of care required of soccer players once the goalie has possession of the ball in the penalty area.

It should not be inferred, however, that someone is liable for all injuries sustained by users. A park, recreation, and sport agency is not the insurer of the safety of users but owes them only the duty of reasonable care. It behoves the employee to understand and conform to this standard of care for their own protection and for that of the agency.

The best defense against an allegation of negligence is to prove that one of the four elements required for negligence is not present. Beyond the absence of negligence the law recognizes a number of other defenses to negligence liability. These include the big three, consisting of contributory and comparative negligence, assumption of risk, and governmental immunity and the lesser known defenses of notice of claim, statute of limitations, and waiver of liability. The big three are so noted because they are most often raised in negligence lawsuits.

Contributory negligence is the failure of the plaintiff to act as a reasonable and prudent person to prevent unreasonable risks of harm. It is based on the premises that persons are responsible for their misconduct when it is a factor in their injury. By operation of the doctrine, if a plaintiff is 10 percent at fault and the defendant 90 percent at fault, the defendant is not liable. This rule has been so criticized for its harshness and inflexibility in apportioning fault that it has resulted in the adoption of the comparative negligence rule in most states (only the states of Alabama, Arizona, Delaware, Indiana, Kentucky, Missouri, North Carolina, Tennessee, and Virginia still follow contributory negligence). *Harrison* v *Montgomery Co. Bd. of Education,* 456 A.2d 894, 901 (MD 1983). The comparative negligence rule follows the contributory negligence concept but differs in that the fault can be apportioned between the plaintiff and defendant. Thus if a plaintiff is seeking $100,000 in damages and the court determines the plaintiff was 25 percent at fault, the damages award is $75,000.

If a person is cognizant of a risk or hazard and voluntarily continues with an activity and is thereby injured it is presumed that the person assumed the risk of harm. This is the basis for the doctrine of assumption of risk. Several criteria must be satisfied before the doctrine operates as a defense. The danger must be known and obvious to the plaintiff and of the type inherent in the facility or program. Extraordinary risks, not normally associated with the activity, are not assumed. In addition to the knowledge criteria the plaintiff must voluntarily agree to take the risk. Forced or coerced participation is not voluntary, thus there is no assumption of risk. When all criteria are met this doctrine is a valid defense and there is no apportionment of damages. It is therefore incumbent on an agency and its staff to make all users aware of all possible risks and dangers. The more knowledgable the user the greater the risk assumed.

The judicially created doctrine of governmental immunity, protecting public agencies from liability for the torts of their employees, has been supplanted by state tort claim statutes. Nevertheless, it is still an issue in park, recreation, and sports injury lawsuits, but most litigation focuses on the application of the statutes or upon judicially created exceptions. It is safe to say that the blanket of immunity enjoyed by these agencies is history. Because the pattern of protection is so varied among the states the reader is referred to a local attorney to determine application in a particular state.

Of the lesser known defenses perhaps the most significant to agencies and their staffs is the liability waiver or release. Among other things these forms attempt to absolve the program sponsor and its staff from liability associated with user injuries. As a general proposition, these documents can be upheld as a valid defense when the sponsor is a private agency. Liability waivers and releases are not valid to protect the public sponsor for various reasons.

Perhaps the best advice for park, recreation, and sports professionals to minimize negligence lawsuits is to avoid actions that subject users to unreasonable risks of harm. Acting as a reasonable and prudent professional by complying with the accepted standards and practices is positive proof that the standard of care required by the law is satisfied.

DISCUSSION QUESTIONS

1. What must a person prove in order to recover damages for an injury that occurred in a recreation program?

2. What are the characteristics of the reasonable and prudent man described

in negligence law and how does the plaintiff establish that the defendant failed to act as this hypothetical figure?

3.   Distinguish a legal duty from a moral duty. Is there a liability for breaching either duty?

4.   How is a legal duty of care established between the recreation and sports agency and participant?

5.   Many doctrines are recognized as defenses to negligence claims. What are the distinctions between contributory and comparative negligence? How does this difference affect the recreation and sports enterprise?

6.   In injury cases involving children the failure of a parent to supervise the child is often alleged to be a reason for the injury. Under what circumstances may parents be contributorily negligent for an injury to their child so that they will be barred from recovery?

7.   Do "liability waivers" protect the sponsor and employee from liability for user injuries? If they do not why should they be used?

8.   If an employee is negligent in the supervision of a program will the agency be responsible? Why or why not?

9.   What risks of injury does a participant assume in a recreation program or an athletic contest? What risks are assumed at these events?

NOTES

[1]Restatement (Second) of Torts §282.
[2]WILLIAM PROSSER, *Law of Torts,* 4th ed. (St. Paul: West Publishing Co., 1971). p. 143.
[3]*Elbert v Saginaw,* 109 N.W.2d 879 (MI).
[4]PROSSER, *Torts,* p. 326.
[5]SEAVEY, *Negligence—Subjective and Objective.* 41 Harv. L. Rev. 1 (1927), pp. 5–7.
[6]A. P. HERBERT, *Misleading Cases in the Common Law* (New York: G.P. Putnam's Sons, 1930), pp. 12–16.
[7]Restatement (Second) of Torts, §283A.
[8]PROSSER, *Torts,* p. 236 citing 24 separate law review articles.
[9]Restatement (Second) of Torts §924 (1965).
[10]PROSSER, *Torts,* p. 182.
[11]Restatement (Second) of Torts §500.
[12]PROSSER, *Torts,* p. 454.
[14]BETTY VAN DER SMISSEN, *Legal Liability of Cities and Schools for Injuries in Recreation and Parks* (Cincinnati: W.H. Anderson Co., 1968), p. 7.
[15]See 33 A.L.R.3d 703, 35 A.L.R.3d 725, 36 A.L.R.3d 361, 37 A.L.R.3d 738 for a discussion.
[16]*South Dakota v North Carolina,* 192 U.S. 286.
[17]Vermont, 12. V.S.A. §513.
[18]McQuillin Mun. Corp., 3rd ed. §53.
[19]66 Am. Jur. 2d, Releases §1.
[20]*Morrow v Auto Championship Racing Assoc., Inc.,* 291 N.E.2d 30. (IL 1972), *Lee v Allied Sports Assoc.,* 209 N.E.2d 329. (MA 1965).
[21]*Schnackenberg v Towle,* 123 N.E.2d 817 (1954).
[22]*Ciofalo v Vic Tanney Gyms,* 177 N.E.2d 925 (NY 1961).
[23]N.Y. General Objections Law, §5–326.
[24]*Fedor v Mauwehu Council of Boy Scouts,* 143 A.2d 466 (MA 1958).

six

liability
of recreation
and sports facility
owners

The American land ownership ethic is so strong that preferential liability rules favoring a landowner have been established. Recent judicial attempts to abolish these special rules and establish a single standard of care have met with limited success. This chapter outlines the standard of care that owners and operators of recreation and sports facilities generally owe to their users.

STANDARD OF CARE

In dealing with user injuries caused by conditions in recreation and sports facilities, courts have extended by case and statutory law special rules to public and private enterprises. The legal duty owed to visitors by landowners is generally determined by the status of the visitors. Visitors are divided into three fixed classes of *invitee, licensee,* or *trespasser.* Basically, an invitee receives the most protection, a licensee moderate protection, and a trespasser minimal legal protection. A great deal of confusion and controversy has surrounded the classification of visitors, especially between invitees and licensees. The term *invitee* can be confusing unless it is noted that not all persons who come into the premises at the possessor's invitation are invitees. The following sections outline the definitions of users and summarize the legal duty of care that recreation and sports enterprises owe to visitors who use their facilities.

Invitees

At one time only the business customer was classified as an invitee. Invitees were patrons of restaurants, stores, banks, theaters, bathing beaches, fairs, and other places of amusement and business open to the public. To this business invitation test has been added a public invitation test. As outlined in the Restatement (Second) of Tort §332

1. An invitee is either a public invitee or a business visitor.
2. A public invitee is a person who is invited to enter or remain on land as a member of the public for a purpose for which the land is held open to the public.
3. A business visitor is a person who is invited to enter or remain on land for a purpose directly or indirectly connected with business dealings with the possessor of the land.

When a public or private enterprise invites the public into a park or to use a recreation facility, the visitors accepting such invitations are invitees. An invitee's status, however, may be limited by time and location. The position taken in the Restatement (Second) of Torts is that the invitation extends only to those uses "for which the land, park, or recreation facility was established." For example, bathers using a swimming pool during open hours are invitees, but if their use is beyond that open time period they may become trespassers. Correspondingly, the pool use may be restricted to selected areas, and a patron entering a filter equipment room may be classified as a trespasser to that area. If a patron is injured in that restricted area the duty of the pool owner may be reduced.

A landowner owes the highest duty of care to invitees and must act as a reasonable and prudent operator to make the premises reasonably safe for invitees. Translated into management practices, the landowner has a duty to

1. Keep the premises in safe repair,
2. Inspect the premises to discover hidden hazards,
3. Remove the hazards or warn of their presence,
4. Anticipate foreseeable uses and activities by invitees and take reasonable precautions to protect the invitee from foreseeable dangers, and
5. Conduct operations on the premises with reasonable care for the safety of the invitee.

When a hidden hazard is discovered and cannot be reasonably reduced or eliminated, the possessor must use reasonable care to warn invitees of the danger. A frequently litigated question concerns the adequacy of warnings given to the user. Depending on the facts and circumstances, a warning sign in one case may not be adequate in another. For example, a "No Swimming" sign written in English and posted in an area used by non-English speaking users is not an adequate warning. Many of the case examples used in the remaining chapters of this book concern *inter alia,* the adequacy of warnings. It must be noted, however, that the landowner or facility operator is not the guarantor of an invitee's safety and the law imposes a burden on the user to avoid known and obvious dangers.

Another interesting question which frequently arises is the extent of the owner's duty to a business invitee to protect against criminal violence by third persons on the premises. The authorities are divided on this issue. Some courts have held there is no duty to accede to criminal demands even at the risk of harm to an invitee. In other cases the possessor's negligence has been held a question of fact for the jury.[1] In some cases, hotels have been held liable for the criminal acts of third persons against guests, while in others there has been no liability.[2]

The following cases illustrate some of the problems courts have faced in resolving issues associated with the "invitee" status of users. In the *Phillips* case the status of the user was in issue, in *Nunez* the degree of danger posed by a facility, and in *Zaepfel* the adequacy of warning.

PHILLIPS v UNITED STATES
United States Court of Appeals
590 F.2d 297 1979

Per Curiam

Phillips appeals from a summary judgment granted against him in his action, under the Federal Tort Claims Act (28 U.S.C. 2671 et seq.), to recover damages for serious personal injuries that he sustained when he fell seventy feet to the base of San Antonio Falls while hiking in Angeles National Forest. The district court held that California Civil Code 846, immunizing real property owners from liability for injuries to persons who permissively use property for recreational purposes, precluded the Government's liability to Phillips. The question on appeal is whether there was a triable issue of fact presented by Phillips' claim that he was an "express invitee" within an exception to Civil Code 846 immunity. We agree with the district court that Phillips was not an express invitee within the meaning of the exception.

This tragic accident occurred on October 13, 1971, when Phillips and a friend were hiking up the side of the San Antonio Falls. The falls are in the Mt. Baldy recreation area of Angeles National Forest. Sometime before the date of the accident, a sign warning of the danger of climbing in the falls had been destroyed by vandals, and no warning sign appeared in the San Antonio Falls area when Phillips was injured. He claimed that the United States was negligent in failing to give warning of the known hazardous conditions near the falls and that the Government's negligence proximately caused his injury.

Discovery had been completed before the Government moved for summary judgment. The only factual basis upon which Phillips based his claim that he was within an exception to the immunity statute is that promotional literature from the Forest Service, describing the attractions of Angeles National Forest and its facilities, constituted an "express invitation" within the meaning of exemption (c) of section 846 of the California Civil Code, which provides that landowners owe no duty of care to persons who permissively use the property for recreational purposes, including hiking, but it "does not limit the liability which otherwise exists . . . (c) to any persons who are expressly invited rather than merely permitted to come upon the premises by the landowner." The precise issue is a question of law: Does promotional literature published by the Forest Service constitute an "express invitation" to the general public to hike in the advertised national park?

The purpose of section 846 was to encourage landowners to let members of the general public use their land for recreational purposes. That purpose could not be achieved without sharply restricting potential liability to landowners for injuries that might be sustained by persons who were given permission to use the land for recreation. To accomplish that purpose, the Legislature eliminated the common law concepts of invitee and licensee as to landowners who gave permission to members of the general public to use the land for recreational purposes. In ordinary parlance, an advertisement to the general public is not considered an "express invitation" to each member of the public to whom the message is beamed. Nothing in the sparse legislative history of Civil Code 846 suggests that a more encompassing reading of the term "expressly invited" was intended. To the contrary, the little history available indicates that the Legislature intended the term "expressly invited" to include only those persons who were personally selected by the landowner. That intent can be gleaned from an explanation of the legislation when the statute was initially enacted in 1963. In 38 State Bar Journal 647 (1963), the history of the section was briefly discussed: "As originally drafted, the section would have exempted the landowner from all liability to a person expressly invited on the premises. However, under section 846 as enacted, if a person has been expressly invited the landowner will owe the same duty of care owed a licensee or invitee, depending on the person's legal status. . . In order to vitiate any claim by a 'permittee' that he has been expressly invited or has paid consideration the landowner can now record a notice of consent to the use of his land for specified purposes under new Civil Code 813."

The record shows that no personal invitation was ever issued to Phillips. We do not reach the question whether promotional literature mailed to a person who thereafter visits the advertised park can be an express invitation within the meaning of section 846. The advertisements were never sent to Phillips, and there is no evidence that he had even seen the advertisements before this accident. Under these circumstances, we conclude that the brochures and other promotional literature published by the Forest Service did not constitute an express invitation to Phillips within the meaning of section (c) of section 846.

Affirmed

NUNEZ v ISIDORE NEWMAN HIGH SCHOOL
Court of Appeals of Louisiana
306 So.2d 457 1975

Boutall, Judge

This is an appeal from a judgment of the lower court dismissing plaintiff's suit for personal injuries to his minor son.

The facts are these: Plaintiff's son was a senior basketball player for St. Bernard High School. St. Bernard had been invited to participate in the Isidore Newman School Invitational Tournament, an event held annually at the Newman gym around Christmas time. Admission is charged the spectators at the tournament and these revenues go entirely to Newman School. On December 20, 1968, St. Bernard was scheduled to play Country Day for third place in the tournament.

The weather conditions on the day of the game were very unseasonal for a December evening. It was hot, very humid and had rained earlier in the day. Due to the high humidity water had condensed on the floor of the Newman gym. Prior to the start of the game porters from the Newman School had mopped the floor and someone had turned on the fans and heaters in an attempt to dry the floor.

The game was started on time and continued normally, except for the fact that several times Newman porters mopped some areas of condensation on and off the playing surface. At some point in the third quarter of the game plaintiff's son, Martin Nunez III, jumped in the air attempting a lay-up shot and upon coming down he slipped and fell, seriously injuring his back. This suit was brought to recover for these injuries.

The record in this case is voluminous, in all nineteen witnesses were called to testify. The record reveals contradictory testimony on the one essential point in controversy—the condition of the floor during the St. Bernard–Country Day game.

Plaintiff's witnesses basically testified that the floor was wet and slippery as early as the warm-up period before the game and this wet condition worsened as the game progressed. This position is strengthened by the fact that the second game to be played that night was called off because of moisture on the floor. Plaintiff's witnesses fall into two classes; basketball players for St. Bernard High School and spectators at the game, comprised of Nunez's relatives, teachers, and coaches.

Defendant's witnesses testified that the floor was in a playable condition throughout the game and that only late in the forth quarter did any water begin to seriously accumulate. This accumulation of water was not on the playing court itself but off the court by an entrance to the gym. Defendant's witnesses also fall into two classes: the game referees and Newman personnel, the principal, and the athletic director.

Plaintiff contends that Martin Nunez III was a business invitee of Newman, since Newman was deriving revenue from his participation and presence at the gym that night. The defendant does not seriously contest this assertion and we agree with plaintiff's view of Nunez's status.

Plaintiff further maintains that as a business invitee Nunez is owed a certain duty by Newman and that Newman has breached that duty. A fair statement of that duty is: An owner or occupier of lands or buildings must take reasonable and ordinary care to protect invitees from any dangerous conditions on the premises. He must also warn them of any latent dangerous defects in the premises and inspect the premises for any possible dangerous conditions of which he does not know. This statement of the duty Newman owed presupposes one important fact which the trial court must have found to be lacking—the condition must actually be "dangerous." Unless a condition of the building can be termed dangerous then this duty owed to invitees will never arise; to hold otherwise would mean that the building owner was the insurer of his patron's safety.

The testimony of the witnesses actually on the floor and moving about is clearly contradictory. Nunez and the other St. Bernard basketball players claim the floor was wet and slippery throughout the game. Most claim to have complained to their coach and even to the referees, about this condition. The referees claim the floor was "definitely playable," that they had no trouble with their footing and no one brought the floor conditions to their attention until the second game was about to start.

Newman has the duty to employ reasonable care in discovering defects on its premises. This duty generally cannot be delegated to others, however, we are compelled to consider all the circumstances of the case in determining if Newman acted reasonably.

Present at the gym that night were the two game referees and the two coaches of the teams playing. These four men were men of great experience in high school athletics and each had some authority over the game and players. Mr. Frank Spruiell, the Commissioner of the Louisiana High

School Athletic Association and Mr. Charles Meyers, Assignment Secretary for the Greater New Orleans Basketball Association, each testified that the referees have complete control of a basketball game from thirty minutes before a game starts until the final score is recorded in the scorebook. The referees are also responsible for inspecting and approving the playing conditions. The coaches of the teams have, of course, authority over the players' actions and a corresponding obligation to look out for their welfare. We hold that the gym floor was not a dangerous condition.

Affirmed

ZAEPFEL v CITY OF YONKERS
Supreme Court, Appellate Division
392 N.Y.S.2d 336 1977

Memorandum by the Court

In a negligence action to recover damages for personal injuries, plaintiff's appeal from a judgment of the trial court's dismissal of the complaint at the close of plaintiff's case.

On December 31, 1970, at approximately 1:00 P.M. the infant plaintiff, Kenneth Zaepfel, then about six weeks shy of nine years of age, sustained personal injuries while sledding on the grounds of Roosevelt High School in the City of Yonkers. The trial court held that he was on the premises lawfully as an invitee.

The neighborhood children had the option of using either of two hills. Kenneth first went sleigh riding at "the big hill that most of the kids went" on, which had no natural or artificial physical obstructions. Later, he and two friends took their sleds to the other hill. There the three boys devised a sled train, that is, with each one lying prone (belly whopping), the feet of the child on the first sled locked into the front of the one behind; and the boy on the second sled (Kenneth) hooked his feet to the front of the third.

Using this contrivance they negotiated the decline without incident on the first occasion. The accident that befell Kenneth occurred on the second descent. He was aware that the school authorities had left a snow fence near the foot of the hill. Oddly enough, the fence was not used for snow purposes but was employed to contain the spectators at football games during the fall season. The fence would normally have been dismantled by the school maintenance crew shortly after Thanksgiving Day, but for some unexplained reason it had been left standing.

In any event, the three sleds disengaged on the second ride. Kenneth passed successfully by an open portion of the fence, but his right leg caught on a bent rusty pole which was embedded in the ground and supported a portion of the fence. Even though aware of its existence, Kenneth testified "I just didn't notice it." This can be explained under the theory of momentary forgetfulness, which does not constitute negligence as a matter of law.

On the issue of constructive notice, the superintendent of an apartment building adjoining the school grounds testified that he had observed the bent condition of the fence as early as December 1, 1970, thirty days prior to the accident. And as to giving warning to the neighborhood children of possible dangers, no sign was posted; nor did the school authorities affirmatively attempt to dissuade the children from using this second slope in favor of the other "safer" one.

The trial court dismissed on the ground that Kenneth was contributorily negligent as a matter of law as well as upon the ground of failure to establish a prima facie case.

"The question of contributory negligence ordinarily is a question of fact. It is only when there is no dispute upon the facts and only one conclusion can be drawn therefrom that it may be decided as a question of law."

At bar we have the natural propensity of children to venture into areas of questionable danger; permission by the school authorities for children to use the premises; and the actions of a soon-to-be nine year old, who is not to be charged with the same standard of care and caution to be expected of an adult. All of these factors must be given consideration in appraising the factual circumstances of this case.

Thus, on the basis of the testimony adduced upon the trial, questions of fact were presented which, in our view, should have been presented to the jury for determination.

Judgment Reversed

Licensees

A licensee includes anyone who enters the premises by permission only, without any enticement, allurement or inducement being held out by the owner of the recreation and sports facility.[3] As commonly used, this status is used to describe those who are mere social guests. They are invited on the premises but not for any business purpose but only for social purposes.

The owner's duty to a licensee is to keep the facility in reasonably safe condition and to warn of hidden dangers. There is no duty to inspect the facility to discover hidden dangers or to warn of obvious and known dangers. The owner may assume that the licensee will be vigilant as to any dangers on the premises. A licensee is presumed to take the premises as he finds them with all known and obvious dangers.

Two types of cases arise in recreation and sports wherein the status of the user is in issue. In the first, a person comes on the property as an invitee but then, because of unauthorized actions becomes a licensee. Such a fact pattern is found in the *Cox* v *Des Moines* case. The second type of case, although not without some contrary decisions is in the area of the social guest. In this type of case the invitee is not truly an invitee but a bare licensee, even though he was expressly invited on the premises. For example, in *Vogel* v *Eckert*, 91 A.2d 633 (NJ 1952), a guest was injured by the collapse of a rotted bench she was sitting on. It was one of several pieces of outdoor furniture made by the defendant. The court denied recovery because the defendant didn't know of the condition and had no duty to the guest to acquire such knowledge. Such a limitation of duty probably conforms to reasonable expectations in the ordinary host-guest relations.

COX v DES MOINES
Supeme Court of Iowa
16 N.W.2d 234 1944

Mulroney, Justice

Suit for personal injuries suffered by plaintiff when he fell into the well of an outside basement stairway located at the club house of a municipal golf course. Judgment was for plaintiff and defendant city appeals.

The undisputed evidence in the case shows that on the night of May 17, 1941, plaintiff attended a dance at the Waveland Park Club House in Des Moines, Iowa. This club house is located upon the Waveland municipal golf course and it is often leased to individuals and clubs for dances and parties. On this night it was leased to a dancing club of which plaintiff was a member. Plaintiff and his wife and another couple, Mr. and Mrs. Burke, went first to the home of Mr. and Mrs. George Murphy and they all rode to the dance in Mr. Murphy's car. They arrived at the dance about 9 or 9:30 P.M. and when the dance was over, some time around midnight, plaintiff's group, with the exception of Mr. Murphy, congregated outside the club house at the east or street entrance near an outside light. They were waiting for Mr. Murphy to return with the car, for he had left the dance to take a girl, who had been staying with his child, to her home. The persons in charge of the club house had closed it up and turned out the lights. After standing around in the group for about half an hour Burke and the plaintiff walked around to the north side of the club house upon a cement sidewalk to seek a place to answer the call of nature. The cement sidewalk was level, and smooth and five feet wide and plaintiff was walking on the building side of the walk. There is no street along this side of the building and, with the lights turned off inside the club house, it was dark here, but, of course, both Burke and plaintiff testified they were seeking a dark place. Upon the inside of the walk there was a practically level grass shoulder about four feet wide, then a steep grass embankment down to an open basement entrance to the club house. This basement entrance which is seven to nine feet south of the sidewalk has steps along the west end. It is about four feet wide with a cement floor east of the steps and the pit or well, as it is called in the testimony, is about eight feet deep, with the north wall, that is parallel to the sidewalk, flush with the bottom of the steep grass embankment.

Plaintiff testified: "Mr. Burke and I were walking on the north side of the building on the sidewalk. I stepped on the edge of the sidewalk, turning my ankle, and was thrown south of the sidewalk. It was in utter darkness. I maintain while walking down the sidewalk I stepped too close to the edge of the sidewalk, which turned my ankle and caused me to step in the direction of the pit. I fell into the pit. I did not fall at the edge of the walk. I did not roll down this terrace. I maintained my equilibrium. I kept running down the terrace. I was standing up straight. The walk was smooth. There were no defects in it. It was not out of repair in any particular. There was no obstruction on the walk that evening. I would say that if my ankle had not turned this would not have happened. The turning of the ankle is what set in motion the train of events that ended up in my injury. The grass at the edge of the walk that night was not wet. There is a lighting fixture over the basement door but it was not lighted."

The trial court submitted two grounds of negligence to the jury, namely failure of the defendant to erect a barrier at the wall of the basement pit and failure of the defendant to maintain the light near the pit.

But plaintiff's chief reliance is upon his argument that he was "both an invitee and a paying customer of the city of Des Moines (and) before his invitation or business had been concluded he walked from the east side around to the north side of the city's building for a legitimate purpose." The argument then proceeds on the theory of the defendant being negligent in maintaining this unguarded and unlighted open basement stairway along the north side of the building, in close proximity to the sidewalk down which plaintiff, as an invitee, fell.

We fail to follow the argument. True, plaintiff was an invitee to the club house and as such the city owed to him the duty of exercising due care in maintaining the premises in a reasonably safe condition.

In order for plaintiff to recover upon the theory of an injured invitee not contributorily negligent, it was incumbent upon him to show (1) *that he was injured during the time covered by the invitation,* (2) *at a place where he was invited,* and (3) *the unsafe condition of the premises, negligently allowed to exist, that was the proximate cause of the accident.* In our opinion the undisputed evidence does not establish any one of these three requisites.

The plaintiff was invited to a dancing party in the club house. The party was over. Plaintiff and his party were the last to leave. Indeed the evidence shows that the city's employees had some trouble getting the plaintiff and his party out of the club house so they could lock up after the party was over. The lights in the building had been turned off. The club house had been locked. The park employees had gone home. The plaintiff and his party stood in the lighted vehicular drive for half an hour waiting for the car to come back and take them home. The plaintiff's invitation to the city's club house building and grounds had expired. He would no longer be considered an invitee if he attempted to reenter the building or walk around the darkened grounds. The city had provided a lighted area in front of the club house where the plaintiff could wait for his transportation, but the invitation for plaintiff to the building and building premises had definitely ended. During the period that the invitation was in force the building and premises were lighted. The very basement entrance down which plaintiff fell was lighted by an outside light while the party was in progress. Because plaintiff was an invitee when he came to the building and the club house premises, he did not remain an invitee after he left the building at the conclusion of the party.

Plaintiff was not injured at a place where he was invited. Of course the time and place must be considered together. Plaintiff's status at the conclusion of the party to which he was an invitee might well continue as he proceeded to leave. This is the case he pleaded, but his proof is otherwise. He was not injured "as he was leaving the building" as he stated in his petition. He was injured a half hour after he had left the building while wandering around the building in the dark to seek a place to relieve himself. The invitation extended to him to come to the lighted building for the dance did not include an invitation to walk around the building after the dance was over and the lights extinguished.

The plaintiff was not the city's invitee when he walked around to the north side of the building a half hour after the party was over. It cannot be said that the city could reasonably expect that plaintiff, whom it had invited to the dance, would go walking around the darkened building a half hour after the dance was over.

Proof that the city constructed this smooth level cement walk with an almost level grass shoulder four feet wide with a steep grass embankment beyond the shoulder leading to the well of an open basement entrance is no proof of negligence. There is nothing particularly dangerous about such construction. Plaintiff argues that the negligence lies in the failure to erect a barrier and maintain a light and he leads us into the cases that discuss a municipality's liability for a defect, not in the walk itself, but so close to it as to endanger persons properly using the walk.

The city could not be held negligent in failing to maintain a light after the club house was closed for the night. The walk ordinarily served the club house in the sense that it was used as a way to and from the side door entrance. There would be no legal duty to maintain the light at night when the club house was closed.

It is our conclusion that plaintiff failed to prove he was an invitee at the time and place of the accident and that in any event there was no proof of negligence.

Reversed. Judgment for Defendant

GOLDSTEIN v BOARD OF EDUCATION OF UNION
Court of Appeals of New York
278 N.Y.S.2d 224 1966

Memorandum Opinion

Action was brought against the board of education of school district of town and defendant corporation, which had been employed to install playground equipment, including a horizontal ladder held in the air by two risers and weighing more than 250 pounds, on school premises, for injuries sustained by infant plaintiff and for medical expenses and loss of services incurred by plaintiff father when the horizontal ladder, which the infant plaintiff and other children were attempting to lift, fell on the infant plaintiff at grade school. There was evidence that defendant company's employees assembled the ladder and dug holes for its installation, and that, at the end of their workday, they left it lying on its side because it was too heavy to move, and that on the same day the principal of the school told the children they were to stay away from the playground area until they were told that the playground equipment was completely installed, and that on the following day, a holiday on which the school was closed and on which the company's employees did not work, the plaintiff who was then eight years of age, and other children went to the playground area and attempted to lift the ladder off the ground, and that they dropped it and it fell on the infant plaintiff, and that prior to the accident the infant plaintiff had seen or been told about attempts of other children to lift the ladder and that the ladder fell and injured at least one other child.

The trial court, Nassau County, entered a judgment for the plaintiff. The Appellate Division entered an order which reversed, on the law and facts, the judgment of the trial court and the plaintiffs bring this appeal. The Appellate Division held that the infant plaintiff was a licensee on the school property and that the defendant owed the plaintiff no greater duty than to avoid the maintenance of traps, hidden dangers, or wanton and reckless conduct, and that the horizontal ladder, while lying on the ground, was not an inherently dangerous article, and that evidence of the plaintiff was, as a matter of law, insufficient to the creation of a trap. We affirm the findings of the Appellate Division.

Affirmed

Trespassers

The adult trespasser is lowest in the legal scale of protection. The invitee and licensee are invited or have the consent to enter land, but the trespasser has neither. A trespasser has been defined as

> a person who enters or remains upon land in the possession of another without a privilege to do so.[4]

Although minors may be trespassers, the law extends special privileges to them and adds extra burdens to the landowner. The doctrine commonly known as attractive nuisance has been applied when minor trespassers are injured by conditions or facilities on the land.

A possessor of land owes an adult trespasser no general duty of care, except to avoid injuring the trespasser through intentional or reckless misconduct. There is no duty to make the premises reasonably safe or to discover, remedy, or warn of dangerous conditions. But where danger to the trespasser arises from activities of the possessor rather than conditions of the land or facilities, the possessor is to exercise reasonable care for the protection of the trespassers. For instance, if the presence of a trespasser is known in a park area where construction equipment is being operated, the possessor may be liable for failing to stop the equipment.

In the absence of evidence that the possessor is aware of trespassers, there can be no recovery where the possessor's conduct is not intentional, willful, or wanton. Where a trespasser is discovered, the modern view requires the possessor to exercise reasonable care to warn him of dangerous hidden artificial conditions.[5] The possessor's duty to a discovered trespasser is not a duty of reasonable care to make the premises safe but merely to use reasonable care to warn of hidden dangers.

Attractive Nuisance—Trespassing Children

When the trespasser is a child, at least forty-three states have adopted special liability rules which impose on landowners a greater duty of care.[6] Under the doctrine of attractive nuisance, a possessor of land may be liable for injuries to trespassing children if their presence should have been reasonably anticipated and there is a likelihood that a child would be enticed by the artificial condition. Gradually courts modified this general rule and rejected the notion that a child must be enticed into trespassing. According to Prosser, the logic and rules of the earlier cases have been discarded by the courts and the better rule of law is the view taken by the Restatement (Second) of Torts §339.[7]

1. The place where the condition exists is one upon which the possessor knows or has reason to know that children are likely to trespass leaders.
2. The condition is one of which the possessor knows or has reason to know and which he realizes or should realize will involve an unreasonable risk of death or serious bodily harm to such children. . . .
3. The children because of their youth do not discover the condition or realize the risk involved in intermeddling with it or in coming within the area made dangerous by it. . .
4. The utility to the possessor of maintaining the condition and the burden of eliminating the danger are slight as compared with the risk to the children involved and . . . the possessor fails to exercise reasonable care to . . . protect the children.

Thus, it is not necessary that the child be lured onto the premises by the condition. The landowner must have actual knowledge of the presence of children or that their presence is foreseeable. Past trespasses or proximity to places where children are likely to be may establish foreseeability of trespass.

Courts have generally held that the doctrine applies to artificial or manmade conditions and not to natural conditions. Therefore, natural waters, geologic formations, vegetation, or other natural conditions causing injury to the child are exempt from the rule. The creation and maintenance of the manmade condition by the landowner is not necessary for liability. It has been held that a possessor is liable for conditions created by adjoining landowners or previous occupants if he knows of the condition, can easily take precautions against it and can reasonably anticipate that it will injure children. A landowner is not required to childproof the property from all conditions, but only those which involve a foreseeable risk of injury.

Recovery will be denied if the child knew of the condition and fully understood the danger. The age and experience of the child is an important factor in determining comprehension of danger. It is the appreciation of danger that bars recovery rather than mere knowledge of the condition itself. As might be expected, most cases involved very young children, usually under twelve years of age. Although the Restatement does not limit the doctrine to "young" children, obviously the older the child the greater the comprehension and understanding of dangers.

The doctrine of attractive nuisance has limited application to parks, recreation, and sports facilities. The doctrine does not apply to a child in a public place through invitation. It is only applicable to trespassing children. Attractive nuisance, however, could become an issue in public areas and facilities when children enter closed areas or areas restricted to public access.

LATIMER v CITY OF CLOVIS
Court of Appeals of New Mexico
495 P.2d 788 1972

Wood, Chief Justice

This is a wrongful death case. The trial court granted defendant's motion for summary judgment. The issue is the propriety of the summary judgment. We discuss each of the reasons the trial listed in granting the summary judgment.

Facts and inferences supported by the record are:

Mack Allen Grayes, age five, drowned after falling into water in a fenced swimming pool located in defendant's park. The park was across the street from where Mack lived with his mother, brothers, and sister. The family had lived at this location for approximately five years.

The park is open the entire year; the pool is open from June to September. A contractor, in connection with submitting a bid for construction work at the pool, inspected the pool on or about April 7, 1969. At the time of this inspection there was no collection of water any place within the pool area. On the accident date, April 18, 1969, water had collected in the deep end of the pool to a depth of slightly less than six feet. There is an "estimate" that the water had collected after a rain.

On the accident date the mother, accompanied by her children, went to the park to play softball. She gave her sons permission to play on the swings. After playing on the swings, monkey bars, and seesaw, running some races and wrestling with one another, the boys' attention was directed to a hole in the fence around the pool.

The boys were Mike Grayes, age seven, Mack and his twin brother Mark, and a friend named Gregory. Mike saw the hole in the fence and asked the other boys if they wanted to come into the pool with him. They went through the hole in the fence. They went down into the dry portion of the pool, threw rocks into the water in the deep end and played around the edge of the pool before Mack fell in. The estimated time from entry into the pool area until Mack's fall is ten minutes.

The estimated distance from the pool to where the mother was playing softball varies from fifty feet to one-half block. The pool area was visible from where the mother was playing softball. The mother could have seen the boys enter the pool area if she had kept an eye on them.

The Grayes children had been specifically warned about the hazards of water. According to the mother, they knew or should have known of the dangers related to water. The mother had told Mike to stay away from the pool; that the water was not safe.

Mike had seen other, and older, children climb the fence and go into the pool area, but the time and date of this observation is not clear. On the day of the accident, the mother did not know the boys had entered the pool area, and Mike had forgotten he wasn't supposed to be in the pool area. According to the grandfather, he had explained the danger of water but Mack, the deceased, "wasn't aware of it because he was too young"; he had no knowledge of danger.

There is nothing indicating that prior to April 18, 1969, anyone knew that water had collected in the deep end of the pool. The boys saw the water after entering through the hole in the fence. The affidavit of defendant's superintendent of parks states that he is in charge of the upkeep and maintenance of the park and pool, that he had been in and around the park pursuant to his duties as superintendent and was unaware that water had collected in the deep portion of the pool until subsequent to the drowning.

There is nothing indicating how long the hole had existed in the fence. The grandfather characterized the hole in the fence as a three foot opening and stated that anybody that had been there should have seen the opening. The mother and Mike stated they were unaware of the hole prior to the accident. The park superintendent made no statement in his affidavit concerning the hole. There is nothing in the record indicating either knowledge or lack of knowledge on the part of the City concerning the hole.

The mother and the father of the Grayes boys were divorced; the father had abandoned his family; the father's whereabouts were unknown; the mother had custody of the children.

Is there liability under the doctrine of attractive nuisance?

The elements of the doctrine of attractive nuisance are stated in *Saul v Roman Catholic Church of Arch. of Sante Fe,* 75 N.M. 160, 402 P.2d 48 (1965), and *Klaus v Eden,* 70 N.M. 371, 374 P.2d 129 (1962). Defendant asserts that three of the elements are absent. Since all elements must concur if the doctrine is to be applied, we consider each of the allegedly missing elements.

One element is: The place where the condition is maintained is one upon which the possessor knows or should know that children are likely to trespass. Defendant asserts the question is whether the City had knowledge or should have had knowledge that children came into the pool area to play at a time when the pool was closed. It asserts: "There is nothing in the record to indicate any actual knowledge of trespassing children on the part of the representatives of the City of Clovis."

In the absence of evidence showing how long the hole in the fence had existed, we agree that there is nothing in the present record showing that the City knew or should have known that children were likely to trespass in the pool area. However, there is also nothing in the record showing the absence of the requisite knowledge.

Defendant had the burden of showing an absence of the requisite knowledge. Since no such showing was made, summary judgment on the basis of this element of the doctrine of attractive nuisance was improper.

Another allegedly missing element is: The condition is one of which the possessor knows or should know and which he realizes or should realize as involving an unreasonable risk of death or serious bodily harm to children.

Defendant states: "For the City of Clovis to be held liable, under this element, the knowledge, actual or implied, had to be of the accumulation of water. The undisputed facts clearly show that there could have been no such knowledge." Further: "It is obvious that the collection of water had accumulated only a very short time prior to the accident, that the water could not be seen unless an individual actually entered the pool area and certainly, under these circumstances, knowledge of the water cannot be imputed to the City of Clovis."

Assuming, as defendant contends, that the hole in the fence is of no consequence in considering this element (a point we do not decide), the issue is not whether plaintiff has shown that the City knew or should have known of water in the pool. The issue is whether defendant made a showing that the City did not know or should not have known about the water in the pool.

Defendant's showing is that no water was in the pool on or about April 7th, that almost six feet of water was in the deep end of the pool on April 18th, and an "estimate" that the water collected after a rain. The superintendent in charge of upkeep and maintenance of the pool states he was unaware of the water prior to the accident. This is an affirmative indication of lack of knowledge by the City. It is not a showing that the City should not have known about the water since the superintendent states that he was in and around the park pursuant to his duties. Those duties included the maintenance of the pool. There is a factual issue as to whether the City should have known about the water in the pool.

Defendant asserts it had no duty to inspect or police the pool ". . . in order to discover whether there is any condition which will be likely to harm trespassing children. . . ." We agree; however, the statement does not conflict with this element of the doctrine. This element is not concerned with "any condition" but with conditions involving unreasonable risks. The test of foreseeability of harm to a child under the particular circumstances is the crucial consideration. If the water hazard in this case was not an unreasonable risk as a matter of law, certainly a factual question exists concerning that risk.

The third allegedly missing element is: The children, because of their youth, do not discover the condition or realize the risk involved in intermeddling in it or coming within the area made dangerous by it.

Defendant asserts that Mack, the deceased, knew or should have known of the perils of water. It asserts that this knowledge is affirmatively shown by the deposition testimony of the mother as to the warnings she gave to her sons, and by Mike's admission that such warnings had been given. The fact that warnings had been given does not eliminate the question of whether there was a realizatioi of the risk.

Although warnings had been given, Mike states that he had forgotten he wasn't supposed to go in the pool (area). Further, the grandfather stated that Mack, the deceased, didn't know of the danger because he was too young. A factual issue existed as to the deceased's appreciation of the risk.

The third element was not missing as a matter of law. There being a factual issue as to this element, summary judgment was improper. The trial court erred in granting summary judgment on the basis there was no liability under the attractive nuisance doctrine.

The trial court ruled that decedent "assumed the risk and was negligent."

In discussing the elements of the attractive nuisance doctrine, we held that defendant failed to show that Mack, age five, realized the risk involved.

Reversed

Abolition of User Categories

Dissatisfaction with the categorization of visitors as trespassers, licensees, or invitees has been expressed by legal writers urging their elimination. In 1968, the California Supreme Court in *Rowland* v *Christian*, 443 P.2d 561 (CA 1968), abolished the user categories, holding that whether the plaintiff was an invitee, licensee, or trespasser was immaterial as there was a duty to use reasonable care under any circumstances. By 1976, seven states followed the California lead to varying degrees.[8] Decisions in these cases cite with approval *Rowland* v *Christian* to the extent that it abolishes the distinction between licensees and invitees. Courts have been reluctant to abolish the trespasser category and upgrade the standard of care owed to this class of visitor. The abolition of the trespasser, licensee, and invitee classes is still a minority position in a number of jurisdictions which have elected not to follow the trend.[9]

Recreation Liability Statutes

While the judicial trend is to abolish user categories and raise the standard of care, there is a legislative trend affirming the judicially created classes. Forty-six states have enacted statutes providing a degree of legal protection to private and public landowners who allow their property to be used for public recreation purposes.[10] Although legislative histories are scarce, it is assumed that this proliferation of statutes was the result of a perceived need for public access to private lands coupled with a willingness on the part of the user to forego a recovery for injuries for the opportunity to use the land. Many of the statutes were patterned after a 1965 Council of State Governments suggested Model Act entitled "Public Recreation on Private Lands—Limitations on Liability."[1] The Model Act reverses the judicial trend of raising the standard of care owed to recreation users on private lands. However, the paucity of appellate cases construing these statutes makes it difficult to suggest a trend in resolving this apparent conflict. One court which has reviewed these statutes has suggested that they be narrowly construed so as to have the least possible impact on the law prior to enactment.[12]

In a few cases involving ambiguities in statutory definitions, the courts indicated a decided preference for strict construction. For example, a New Jersey statute was held not applicable in a recreation rescue case when a Good Samaritan, in attempting to rescue two teenagers who fell through the ice while skating, also fell through the ice and drowned. The court refused to apply the statute despite the fact that the rescue attempt involved skating, an activity specified in the statute.[13] Application of these statutes to public park and recreation agencies was an issue in Wisconsin and Michigan. In *Goodson* v *Racine,* 213 N.W.2d 16 (WI 1973), the Wisconsin court held that the statute is limited to private individuals and does not protect a municipality. This rule was also followed in Michigan when the court held that the statute was not designed or intended to apply to the recreation lands of a municipality.[14] An opposite position was taken by the federal courts in finding a Nevada statute extended coverage to the federal government in prescribing liability to a sightseer injured while exploring an abandoned mine on federal lands.[15]

Despite attempts at uniformity, the law concerning landowner liability for injuries to recreation users remains uncertain. The sparsity of appellate court decisions interpreting language of these statutes adds to the uncertainty. Application of these statutes to public park and recreation agencies is also unclear. Given the rationale for passage of the statutes—to increase private land available for public recreation without public purchase—there seems to be little reason to extend this statutory protection to public agencies.

LEGAL RISK
IN SELECTED FACILITIES

Accidents can and do happen everywhere—in parks, playgrounds, recreation centers, health clubs, athletic fields, swimming pools, beaches, campgrounds, and every other area owned or operated by public and private recreation enterprises. For instance, between 1975 and 1982 more than one-half of all Texas municipal park and recreation departments were involved with lawsuits or injury claims resulting from accidents.[16] Recognition of the legal risks associated with accidental injuries is reflected in the fact that 70 percent of Texas park and recreation departments purchased some type of insurance policy in this time period.[17] The accidents affecting park and recreation departments and the rules of law concerning liability are not unique to the public agency. Indeed, the law applies to public and private owners of land, albeit the focus of this chapter is on the recreation facility operator. The cases cited involve six specific recreation facilities: (1) beaches, (2) swimming pools, (3) recreation centers, (4) playgrounds, (5) ball diamonds, and (6) campgrounds. In total, these facilities generate more than 70 percent of the recreation tort litigation.[18] Although these facilities are the litigation generators this does not mean that they are highly dangerous facilities but only that there is a need for specific risk management strategies.

Beaches and Lakes

Actions against swimming facility operators to recover for injuries or death of visitors are usually decided under premises liability rules. Thus, operators are held to a negligence law duty of ordinary and reasonable care for the safety of *invitees* and a lesser standard with respect to *licensees* and *trespassers*. These standards apply to public and private operators of swimming facilities, although in the older line of cases recovery against public operators was based on maintaining a nuisance. In the multitude of actions involving beaches and lakes the factual basis for the lawsuits generally involved hazardous conditions in the waters or adjacent land, inadequate lifeguard protection and rescue equipment, or the failure to warn users that the area was closed to swimming.

Hazardous hidden conditions   A nearly infinite number of conditions exist at most swimming facilities that are or may be hazardous to the user. The bulk of dangerous conditions cases concern water depth or submerged objects as the hazardous condition.

In *deep water* cases, where the injury or death allegedly resulted from the operator's failure to warn against a hole, drop off, or adjacent deep water, the courts have held that were the area of deep water was marked by signs, ropes, buoys, or some other warning device the operator was not liable. Thus in *Cortes v State*, 218 N.W.2d 214 (NE 1974), where a fifteen year old patron of a state park beach used a tube to float into deep water beyond a marked swimming area and upon realizing that he was in deep water, panicked, causing the tube to capsize and the patron to drown, the state was not liable for the boy's death on the ground that it had failed to warn of the condition. Moreover, the court found that decedent was guilty of contributory negligence, noting that the use of such floating devices in deep water by patrons who do not know how to swim is generally recognized as unusually dangerous. Other cases in which the operator was not liable for drownings occurring in deep water beyond a designated wading area include: *Tuerck* v *State*, 91 N.Y.S.2d 847 (NY 1947), drowning of a 5 year old in a deep portion of the pond beyond marked swimming area; *Pope* v *State*, 96 N.Y.S.2d 708 (NY 1950), drowning of a state park patron in deep water beyond a marked swimming area while attempting to rescue two nieces; *Dandurand* v *Chebanse Recreation Center*, 290 N.E.2d 276 (IL 1972), drowning of a nineteen-year-old nonswimmer who attempted to reach a raft in deep water outside a clearly marked shallow water beach area, and *Rodrique* v *Ponchatoula Beach Dev. Corp.*, 152 So.2d 562 (LA 1963), drowning of a seventeen year old after falling from an innertube in deep water.

Where the deep water occurs within a marked swimming area and the danger is not apparent, findings of operator liability have been reached. Illustrative of the duty to warn of deep water in these instances is *Ide* v *St. Cloud*, 8 So.2d 924 (FL 1942), where the city was liable for failing to warn of a deep hole (ten feet deep) within the confines of a bathing beach that averaged three feet in depth. For other cases imposing liability for the failure to warn of deep water as a hidden danger see *Carsoni* v *Islip*, 103 N.Y.S. 435 (NY 1951), *Brevard County* v *Jacks*, 238 So.2d 156 (FL 1970), and *Roth* v *Heer Contracting Co.*, 284 N.Y.S. 372 (NY 1935). In some cases, courts have found no operator liability for failure to warn of hidden dangers based on a defense of contributory negligence or assumption of risk.[19]

The *shallow water* cases involve the operator's failure to prohibit diving, warn of the hidden dangers, or inspect the diving area to discover changes in the bottom conformation and to warn of or remove these hidden dangers. Several cases can be cited under either pattern supporting the responsibility of the operator to inspect and warn.[20] The most troublesome cases to resolve are those where diving has occurred outside a designated swimming area with the operator's knowledge. Operator inaction in warning or preventing the dive may lead to liability. Thus in *Hawk* v *Newport Beach*, 293 P.2d 48 (CA 1956), where a seventeen-year-old boy was injured when he dove from a rock in a cove adjacent to the beach and struck his head on the bottom, the city was held liable. It appeared that the city knew that beach patrons used this rock as a diving platform but did not provide adequate warnings of shallow water. These shallow water cases turn on the question of concealment of the danger. Clearly, an operator has no duty to warn of known and obvious dangers but must inspect the premises to discover and warn of hidden dangers. Thus an operator with knowledge that users dive in an area not designated as such has a duty to warn of shallow water or preferably to prohibit the activity.

In the *submerged objects* cases the issue is generally not operator failure to warn, but operator failure to conduct reasonable and timely inspection to discover the hidden danger. When the objects were floating or clearly visible to the swimmer, the majority rule absolves the operator from liability, but where their presence is unknown there is liability.[21] The type and size of the submerged object is significant in these cases. Obviously the smaller the object the greater the difficulty in discovery and the lesser the potential for operator liability. Where swimmers have been injured by submerged pieces of glass, for example, the courts have frequently denied liability rationalizing that reasonable inspection could not have prevented the injury.[22] But where the swimmers have struck larger objects, such as pipes, anchors, piers, or a barbed wire fence, courts have held the operator liable.[23]

Lack of proper supervision and rescue equipment   Operators of public and private swimming facilities may have a duty to provide adequate lifeguarding supervision and to rescue and resuscitate those in danger of drowning.[24] In those cases where recovery has been allowed for the drowning of a swimmer following an observed disappearance which occurred when no lifeguard was on duty, the courts have usually concluded that the victim was an invitee to whom the operator owed a duty to provide a lifeguard. For example, in *Ward v United States,* 208 F. Supp 118 (CO 1962), the Federal Government was held liable under Colorado law for the drowning of a sixteen year old girl at an unguarded public swimming facility, and in *Perkins v Byrnes,* 269 S.W.2d 52 (MO 1954), the operator of a private resort was liable for the death of a nineteen year old who drowned in a strong undercurrent of the river. The court found that the deceased was an invitee and the operator was required to warn him of the dangerous undercurrent and to provide a lifeguard to prevent unreasonable risk of harm.[25]

Contrary results have been reached in a number of cases where the courts decided that the victim was a licensee or trespasser to whom the operator owed no duty of providing a lifeguard. Thus, in *McCallister v Homestead,* 185 A. 583 (PA 1936), the court found that a four-year-old child who drowned while playing on a float at the time when the lifeguard was not on duty was a licensee with no expressed invitation to use the swimming facility and the city was not guilty of a breach of duty. In concluding that the failure to have a lifeguard was not the proximate cause of the drowning, the court in *Rodrique v Ponchatoula Beach Development Corp.,* 151 So.2d 157 (LA 1963), determined that the drowning of a seventeen year old who fell off an innertube in deep water beyond the swimming area was a result of contributory negligence on his part and therefore the operator was not liable.

Closely related to the absence of lifeguard cases are those where there was an allegation that a swimming facility was without lifesaving or rescue equipment. A review of the cases suggests that the operator of a public swimming facility has a duty to provide lifesaving equipment and the failure to do so renders the operator liable for the drowning of an invitee.[26] In those cases wherein the drowning was unwitnessed, the courts have concluded that the failure to provide rescue equipment was not the proximate cause of the accident because no person was available to conduct a rescue attempt.

Failure to prohibit swimming   A third line of cases concerns the failure of an operator to prohibit swimming in certain sections of the lake wherein there are hidden dangers or to provide warnings of those dangers. Where the operator of a facility knows or has reason to know that swimming is occurring in unguarded or in nondesignated areas the potential for liability is great where the operator takes no action to prohibit swimming.

DAVIS v UNITED STATES
U.S. Court of Appeals—Seventh Circuit
716 F.2d 418 1983

Posner, Circuit Judge

Scott Davis was injured in September 1978 while diving into Devil's Kitchen Lake in the Crab Orchard National Wildlife Refuge. The Refuge is owned and operated by the United States, and is heavily patronized—it had one and a half million visitors in 1978—especially students at the nearby campus of Southern Illinois University (SIU). In the nine years preceding the accident there had been five diving accidents at another lake in the Refuge, Crab Orchard Lake. One of the accidents had been fatal; two others had rendered their victims quadriplegics. Knowing there was swimming in Devil's Kitchen Lake too and fearing lest the subsurface rocks in the lake cause serious diving injuries such as had occurred at Crab Orchard Lake, the government in 1975 had closed Devil's Kitchen Lake to swimming except at a beach at one end of the lake, and had posted along the Refuge's roads leading to the Lake, near the entrances to the Refuge, signs of moderate size reading "No Swimming in Devil's Kitchen Lake." Beneath each sign had been erected a slightly smaller one reading "No Diving." Neither the size nor the color of the signs (white on blue) indicated danger, and there was no reference to the subsurface rocks or to any other possible hazard to a swimmer or diver—or, for that matter, to the fact that swimming was permitted at the beach. At first no effort was made to enforce the prohibition, but in 1976 the rangers who patrol Crab Orchard Refuge began issuing citations, accompanied by oral explanations of the danger, to people caught swimming in the lake. The government also made an effort to publicize the prohibition with local radio spots and notices in the SIU campus newspaper.

It was against this background that Davis, a twenty-three-year-old student at SIU, went with three friends to swim in Devil's Kitchen Lake one summer afternoon. One of the young men, Ellison, had swum in Devil's Kitchen Lake before and had not noticed any hazardous rocks. As the group drove into Crab Orchard Refuge, Davis was seated on the lefthand side of the rear seat of the car and did not see the no-swimming and no-diving signs. One of the young men asked Ellison whether it was okay to swim in Devil's Kitchen Lake and he replied, "you're not supposed to but everyone does." Davis testified that he did not hear this exchange. The group parked in a gravel "widened spot" and walked to the shore. There was no one in the water and no indication that it was an authorized swimming area. Ellison inflated a rubber raft and floated out on it. Davis and another young man swam about for a short time without incident and then got out and walked some feet to a point on the shore opposite Ellison on his raft. The shore here was a stone ledge about three feet above the surface of the lake. The lake seemed clear to Davis, but he also testified, "There was glare from the sun. So that if you looked down at the water the sun was reflected into your eyes." Davis and his companion decided to swim out to Ellison and tip him into the water from his raft. They took running dives and while in the air David dropped his arms to his side. He landed head first on a rock outcropping that protruded from the bottom of the lake to a point about a foot and a half below the surface, and broke his neck. His companion struck the same outcropping but just scraped his chest.

The accident rendered Davis a quadriplegic. He brought this suit for damages against the United States under the Federal Tort Claims Act, 28 U.S.C. 1346(b), 2671 et seq. The district court determined his damages to be $4,047,000, and the amount is not contested. The district court also determined that the accident was due 75 percent to Davis's own negligence and 25 percent to that of the United States, and therefore awarded him $1,012,000. He has appealed, contending that he is entitled to his full damages or at least to more than 25 percent; the government has cross-appealed, contesting liability.

We think it clear to begin with that under Illinois law (which governs the substantive issues in this case, see 28 U.S.C. 1346 (b) because the accident occurred in Illinois) the government was at least negligent in failing to warn the public of the danger of subsurface rocks more effectively than it did. From the photographs in the record, Devil's Kitchen Lake, despite its faintly ominous name, presents a placid, unthreatening appearance. Although the shoreline is rocky, the lake looks deep and there is no indication that there might be sinister stilettoes jutting up from its bottom. Even to one swimming in the lake there is no suggestion of danger, for Davis and his companion swam about, and Ellison floated about on his rubber raft, for some minutes—how long is unclear—without noticing any subsurface rocks. The "No Swimming" sign was not much good as a warning of danger; the prohibition it laconically announced could just as well have been intended to protect the lake from swimmers as vice versa. The "No Diving" sign was a little better—for what could be its purpose but to warn of danger?—but still left too much to the imagination. For rangers to give oral warnings to people they caught swimming or diving was fine as far as it went, but did Davis no good, for no ranger saw these young men swimming; nor had they gotten the message by word of mouth from fellow students who had been caught, or from the occassional radio spots or occassional notices in the campus newspaper.

The history of diving accidents at Crab Orchard Lake showed that people were diving despite the prohibition against swimming and diving and were getting seriously hurt doing so; and the government was aware of unauthorized swimming, and similar danger, at Devil's Kitchen Lake. It could not have cost much to amend the "No Diving" sign to add "Danger: Subsurface Rocks," and to have posted these signs where swimmers could be expected, such as at the gravel-widened spot where Davis and his friends parked their car, as well as at the entrances to the Refuge. Of course the cheapness of a precaution is not the only consideration in deciding whether its omission is negligent; the benefit from the precaution must be commensurate.

In this case it would have been, in view of the gravity of diving accidents, their incidence at the nearby Crab Orchard Lake, and the possibility, well illustrated by this case, that swimmers might simply be oblivious to the danger of subsurface rocks—especially since the refraction of light in water can cause a person to misjudge depth—signs such as we have described might well have been highly beneficial. If they had been posted and had prevented this accident, their benefits would have measured in the millions of dollars and their costs in the thousands or less. Even if such signs would have reduced the probability of the accident by only one percent, they would have been a bargain in an expected-value sense, for one percent of four million is $40,000, which must be more than what the signs would have cost to buy, install, and maintain. And this understates the benefits of the signs, since other potential accident victims, not just Davis, would have been warned.

The government could have prevented this accident (if at all) only by erecting signs warning of the danger of subsurface rocks, or by stepping up patrols of its rangers, and neither form of prevention would have been of certain efficacy. But to stop with this observation would be to let the government off the hook too easily. As the signs and increased ranger patrols would not have benefited just Davis but all potential victims of swimming and diving accidents, the cost to the government of preventing the accident to Davis would have been much less than the total costs of those measures. The government also had more information than Davis about the hazards of diving into Devil's Kitchen Lake.

But Davis's own fault was grave. He could have prevented the accident by just not diving. This would have been a trivial sacrifice. He still could have swum out to tip Ellison off the raft; it would just have taken him a few seconds longer. If he derived particular pleasure from diving, he could have pursued the sport in areas marked safe for diving; but it appears he dove just to get to the raft faster. Furthermore, had he not insisted on taking a running dive—and from a ledge three feet above the surface of the water— the danger would have been less. By running and diving from a height he made certain that he would dive into a part of the lake the depth of which he could not gauge from his position on the shore.

Davis's conduct was, therefore, not minimally negligent but willful and wanton. But it does not follow that Davis's willfulnes and wantonness was three times as great as that of the government. Although the scope of judicial review of such a determination is limited, the determination is not committed entirely to the discretion of the trier of fact and we must reverse if we have a firm conviction that it is wrong. It would be easy to uphold the district court's allocation of fault if the government were guilty of only minimal negligence. But since both parties were willful and wanton under Illinois law, the natural division of fault would have been fifty-fifty; and giving all due deference to the district court's superior ability to make the comparative negligence determination, we cannot find any basis in the district court's opinion or in the record for regarding Davis as having been more than twice as blameworthy as the government. This means that, at the most, he should bear two-thirds (not three-fourths), and the government one-third, of the cost of the accident.

We shall therefore reverse the judgment of the district court insofar as it failed to award Davis more than one-fourth of the $4,047,000 damages that the parties agree is the proper measure of his injury, and remand the case for a new trial limited to the proper apportionment of the parties' fault.

Reversed

KESNER v TRENTON
Supreme Court of Appeals of West Virginia
216 S.E.2d 880 1975

Haden, II, Chief Justice

The Circuit Court of Grant County, West Virginia, set aside a jury verdict and awarded the father of two girls drowned in the defendants' boating marina new trials in two consolidated wrongful death actions on the ground that only the verdicts rendered in favor of the plaintiff for funeral expenses were adequate.

The Supreme Court of Appeals of West Virginia, affirmed the judgment awarding new trials, holding that the marina operators were liable for the drowning deaths of the girls, where the girls drowned when they stepped into a ten-foot deep culvert which dropped precipitously from an area which was otherwise only "knee deep," where neither they nor anyone in their party were aware of the existence or location of the culvert, and where there were no markers, buoys, or other indicators of the existence of the culvert.

Plaintiff's decedents, Dianna and Carol Kesner, drowned at VEPCO lake in Grant County, West Virginia, on July 7, 1968. On that Sunday Gleason Kesner, the plaintiff administrator, took his family to the lake for the purpose of a family outing. The defendants and appellants operated a boat marina on the lake. As lessees of Virginia Electric Power Company, they offered at their establishment rental spaces for private boats, camping spots with electricity, water, and toilet facilities, and boat sales and rentals to the general public. Coincident with these commercial enterprises, the marina operation also provided, without charge to the general public, areas for picnicking and swimming in the waters adjacent to the defendants' boat dock and marina.

The Kesner family visited the lake so that, among other things, Mr. Kesner, the plaintiff, could rent a boat for the purpose of going to the mouth of Stoney River for fishing. Upon arrival at the marina area, the family had a picnic lunch. The Kesner girls, in the company of their sisters and two friends, decided to go wading in the lake within twenty minutes to one-half hour after they had eaten lunch. At approximately the same time, their father was on the boat dock awaiting his turn to rent a boat from the operator of the marina. Shortly after the girls entered the water they slipped or stepped into a culvert or excavation which had been dug from the lake bottom for the purpose of channeling water to a run-off culvert at the dam site on the lake. This culvert was approximately ten feet deep and dropped off precipitously from an area which was otherwise only "knee deep." Evidence disclosed that the plaintiff's decedents were fifteen and sixteen years old, were less than five feet in height and were nonswimmers. Neither they nor anyone in the Kesner party was aware of the existence or location of the hidden excavation or culvert. There were no marker buoys, signs, or other indicators alluding to the existence of the culvert or to the hazards of swimming in the area; however, defendant Arthur Trenton revealed that he had roped off the area previously in order to restrict swimmers or waders from proceeding into the area of potential danger. Apparently, boats using the area had cut or destroyed the nylon rope one or two weeks prior to the accident, but Trenton had not replaced any type of markers to warn of the hazards at the time of the drownings.

The bodies of the two Kesner girls were recovered some twenty-five to thirty-five minutes after they fell into the excavation. Unfortunately, efforts to resuscitate the victims were unsuccessful.

The trial court instructed the jury on the theory that plaintiffs were owed ordinary care by the landowner in their capacity as invitees. This Court in *Smith* v *Sunday Creek Co.,* 82 S.E. 608 (WVA 1914), recognized a landowner's common-law duty to an invitee when it stated that " . . .where the person injured was induced, allured, or enticed by the owner to enter upon the premises, or was thereupon by his express or implied invitation, a higher degree of care is imposed to have and to keep the premises reasonably safe." The Court in *Smith, supra,* also explained that:

"An invitation to enter upon premises, within the meaning of the law of negligence, will be implied where entry thereon at the instance of the owner is in connection with his business or for his benefit."

More specifically, see *Morgan* v *Price,* 150 S.E.2d 897 (WVA 1966), wherein this Court held that a boat dock owner and operator owed an injured woman the duty of exercising ordinary care in maintaining his premises in a reasonably safe condition, when she fell because of an alleged defect in a board on the owner's boat dock.

Consequently, we are of the opinion that the trial court did not err in refusing defendants' motions for directed verdicts or in refusing to give defendants' proffered instructions which would have limited the marina operators' duty of care toward plaintiff's decedents.

Affirmed

Swimming Pools

When the operator of the pool is a state agency or a municipal corporation, the courts must deal with the issue of governmental immunity. There is a split of authority on this issue. The majority of jurisdictions have adopted the rule that a pool operated by a public entity *free of charge* for public use is a governmental service.[27] However, where a fee is charged for public use the majority of states view the activity as proprietary in nature and thus without immunity.

Swimming pool litigation falls into one of the following groupings: (1) inadequate supervision, (2) dangerous water conditions, (3) slippery surfaces, (4) inadequate rescue equipment, and (5) accidents caused by other pool patrons. As with other recreation facility litigation the legal status of the user establishes the operator's duty of care. To the extent that the defenses of contributory negligence and assumption of risk are available, courts have held that such defenses may be imposed by the operator to escape liability.

Inadequate supervision   The overwhelming weight of case authority provides that operators of public and private pools are liable for drownings which follow an observed disappearance or struggle in the water at a time when there is no lifeguard on duty. In such cases the courts have concluded that the victim was an invitee and had a sufficiently staffed lifeguard crew been on duty they would have observed the accident and had time to rescue the decedent. Indicative of this line of cases is *Longmont* v *Swearingen,* 254 P. 1000 (CO 1927), where a sixteen-year-old boy drowned in a municipal pool at a time when there were a number of patrons in the pool and on the deck but no lifeguard on the premises. Evidence indicated that over a period of nine minutes the boy went down three times and efforts by other patrons to locate a guard were unsuccessful. Judgment was rendered against the city on the ground that its failure to provide a lifeguard or assistant in time of need was the proximate cause of the drowning. For other cases and jurisdictions following this view see Ill. *Griffin* v *Salt Lake City*, 176 P.2d 156 (UT 1947), *Collins* v *Riverside Amusement Park Co.*, 145 P.2d 853 (AZ 1944), *Rovegno* v *San Jose Knights of Columbus Hall Assoc.*, 291 P. 848 (CA 1930), *Brown* v *United States*, 99 F.Supp 685 (FL 1951), *De Simone* v *Philadelphia*, 110 A.2d 431 (PA 1955), *Williams* v *Delta Swimming Pool, Inc.*, 5 P.2d 583 (CO 1931), *Decatur Amusement Park Co.*, v *Porter*, 137 Ill. App. 448 (IL 1907), *Brotherton* v *Manhattan Beach Imp. Co.*, 67 N.W. 479 (NE 1896), and *Sneed* v *Lions Club of Murphy, North Carolina, Inc.*, 159 S.E.2d 770 (NC 1968).

In cases where the courts reached a finding of no liability the decision was often based on the fact that the decedent was a licensee or trespasser to whom the operator owed no duty of providing a lifeguard, guilty of contributory negligence in placing himself in a position of peril, or that there being no evidence as to how the drowning occurred the element of proximate causation was not established. Thus, in *McCallister* v *Homestead*, 185 A. 583 (PA 1936), and *Sroufe* v *Garden City*, 84 P.2d 845 (KS 1938), where young children drowned in swimming pools when lifeguards were not on duty, the courts concluded the children were not invitees and the operator owed them no duty to provide lifeguards. Where the body of a seventeen year old was found in six feet of water, approximately fifty feet from shore, it was held in *Luck* v *Buffalo Lakes, Inc.*, 144 S.W.2d 672 (TX 1940), that the proximate cause of death was not the failure to have a lifeguard on duty.

The number of lifeguards on duty during the time of the accident is frequently raised as an issue, usually without much success. Except in those cases involving drownings at crowded pools, inattentive lifeguards, or swimming and diving lessons, the courts have uniformly absolved operators from liability when two or more guards were on duty.[28] Recovery has been allowed in those cases were the attentiveness of lifeguards is an issue. In *Carter* v *Boy's Club of Greater Kansas City*, 552 S.W.2d 327 (KS 1977), the court rejected the Boy's Club request for a directed verdict in the drowning of a twelve year old finding that the Club's two lifeguards failed to keep a lookout over twelve boys, some of whom were nonswimmers. Observing that one of the lifeguards knew of the decedent's presence in the deep end of the pool but failed to make sure that the decedent returned to the safety of shallow water, the court concluded that lifeguard inattentiveness was the proximate cause of the drowning. The cases of *Naber* v *Humbolt* and *Pickett* v *Jacksonville* are indicative of the liabilities of inattentive lifeguards.

Hazardous conditions in water Recovery has been sought in a number of cases for an injury which allegedly resulted from inadequate depth of water for diving, cloudy or dark water, electrified water, floating objects in the water or defects in the pool. With the exception of inadequate depth for diving cases, which turn on the question of adequacy of warning, the other categories of cases deal with the operator's affirmative duty to inspect and test the water to discover and remove the hazardous condition. Recent case decisions have imposed liability on pool operators for drownings which were allegedly caused by cloudy, dark, discolored water or the presence of electrical current in the water at the time of the drowning. Thus in *Bugert* v *Tietjens*, 499 F.2d 1 (KS 1974), the operators of a swimming pool were held liable for the death of a twelve year old boy whose body was found in six feet of water on a day when the water visibility was only three feet. The court concluded that the pool operators were negligent in opening the pool when they knew that the cloudy water interfered with the lifeguard's ability to observe swimming and that this condition was the proximate cause of the drowning. For other cases dealing with cloudy or dark water see *Sneed* v *Lions Club of Murphy*, 159 S.E.2d 770 (NC 1968), *Newport* v *Ford*, 393 S.W.2d 760 (TN 1965), *Honeycutt* v *Monroe*, 253 So.2d 597 (LA 1971), *Mock* v *Natchez Garden Club*, 92 So.2d 562 (MS 1951), and *Guthrie* v *Monumental Properties, Inc.*, 232 S.E.2d 369 (GA 1977).

The floating objects and defects in pool structure cases indicate a pronounced trend to require that operators conduct reasonable and periodic inspections of the pools and to act expeditiously in removing these hazards. It is generally not sufficient only to warn of their existence.[29]

Slippery surfaces   Slip and fall accidents resulting from slippery or wet surfaces are the bane of all recreation facilities; however, the pool operator is most susceptible to this malady. The bulk of these cases involve the floors, decks, or walkways adjacent to the pool, diving platforms, or ladders in the pool and floors and stairwells in bathhouses and shower rooms. In resolving lubricious surface cases the courts often examine such factors as the absence of nonskid material on known slippery surfaces, or the presence of some substance, such as algae, soap, scum, or tanning oil on the surface which made it more slippery than it would have been had it been merely water soaked.[30] Where the cost to the operator is minimal to install nonskid surfaces or to remove the slippery substance, and the risk of injury is high, the operator is under an affirmative remedial duty to protect the user. Contrary results have been reached in a number of older cases where the courts have stressed the impossibility of preventing areas adjacent to swimming facilities from becoming water soaked.[31] Slip and fall cases should be a thing of the past with the availability of nonskid products for slippery surfaces.

Inadequate rescue equipment   The cases in this category logically examine the unavailability or inadequateness of rescue equipment as the proximate cause of the drowning. Where the drowning victim was a trespasser or knowingly placed himself in a position of peril, the failure to provide lifesaving equipment does not render the operator liable for the drowning.[32] Where a statute or ordinance requires equipping pools with certain lifesaving devices, courts have uniformly concluded that operators are liable for witnessed and unwitnessed drownings when such equipment was missing. See the *Harris* case for an example.

Injuries inflicted by other patrons   Recovery has been sought against pool operators for injuries resulting from diver/swimmer collisions or boisterous patron conduct. Liability of the operator has been sustained in the collision cases where it appeared there was no lifeguard in the area to separate the swimming and diving patrons.[33] It is apparent from these cases that the pool operator has a duty to post a lifeguard at the interface of swimming and diving activities to keep the two uses separated and to regulate diver sequencing. However, the operator is not the absolute guarantor of the patron's safety and when it can be shown that the injury resulted from the sudden and unexpected entry of a swimmer into the diving area, it has been held that the operator was not liable.[34]

Pool operators have a duty to post rules prohibiting boisterous patron conduct and to reasonably enforce these rules. Thus patrons injured by the boisterous conduct of others may recover damages from pool operators. In *Shields* v *Watervliet*, 341 N.Y.S.2d 699 (NY 1973), the court concluded that the city's failure to prevent rowdy behavior was the proximate cause of the injury to a patron who sustained damage to her two front incisor teeth when a boy picked her up against her will and jumped into the pool with her. The city was held liable in *Stillwell* v *Louisville*, 455 S.W.2d 56 (KY 1970), for the failure to strictly enforce the rules against flipping when a seventeen-year-old patron was injured when a young man swam between her legs and flipped her over his head.

NABER v CITY OF HUMBOLDT
Supreme Court of Nebraska
249 N.W.2d 726 1977

Coady, Justice

The District Court entered judgment for the city in an action brought by a plaintiff charging negligence in the drowning of a ten year old child in a municipal swimming pool. (Plaintiff Appeals).

This tragedy includes a cast of three lifeguards and, at least, sixty persons of minor age. The Humboldt municipal swimming pool opened on Sunday. On the following Friday, June 1, 1973, the pool opened at 1:00 P.M.

and approximately ninety-eight children entered the pool in the next two and one-half hours according to the pool records. Among the children attending were Glen Naber, age ten, his younger brother, and two younger sisters. They were attending for the first time and were in the charge of a thirteen-year-old female babysitter. The babysitter and the Naber children could not swim.

The pool was eighty-two feet in length. The width was forty feet at the center. The north and south sides tapered from the center to each end so that both the east and west ends were twenty-nine feet wide. At the east end there was a separate wading pool. At the west end there were two diving boards, a one-meter board towards the north, and a three-meter board towards the south. The west end was overlooked by a high, steel lifeguard chair located on the south side of the pool and approximately at the center of the diving area. That chair was unoccupied. There was a second high, steel lifeguard chair on the south side near the center of the pool which was occupied. From that position a guard could see the entire pool, including the bottom of the diving portion. On the north side, there was a building containing the pool entrance, bathhouse, and office.

The pool was cleared of swimmers at 3:00 P.M., and remained closed for fifteen minutes. At that time, a fifty-two year old lifeguard-operator testified that she visually checked the bottom of the pool. This lifeguard was the pool manager or operator and will be hereinafter referred to as the operator. After the 3:00 break, a seventeen-year-old lifeguard took the mobile position, called walking duty, on the north side of the pool, and will hereinafter be referred to as the north guard. A twenty-one-year-old lifeguard climbed and seated herself in the chair located at the center of the pool and on the south side. She will hereinafter be referred to as the south guard. The operator had a senior Red Cross life saving certificate and a pool operator's certificate from the State of Nebraska. Both the north and south guards were holders of the Red Cross senior life saving certificate.

At approximately 3:15 A.M., the break was ended and the children resumed swimming. Sometime thereafter, the operator adjusted an umbrella above and for the south guard so that the south guard need not take her eyes from the pool. The brother and sisters of Glen Naber were located in the wading pool and being supervised by their babysitter. Marty, an eleven-year-old boy, was located at the bottom of the three-meter diving board where he let Glen Naber climb ahead of him. At the top, Glen inquired as to the depth and let Marty go ahead of him after being told. Marty jumped off the board and into the pool.

Marty climbed the high board a second time. From the board he looked over the diving area in front of him and saw what he thought was someone near the drain and under ten to twelve feet of water. He jumped off and climbed out on the south side of the pool near the unoccupied lifeguard chair. He told his ten-year-old friend, Steve, who dove twice from poolside to determine if it really was someone.

The boys told the operator and the south guard. The operator and the south guard yelled to the north guard then located near the northeast corner of the diving area. The north guard dove, retrieved the body of Glen Naber, and brought it to the south side. After yelling to the north guard, yelling to the office for a doctor to be called, and seeing the body brought up, the operator went to the office to complete the emergency call.

The south guard lifted the boy from the water and laid him on his back. The guards looked for signs of life and, finding none, completed one push or stroke of the chest pressure method of artificial respiration. The operator returned and applied six or seven movements of the back pressure arm lift method. A medical doctor arrived after driving five or six blocks on a motorcycle. He checked for vital signs and he ordered the operator to apply mouth to mouth respiration. She administered four or five breaths, at which time the emergency squad arrived with oxygen. All these events were reported by the witnesses to have happened in terms of seconds. In any case, Glen Naber's body was not revived.

This is an action brought under the Nebraska Political Subdivisions Tort Claims Act to recover damages by reason of negligence. On trial to the court, judgment was entered for defendant. We affirm the judgment of the District Court.

Plaintiff argues that the lifeguards were inattentive. There was evidence that the guards were attentive and watchful. There was evidence that the deceased acted in such a way that his act should have been noticed and caused alarm. The trial judge specifically stated that he did not believe the principal sources of this latter evidence and set forth adequate reasons.

Plaintiff argues that the guards should have immediately used mouth to mouth respiration. A reader of the bill of exceptions will have no good idea as to whether anything could have been done for the deceased when his body was pulled from the pool. We conceded that time is critical in lifesaving. There was evidence that the mouth to mouth approach is the preferred method. There was evidence that the methods first applied were standard and acceptable methods. There was evidence that foam, mucus, and blood came from the mouth of this poor boy.

Because negligence is relative and the plaintiff has the burden of proof, the findings of the trial court will not be disturbed. On appeal to this court of an action under the Political Subdivisions Tort Claims Act, the findings of a trial court will not be disturbed unless clearly wrong.

Affirmed

HARRIS v LAQUINTA-REDBIRD JOINT VENTURE
Texas Court of Civil Appeals
522 S.W.2d 232 1975

Cornelius, Justice

Appellant filed suit against appellee for damages resulting from the drowning of her son, Ned Harris, in appellee's motel swimming pool. At the close of evidence from both parties the District Court directed a take nothing verdict. The parties will be referred to as in the trial court.

Plaintiff based her case upon the alleged negligence of defendant in failing to provide a lifeguard, failing to warn of the absence of a lifeguard and failing to have a life pole and a separate throwing line available as required by Dallas City Ordinance No. 8479. We have concluded that plaintiff made a case for the jury on the issues of negligence and proximate cause in failing to provide a life pole as required by the ordinance, and that the directed verdict was therefore improper.

The evidence, viewed most favorably to plaintiff's case, was as follows:

Ned Harris was in Dallas with his sister and other young people attending Expo '72. They were staying at defendant's motel which had a small swimming pool as part of its facilities. Several of the group, including Ned, had gone swimming there on Wednesday night without incident, and on Thursday night Ned and others again went swimming. While he was in the pool on that evening Ned encountered some difficulty and began to call for help. Two of his companions, a boy and a girl, successively got in the water and tried to get hold of him but were unable to do so. Mr. Albuquerque, who was a guest at the motel, saw Ned struggling in the water and jumped in to attempt a rescue. By the time he got into the water, Ned had submerged and was at or near the bottom of the pool, and Albuquerque could not get to him because of the resistance of his own clothing and shoes. Albuquerque then got out and a friend of his dived in, but was also unable to reach Ned. These two men then grabbed two aluminum poles which were nearby and used them to reach the victim. As neither pole had a hook, loop, or other pulling facility on it, the men could not get "ahold" of Ned to pull or lift him out of the water, but could only push him in an attempt to move him to shallow water. After some time and considerable difficulty they finally succeeded in pushing the boy to the shallow portion of the pool where he could be reached and was pulled out of the water. Attempts to revive him failed. Albuquerque testified that because the poles had no hook or pulling facility it was difficult to move the boy and it ". . . took some time, I don't know how much, but it took seconds or minutes to do this because the poles, of course, they are long and aluminum, and we use them to push, not to pull, because there was no way to get ahold."

He further testified that if the poles had been equipped with some type of pulling device he could have effected a speedier recovery. One of the poles bent as it was used in an attempt to push Ned to the shallow area.

Ordinance No. 1479 of the City of Dallas regulating the operation of public and semipublic swimming pools, required that one unit of "safety equipment" be available at all such pools at all times the pools were in use. One unit of lifesaving equipment was defined by the ordinance as including ". . . a life pole or shepherd's crook type of pole with minimum length handle of twelve feet . . . ."

There was evidence that the poles which were provided at the pool were merely straight aluminum poles without any hook or pulling device. The court was therefore required to decide whether a straight pole without such a hook or pulling device was a "life pole" within the meaning of the ordinance. If it was not, the jury could have found from the evidence that the defendant violated the ordinance in failing to provide a life pole. Such a violation would be negligence per se. . . .

It next becomes necessary to determine if from the evidence and inferences to be drawn therefrom, the negligence in failing to provide a life pole could have been a proximate cause of the death of Ned Harris.

In this case the testimony of defendant's own witness, Albuquerque, made it clear that the lack of a pole with a hook or pulling device caused a significant delay in the rescue because the poles could only be used to push the boy to the shallow portion of the pool where he could be retrieved by hand. His testimony also made it clear that the retrieval would have been quicker had the pole been equipped with a hook. The testimony also confirmed that the boy had not been submerged long when Albuquerque and his friend began to use the poles. Albuquerque first observed the boy "bobbing up and down" in the water. When Albuquerque made his unsuccessful attempt at rescue by entering the water, Ned had descended to or near the bottom of the pool. Albuquerque and his friend then got out and used the poles. Reasonable minds could infer from this evidence that, had the poles been as required by the ordinance, the boy could have been retrieved quickly enough to prevent his death. Prompt resuscitation efforts are frequently successful even though the victims have already lost consciousness when such efforts are begun. Many cases have held that circumstances similar to those here were sufficient to make a fact issue on proximate cause. The cases cited are not analogous on the issues of negligence but are analogous on the issue of proximate cause.

A careful analysis reveals that in the cases of this type which have held evidence of proximate cause to be insufficient, there was no evidence to indicate the circumstances surrounding the death. A body was simply found lying under or floating upon the water, with no indication how or when death occurred. . . .

For the reasons stated we conclude there was probative evidence of such causal relation and foreseeability as are required for a finding of proxi-mate cause, and that plaintiff was entitled to have such issue submitted to the jury.

Reversed

MANGANELLO v PERMASTONE INC.
Supreme Court of North Carolina
231 S.E.2d 678 1977

Copeland, Justice

The Superior Court of Cumberland County, North Carolina, Clarence W. Hall, J., directed a verdict for the defendant owner of a swimming facility in an action to recover damages for personal injuries brought by a swimmer who was injured when a young man, who was doing back flips from the shoulders of another, fell upon his neck and head, forcing him under the water. The Court of Appeals of North Carolina affirmed the trial court's judg-ment.

Plaintiff instituted this action to recover damages for personal injuries. Plaintiff's evidence tended to show that the plaintiff, along with his family and friends, went to Permastone Lake, owned by defendant corporation, on Labor Day, 1973. The parties stipulated that the defendant was engaged in operating a recreational facility which included a lake for swimming and that defendant charged a fee to members of the general public to use the lake and adjacent facilities. Plaintiff testified that on September 3, 1973, he paid the fee for himself and his family. It was further stipulated that defendant employed lifeguards at Permastone Lake for safety purposes and that life-guards were present and on duty on the day and during the hours in ques-tion.

After plaintiff had been at the lakeside for some time, he entered the water with his children near the sliding boards. Plaintiff's children slid down the board while plaintiff stood by to catch them and otherwise look after their safety. The water was about chest high on the plaintiff in the sliding area. The sliding continued for approximately one hour.

While this was going on, some young men, located about twenty to thirty feet away, began standing on the shoulders of one another and jump-ing backwards into the water. This activity continued for at least twenty min-utes, during which time the young men either gradually or suddenly moved over closer to the slide.

Plaintiff, thinking his children had been in the water long enough, sent them ahead to the pier. While he was swimming behind them to the dock, one of the young men jumped backwards from the shoulders of another and fell upon the plaintiff's head and neck, forcing him under the water. When plaintiff surfaced, he appeared to have been "knocked silly." A friend assisted him to the pier where he rested for about five minutes. Sometime later a man, who was apparently the father of the young man involved, came up and apologized for the conduct of his son.

Earlier, plaintiff had observed the young men doing backflips but stated on cross examination, "I did not see any danger to myself or my children or the people around the slide while I was there with the children. The last time I saw the men they were far enough away that I was not concerned about them."

The lifeguards on duty were sixteen to seventeen years of age and, according to the testimony, at times appeared to be paying more attention to the young female patrons than to the swimmers. These lifeguards did nothing to stop or control what the plaintiff described as "horseplay" and did not come to the plaintiff's aid at any time after he was injured.

The trial court permitted a Physical Education Director of the Fayetteville Y.M.C.A. to testify to accepted standards of aquatic safety as promulgated by the American Red Cross and the Y.M.C.A. The witness testified that it was not an acceptable aquatic practice to allow young men to get on one another's shoulders and do backflips into the water.

Plaintiff offered expert medical testimony to the effect that he had sustained a five percent permanent neck disability which could have been caused by the blow received at Permastone Lake.

At the conclusion of plaintiff's evidence, Judge Hall directed a verdict for the defendant and dismissed the action. The sole issue presented by this appeal questions whether the trial court erred in directing a verdict for the defendant. We hold that the trial court did commit error.

The duty imposed on the owner or proprietor of a swimming facility used for public amusement is stated generally in *Wilkins* v *Warren,* 108 S.E.2d 230 (NC 1959). The owner is not "an insurer of the safety of his patrons" but he must exercise "ordinary and reasonable care" for their safety lest he be held liable for injury to a patron resulting from breach of this duty. We discussed a proprietor's duty to protect invitees against the acts, negligent or intentional, of third parties in *Aaser* v *City of Charlotte,* 144 S.E.2d 610 (NC 1965). In that case we said: "The proprietor is liable for injuries resulting from the horseplay or boisterousness of others, regardless of whether such conduct is negligent or malicious, if he had sufficient notice to enable him to stop the activity. But in the absence of a showing of timely knowledge of the situation on his part, there is no liability."

While rough or boisterous play in water is not dangerous per se, hazardous consequences to other swimmers and bathers are clearly reasonably foreseeable when such activities are left unattended and unrestricted. If rough or boisterous play is to be permitted at all, it should be confined to a restricted area or, at minimum, closely guarded. We have said that "(t)he law does not require the owner to take steps for the safety of his invitees such as will unreasonably impair the attractiveness of the establishment for its customary patrons." However, this does not alter the proprietor of a public establishment's duty to see that all permitted activities are conducted in a reasonably safe manner.

The activity here in question, backflips done from off another's shoulders, qualifies as a "rough or boisterous" activity. The testimony of plaintiff's witness that this activity was not an accepted aquatic practice under Y.M.C.A. and American Red Cross guidelines is some evidence that dangerous consequences could reasonably be expected to flow from this type of activity.

The nature of the activity was such that its participants could reasonably be expected to change direction and move to different locations posing danger to other swimmers and bathers. The fact that plaintiff testified that, when he first observed the young men engaged in horseplay, "they were far enough away that they weren't causing me any problems," is not a controlling factor in this case.

Presumably, many people were engaged in recreational activity in Permastone Lake on Labor Day; the "acre or two" lake was described as "moderately crowded." Without question, defendant owed a duty to all its patrons, including plaintiff, either to prohibit roughhousing or to closely supervise it. A jury question has been presented as to whether plaintiff's injury was proximately caused by a breach of his duty. The decision of the Court of Appeals affirming Judge Hall's directed verdict for defendant was therefore erroneous and must be

Reversed

Recreation Centers

The defense of governmental immunity has been raised with mixed results in public building visitor injury cases. Governmental immunity has limited application in those states that have passed safe place provision in their tort claims statutes.[35] In abolishing the defense the states extend liability to the operator when the visitor injury was caused by a dangerous condition in a public building. Governmental immunity notwithstanding, the case law imposes a requirement on recreation operators to provide a reasonably safe facility and adequate supervision.[36] Translated into specific actions, the operator has a duty to (1) periodically inspect the doors, floors, walls, halls, stairs and equipment to discover dangerous conditions, (2) remedy dangerous conditions, (3) remove defective equipment, (4) promulgate and enforce rules to maintain order on the premises, and (5) supervise the conduct of those on the premises.[37]

The improper supervision cases involve the failure to protect the patron from actors or the conduct of others. The operator has a duty to maintain order on the premises and may be liable for injuries resulting from the dangerous activities of other patrons if the operator does nothing to restrain or control such conduct. Operators must use due care to protect patrons from assault and battery by other patrons if they might reasonably have anticipated the attack. Liability is not generally imposed for a more or less sudden and direct attack if it could not reasonably be anticipated. Pushing, shoving, and crowding are in the same category of liability provided that the actions are not precipitated by a panic.

WILKINSON v HARTFORD ACCIDENT
AND INDEMNITY COMPANY
Supreme Court of Louisiana
411 S.2d 22 1982

Marcus, Justice

David L. Wilkinson, individually as administrator the estate of his minor son, David Len Wilkinson, instituted this action against Joseph L. Rivers, Rapides Parish School Board, and Hartford Accident and Indemnity Company to recover damages for personal injuries sustained by David Len in an accident that occurred in the gymnasium lobby of the Glenmora High School. Hartford was the general liability insurer of the school board. After trial on the merits, the trial judge rendered judgment in favor of defendants and against plaintiff dismissing plaintiff's suit at his cost. In written reasons for judgment, the trial judge, while finding no negligence on the part of Rivers, concluded that the school board was negligent but denied recovery to plaintiff because of the contributory negligence of David Len. The court of appeal affirmed. On application of plaintiff, we granted certiorari to review the correctness of that decision.

The facts are generally not in dispute. On November 8, 1978, David Len Wilkinson, age twelve, attended his seventh grade physical education class conducted by Joe Rivers, athletic coach, in the high school gymnasium. The gymnasium was originally constructed in 1965 with ordinary glass installed in all windows. When entering the gymnasium through the front doors, the first area encountered is a lobby or foyer extending from left (south) to right (north) about seventy feet with glass panels extending from the floor to the ceiling at each end of the lobby. A concession stand is located immediately in front of the entrance doors, about seven feet back, and rest room facilities are located on either side of the front doors. A water fountain is outside each rest room. To reach the spectator area from the front door of the gymnasium, it is necessary to walk into the lobby, turn left or right and walk about thirty feet in either direction to a door which leads from the lobby to the bleachers. Each door is about five feet from the glass panels at the end of the lobby. There is a wall immediately behind the concession stand with openings or doorless "portages" on either side which provide direct access between the lobby and the basketball court. The panel at the north end of the lobby was safety glass (the original plate glass panel having been replaced several years earlier following an incident in which a visiting coach walked through the glass) and the south panel was the original plate glass. On the day of the accident, the physical education class was being conducted on the east half of the basketball court (side nearer the lobby). Another class was being conducted on the other half. Coach Rivers had divided the boys into six teams of five boys each. Relay races were being conducted between two teams at a time. At the conclusion of each race, the participants were instructed to sit along the inside east side wall of the gymnasium and await their next turn. Coach Rivers was supervising the races at the time. While the boys had been instructed not to linger or engage in horseplay in the lobby, they were permitted to go in the lobby to get water from the fountains. Following one of the races, David Len and the other members of his team went into the lobby to get a drink of water from the north fountain. It was decided at the time to conduct a race of their own between David Len and another boy in order to determine the order they should be positioned in the next race. The race was to be from the north water fountain to the south glass panel and back again. The other boy reached the panel first and turned but when David Len reached the glass panel, running at his full speed, he pushed off the panel with both hands causing the glass to break. He fell through the glass onto the outside. He sustained multiple cuts on his arms and right leg and was bleeding profusely. Coach Rivers came immediately to the scene and administered first aid. David Len was then taken to the hospital for further treatment. After the accident, the school board replaced the south panel with safety glass.

The issues presented are the alleged negligence of Coach Rivers in failing to properly supervise the physical education class and/or that of the school board in maintaining a plate glass panel in the foyer of the gymnasium and if either or both was negligent, whether plaintiff's action is barred by the contributory negligence of David Len.

The trial judge found that Rivers exercised reasonable supervision over the physical education class commensurate with the age of the children and the attendant circumstances. The court of appeal agreed. Our review of the record supports the conclusion reached by the courts below. Hence, we conclude that Coach Rivers was not negligent.

The trial court found that the negligence of the school board was a cause of the accident. A school board is liable if it has actual knowledge or constructive knowledge of a condition unreasonably hazardous to the children under its supervision. The evidence in the record amply supports the conclusion that the school board had actual and constructive knowledge that the existence and maintenance of plate glass in the foyer of the gymnasium was dangerous. An identical panel at the north end of the foyer was broken when a visiting coach walked into the plate glass several years earlier. The panel had been replaced by safety glass. Moreover, we consider that the plate glass in the foyer of a gymnasium less than five feet from the traffic pattern of spectators of all ages and directly accessible to the basketball court was so inherently dangerous that the school authorities should have known of the hazard it created. The court of appeal agreed with the finding of the trial court that the school board was negligent. We agree. Accordingly, we conclude that the school board was negligent.

Having found that the school board was negligent, we must next consider whether David Len, age twelve, was contributorily negligent. While a child of twelve can be guilty of contributory negligence, such a child's caution must be judged by his maturity and capacity to evaluate circumstances in each particular case, and he must exercise only the care expected of his age, intelligence and experience. Defendant bears the burden of proving contributory negligence by a preponderance of the evidence.

The race in the lobby of the gymnasium was simply an unsupervised extension of the relay races being conducted on the basketball court in the main area of the gymnasium. We consider that it was normal behavior for twelve year old boys to do what David Len and his teammates did under the circumstances despite a previous warning to refrain from engaging in horseplay in the lobby. Moreover, David Len had no reason to be aware that the panel through which he fell was plate glass as opposed to safety glass or to anticipate that pushing against this panel would cause it to shatter. Hence, we do not find that defendants met their burden of proving contributory negligence on the part of David Len. The trial judge was clearly wrong in holding otherwise, and the court of appeal erred in affirming the result.

In sum, we find that Joseph L. Rivers was not negligent. However, we do find that the Rapides Parish School Board was negligent but do not find that David Len Wilkinson was contributorily negligent. Hence, the negligence of the Rapides Parish School Board was the sole cause of the accident and the school board is responsible to plaintiff for damages sustained by David Len as a result of the accident.

For the reasons assigned, the judgment of the court of appeal is reversed and the case is remanded to the court of appeal to consider the issue of the amount of damages not reached in its original opinion.

Reversed and Remanded

Playgrounds

Recovery for injuries on playgrounds has been the exception rather than the rule. Although there is conflict as to whether the establishment and maintenance of city and school playgrounds is a governmental or proprietary function, the weight of authority is on the governmental side. While courts have imposed liability on the operators of swimming pools, golf courses, beaches, and other major revenue producing recreation facilities they have been reluctant to impose liability on the municipal operator for an injury to a patron in a playground.[38] This special status accorded to children's playgrounds is exemplified by the court's language in *Williams* v *Red Bark,* 227 A.2d 133 (NJ 1967), wherein playgrounds were held to be a governmental function inasmuch as they are

> intimately related to general welfare and private sources do not and probably cannot fulfill the publics need for such areas. Further . . .such areas are not operated for profit or any other reason but for the public health and welfare.

In the cases imposing liability on municipalities and schools, the basis for recovery is closely related to the length of time the premises defect was allowed to exist. The longer the defect was allowed to exist, the greater the possibility of liability. There is a pronounced trend to classify playgrounds as extensions of buildings and thus bring them within the purview of tort claims statutes.[39]

In the early 1970s, the U.S. Consumer Product Safety Commission, acting on a consumer's petition, began studying playground accidents in an attempt to reduce injuries. While the commission's initial work was oriented toward developing mandatory equipment safety standards, they backed away from the mandatory approach and have opted to issue guidelines for equipment and playground design. These guidelines are incorporated in a two volume handbook for public playground safety.[40] The following information and discussion is taken from that source.

A December 1978 CPSC *Hazard Analysis,* for example, estimates that in 1977 about 93,000 people were treated in hospital emergency rooms for injuries associated with public playground equipment. Children ten years of age or younger suffered four out of five of the injuries. Some of these injuries were caused when children were struck by moving pieces of equipment such as swings and gliders. Other children were injured when they caught an extremity such as a finger at a pivot or pinch point, or ran and fell against protruding bolts, screws, or other hardware on the equipment. Seven out of every ten injuries, however, were caused by falls—the most common playground accident. The type of surface on the playground was a major factor affecting the number and severity of injuries associated with falls. Falls onto paved surfaces resulted in a disproportionately high number of severe injuries. While protective surfaces as wood chips, shredded tires, and sand may not have reduced the number of injuries from falls, these materials could have reduced the severity of the injuries. See Table 6.1.

Traditional categories of playground equipment, such as swings,

TABLE 6.1* Pattern of Playground Injury

CAUSE OF INJURY	PERCENT
Falls to surface	59
Falls to equipment	13
Falls—subtotal	72
Impact with moving equipment	7
Contact with protrusions and sharp edges	5
Fall to other equipment	8
Unknown	8

* From U.S. Consumer Product Safety Commission, *Handbook for Public Playground Safety.*

slides, seesaws, climbers, and merry-go-rounds, are used in many playgrounds throughout the country. Table 6.2 compares the estimated percentage of injuries related to a particular type of equipment with the percentage of that equipment in use.

As indicated, falls are the most common type of playground accident. Nearly half the injuries that result from falls are to the head and range in severity from minor bruises to skull fractures, concussions, brain damage, and even death. Until recently, little information was available on the relative ability of surfacing materials to protect children from head injuries resulting from falls. Analyses of the test results by the National Bureau of Standards indicate that while they may require little maintenance or repair, *hard surfacing materials such as asphalt and concrete do not provide injury protection from accidental impacts and are therefore unsuitable for use under public playground equipment.*[41] More resilient surfacing materials such as bark, wood chips, or shredded tires, for example, appear to provide greater protection to a child in the event of a fall. However, these materials require continuous maintenance to retain their optimum cushioning effectiveness.

TABLE 6.2* Equipment Accident Patterns

	INJURIES BY EQUIPMENT (percent)	TOTAL EQUIPMENT IN USE (percent)
Climbers	42	51
Swings	23	20
Slides	16	12
Merrygorounds	8	5
Seesaws	5	6
All others	6	6

* From U.S. Consumer Product Safety Council, *Handbook for Public Playground Safety.*

The injury data and the playground cases suggest that liability for the operation is based on premises defects resulting from improperly installed equipment, failure to maintain existing equipment, and the use of improper surfacing beneath equipment. The playground operator should take cognizance of these three areas of legal risk in developing and maintaining playgrounds.

HART v WESTERN INVESTMENT & DEV. CO.
U.S. Circuit Court of Appeals
407 F.2d 1296 1969

Phillips, Circuit Judge

Eric Todd Hart, by his guardian ad litem, Milton Dale Hart, and Milton Dale Hart, individually, brought this action against Western Investment and Development Company, Inc. Eric sought to recover damages for personal injuries and Milton, his father, sought recovery for hospital and medical expenses incurred in the treatment of Eric for such injuries, and paid by Milton.

On June 24, 1966, and at all other times here material, Western owned and operated a trailer park in Salt Lake City, Utah, and as a part thereof maintained a playground constructed by it. Such playground was paved with hard asphalt, which contained no substance to soften it or give it resiliency. At such times it maintained thereon several playground devices, among which was a climbing device called a "monkey tree." The device had three vertical, cylindrical elements. The upper ends thereof were eight feet four inches from the asphalt surface paving below. Two of them were joined by a round cross member at their tops and with nine spaced rungs, which together with such two elements formed a ladder from the surface of the pavement to the top of the device. The third vertical element was positioned at a right angle to the ladder, and such third element and the vertical element of the ladder nearest to it were joined together by a round crossbar. Such a third element gave stability to the device and also was intended to be used as a sliding pole. A user of the device could climb to the top of the ladder, move over to the third element, and slide down it to the pavement.

The device had two round arms, one of which extended horizontally from the element which formed one side of the ladder, at a point four feet, ten and one half inches above the surface of the asphalt paving, and the other extended horizontally from the element which formed the other side of the ladder, at a point five feet, eleven and one quarter inches above such surface.

The arms were constructed so they could be used as chinning bars, turning bars, and for other acrobatic acts. An expert witness testified that the arms were so constructed so that a child could get on them and use them as "twirling devices."

Each arm extended thirty-eight inches from the vertical element to which it was attached. The device had no movable parts and was rigidly constructed.

Western purchased the device from Penman, who manufactured it and delivered it to Western on July 1, 1965. Penman had engaged for a period of more than thirty years in designing and manufacturing playground devices like the one here involved. When Penman delivered the climbing device, he suggested to Western that it install the device in a field west of the paved area and over natural earth, rather than "blacktop." Western's representative rejected the suggestion, stating it had paved and fenced the area, so it could close the gates and keep persons out when so desired.

Penman also advised Western that the vertical segments should be set in concrete bases submerged twenty-four inches in the ground; that spaces should be left between the tops of the bases and the surface of the asphalt pavement, and such spaces filled with earth, chips, or sand.

In installing the device, Western constructed the concrete bases so they projected slightly above the paved surface, and the vertical element from which the highest of the two arms extended and the sliding pole element were set in one solid piece of concrete, which extended along the side of the device. Western did not cover either the concrete or any part of the asphalt pavement under or about the device with earth, chips, sand, or other soft or flexible material.

Milton, his wife, Marjorie, Eric, and their older son, Brian, checked in at the trailer court on June 24, 1966, and paid for space to park their trailer. That evening, Eric and his brother Brian, went swimming in the trailer park pool and Eric climbed up part of the way on the ladder of the climbing device, but did not get onto either of the horizontal arms.

On June 25, 1966, Eric was seven and one-half years of age. On the morning of June 25, 1966, Eric and his brother again went to the playground. Mrs. Hart, while returning to the trailer after disposing of garbage, observed Eric sitting on the highest of the two arms on the climbing device. She testified that he was "perched on the bar (arm)." She described what she meant by the statement "perched" by saying, "He was sitting on a bar (arm) like this, with his hands on the bar (arm), sitting there looking around." She stated that as she looked at him, he fell off the bar (arm), and landed face first on the hard surface under the device; that she ran to him, picked him up, found he was quite limp, and carried him to the trailer. She said there was no part of the device he could reach and grab onto from where he was sitting and break his fall.

As a result of the fall, Eric suffered a cerebral contusion, fractures of the left anterior maxillary bone and of the nasal bone, and facial bruises causing tenderness and swelling of the nonosseous tissues in the area around his left eye and mouth and in and around his nasal bone. Later, the areas around his eyes and the exterior of his nose became black and blue. In addition thereto, the fall may have had some effect on his left arm in that he did not appear to use it quite as spontaneously as his right arm.

The law of Utah, which is here controlling, imposed a duty on the part of Western to use greater care for the safety of children of tender years, who, as invitees and paying guests, played upon the devices in its playgrounds, than it would have imposed had they been mature persons. Utah law also requires the owners of hotels, motels, and trailer parks, and their attendant playgrounds to take far greater measures to secure the safety of their paying patrons than a householder would be required to take for the safety of a social or even a business guest; and it requires such owners to possess a greater knowledge of the dangerous qualities of their hotels, motels, and trailer parks and the appurtenances thereto than it requires of such owners' patrons. And it imposes upon such owners the duty to take proper action to protect their patrons from such dangers.

We are of the opinion that the trial court properly applied the law of Utah, and that the evidence afforded ample and substantial support for the court's findings: That Western was negligent in installing and maintaining the climbing device over the "hard surface ground covering"; that Eric's injuries and costs of hospital and medical treatment were proximately caused by Western's negligence; that Eric was not contributorily negligent and did not assume the risk of playing on the device in the manner in which he did; that Eric suffered a cerebral contusion and fractures of his left anterior maxillary bone and his nasal bone and injuries to the nonosseous tissues of his nose and areas of his face adjacent to this nose, and that such injuries caused him permanent disability. And we are of the opinion that such findings are not clearly erroneous.

Affirmed

CATALANO v CITY of KANSAS CITY
Kansas City Court of Appeals
475 S.W.2d 1426 1971

Dixon, Justice

On June 16, 1966, the plaintiff, Richard J. D. Catalano, then ten years old, who had gone to Sunnyside Park to swim, stepped on a piece of broken beer bottle and severely cut his foot. He did not cut his foot in the pool itself. During a rest period he had gone to an adjacent playground area where he received the cut when he stepped off of the hard surface under the swings in rough-housing with another boy. He had a judgment for $3,250 as damages, and the City has appealed, claiming the trial court erred in refusing to direct verdict because the issues of "notice" and "due care" were not submissable. No issue is raised as to the amount of the verdict nor of the instructions in the case. It is conceded that the defendant City operated this park in a proprietary capacity and that it is required to exercise ordinary care to maintain such park in a reasonably safe condition.

For brevity, we summarize only the evidence relating to the issues of submissability. Sunnyside Park, where the plaintiff was injured, is shown to contain a small playground area containing swings and other playground equipment. The swings (and particularly the one near which the plaintiff was injured) have a hard surface under them, either asphalt or concrete. On the morning of June 16, 1966, a young man was present in the park at the exact location where the plaintiff was injured. Called as a witness by plaintiff, he testified that there was a Park Department Supervisor there in the mornings who picked up trash with the assistance of some of the children. He also stated quite a few "parties" had occurred in the park during the evenings immediately prior to this date. He said there was considerable debris scattered around in the park. In response to direct questioning, this witness testified there was glass in the grassy area of the park near the swing; and when asked to describe the glass he could see in the area around the swing, he stated "Most of the glass was beer bottles, and they were broken, and there was quite a few pieces partly imbedded in the ground." He asserted on cross examination that there was dirt and grass on the pieces of glass. This witness apparently remained at the park until the time of the injury to the plaintiff and was approximately twenty feet from the plaintiff when the injury to the plaintiff occurred. When questioned concerning the location of the plaintiff when injured, he testified as follows: " . . . there is a grassy area around the swings and asphalt under the swings. There is grass, you know, right around the asphalt. As far as I can remember, he was on the grassy area almost off the asphalt." He further stated that the grass was not excessively long in the area where the plaintiff was injured. Another witness testified that the condition of glass in the park was quite widespread during the months of May and June of 1966. The plaintiff and plaintiff's father testified that the piece of glass upon which the plaintiff cut his foot was a broken beer bottle, "a dirty beer bottle with mud around the middle of the sides and mud in the center went under the bottle." The piece of broken beer bottle was about six inches long and two to three inches around, "curved like," that it was a "bottle broken in half lengthwise." The time of the incident was between 2:30 and 3:00 in the afternoon, and thus, the condition of broken beer bottles on the ground had existed several hours. The plaintiff also introduced evidence concerning rainfall which indicated no rain had fallen for approximately twenty-two hours.

The City's response to interrogatories which were introduced in evidence showed that on the day in question, twelve employees of the City had been present at some time during the day on June 16, 1966. The occupations of the employees present included two foremen, three trash collectors, five lifeguards, and one supervisor of recreation. The City offered evidence to the effect that there was a daily pickup of trash and daily inspection by a supervisor or assistant, that they urged children to use the park areas and that they wanted to make the parkgrounds particularly safe because they were put there for the children's use. The trash crews were charged with the responsibility of picking up debris, and they concentrated on the playground areas, and there was usually glass in all of the parks. A lifeguard present on the day of the occasion was aware of a general condition of broken glass sometimes even in the pool. He inspected the area around the pool very carefully to protect the children "from the glass we knew was bound to be in the area." Upon this evidence, the City vigorously asserts that the plaintiff has failed to prove notice, actual or constructive, of the broken beer bottle which injured plaintiff. In the interest of simplicity, it may be conceded that there was no actual notice to any particular employee of the City that this particular piece of glass was in Sunnyside Park on the day in question. Nor is it entirely clear that the testimony of City's employees can be taken to be evidence of the actual knowledge of a general condition of broken glass in the park areas, although if that were all the evidence in the case, there might be a legitimate inference that the City's knowledge of the continuing condition of broken glass was sufficient to constitute notice.

In view of all the evidence presented by the plaintiff, we do not consider it necessary to place the resolution of this problem upon an issue of actual notice. The record plainly demonstrates that there was a condition of broken beer bottles in the morning when the City was making its routine inspection of the park. Such evidence supports an inference of notice to the City of this "condition."

The City's contention with respect to the issue of notice is that there was no evidence, actual or constructive, of the presence of "the broken bottle," that the evidence of the rainfall the previous day, coupled with evidence of rain spots and mud on the bottle, does not prove its presence in the area for any period of time. The City continues its argument by asserting that only by "speculation and conjecture" could the jury "deduce just when the bottle was so positioned." If the plaintiff's burden was to show when "the bottle" was deposited in the grass, the City's contention might be sound. Neither logic nor law require that such a burden be shouldered by the plaintiff. If is clear that when the risk arises from a condition as opposed to a specific defect, there is no requirement of notice as to the component parts of the condition.

On the issue of due care, the City stresses the immense size of its park system and argues that to require it to discover this piece of glass in such an immense park system would, in effect, make it an insurer of plaintiff's safety. We do not accept its assumption necessary to this contention that the duty to which it is held embraces all of the area in every park. Here we have a small playground area where the City had, by the erection of playground equipment, directed the activities of the children. The condition which injured the plaintiff arose within this restricted area. The risk of injury to the plaintiff and others similarly situated arose from the condition of broken beer bottles. From the ambit of that risk arose the City's duty to make the premises safe as to that risk. It does not require us to strain reason to say that the City's duty to remedy this condition of which it had constructive notice included the duty of a vigilant enough search to discover a piece of broken beer bottle six inches by two or three inches in size located in grass which had been beaten down by the children and which was, at most, one or two steps from the hard surface where the swings were located.

There was at least one employee present who knew of the very risk which the plaintiff encountered, the lifeguard who testified that he looked very carefully for glass which he "knew was bound to be in the area." It does not require us to find that the City is an insurer to say that the City, having invited the children to the specific area of these swings and having constructive notice of a condition of broken glass, was under a duty during the several hours that such notice existed to have taken steps to remedy the dangerous condition. Under the facts of this case, we feel that the City has failed to perform its duty of ordinary care to keep Sunnyside Park in a reasonably safe condition in the area where the plaintiff was hurt.

Affirmed

RHABB v NEW YORK CITY HOUSING AUTHORITY
Court of Appeals of New York
359 N.E.2d 1335 1976

Cooke, Judge

As the result of a 1973 playground incident, Hampton Rhabb, the infant plaintiff, allegedly sustained a fractured patella requiring open reduction and resulting in permanent disability. In a suit brought on his behalf and by his mother, at the conclusion of their proof upon a trial to determine liability, the complaint was dismissed. The Appellate Division affirmed.

Defendant operated the Williamsburg Housing Project covering sixteen blocks of Brooklyn real estate. Within this space were several playgrounds, all open to the public. One of these play areas, located at or near 164 Ten Eyck Walk, was about a half block in size. There was a fence around part or all of it, with paths leading therefrom to the street and to a basketball court. The playground was equipped with items such as a spider web, rocket, airplane and monkey bars. Children of tender years played there. It was unsupervised. Across the street was a school. I.S. 49, at which Hampton Rhabb, then twelve, was a student.

There was testimony: that every noon hour on nice days from the beginning of school in September 1972 until the day of the accident, a period of about four months, pupils from the school went to the playground; that on each of these occasions an unleashed black, shaggy dog about two or two and half feet tall and belonging to one of defendant's employees was in the playground; that this dog during said period attempted to bite the infant plaintiff five or six times and on diverse instances had chased other children, also trying to bite them. There was also proof: that during the luncheon recess period of January 8, 1873, the infant plaintiff went from the school to the playground with his friends Craig Chapman and Peter Martin; that they were playing tag for about ten minutes when the dog chased Craig and he jumped over a fence; that the animal then chased Peter and he climbed up the monkey bars; that the dog then went towards Hampton who started to run; and that when the dog bit Hampton on the pant leg, he tried to break loose but fell at a point about six feet from the bars and could not get up.

It is the general rule that a municipality is under a duty to maintain its park and playground facilities in a reasonably safe condition. It has been held that his duty goes beyond the mere maintenance of the physical condition of the park or playground and, although strict or immediate supervision need not be provided, the municipality may be obliged to furnish an adequate degree of general supervision which may require the regulation or prevention of such activities as endanger others utilizing the park. When in the discharge of that duty it is or should be apparent, or it otherwise comes to the attention of a municipality, that its park or playground is being used as a site for patently dangerous activities and that such use is likely to be continued, the municipality may not ignore the foreseeable dangers, continue to extend an invitation to the public to use the area and not be held accountable for resultant injuries. Furthermore and more significantly, when practices or activities pregnant with danger take place with frequency and regularity and over an extended period it cannot be said that the condition of the playground is safe. Apart from questions relating to actual notice, when a defective and dangerous condition has existed for such a length of time that knowledge thereof could be acquired by reasonable inspection or supervision, then such party will be held to have known what he should have known as the result of such inspection or supervision.

Upon defendant's motion made at the close of plaintiff's case, the test was whether there was any rational basis on which a jury could have found for plaintiffs, the plaintiffs being entitled to every favorable inference which could reasonably be drawn from the evidence submitted by the. Despite questions of inconsistency of proof and credibility of witnesses, the motion should not have been granted because plaintiffs had by their proof made out a prima facie case. There was evidence that the black, shaggy dog had been in this public playground during the noon hour, when customarily visited by students, over a four month period. During this interval, the animal not only chased these children but attempted to bite them. Under plaintiff's proof, it would be found by the trier of the facts that the defendant had constructive notice of a dangerous condition upon its playground, that defendant ignored this condition and failed in the exercise of the duty case upon it to remove or prevent this danger, that because of the use of the area by youngsters and considering their propensities, the injury to the infant plaintiff was foreseeable, and that defendant was liable.

Reversed

Ball Diamonds

Spectators injured by batted or thrown balls or through other hazards of the game have sought without much success to impose liability on the operator of the facility. The paucity of spectator victories is due in part to the court rule that spectators at sports activities assume, as a matter of law, all of the ordinary and inherent risks of the sport which they are observing.[42] This common knowledge rule applied to spectators of reasonable intelligence is expressed as the *assumption of risk doctrine*. This rule is illustrated by *Hudson* v *Kansas City Baseball Club*, 14 S.W.2d 318 (MO 1942), and involves a paying customer at a baseball double header. He purchased a reserved seat ticket and was escorted to a seat where there was no screen, though he alleged that he wanted a screened seat. He was struck and injured by a foul ball and brought suit against the operator alleging negligence in the failure to screen a specific area and in selling seats without notifying customers as to whether they were screened or not. The court in affirming a judgment for the operator stated that

> the plaintiff says he was "subject to the ordinary impairments of eyesight" of a man sixty-four years of age, but he does not say his vision was so impaired that he could not see which was plainly before him. . . . Assuming that all the plaintiff's allegations are true, yet there is nothing in them indicating that he was not fully aware of the obvious fact that he was sitting in an unscreened area of the grandstand and subject to the well-known personal hazards of a ball game, especially that of being hit by a foul ball. Even though the defendant did not screen a given section of the grandstand, even though there may have been some confusion about the manner of the defendant's selling seats, etc., yet the plaintiff while watching the game "which was then going on" (he does not say how long) must have seen that he was not sitting behind a wire screen. Despite his allegations of negligence we yet have a condition so open and obvious that it was apparent or would have been had he been looking. Because of these allegations he cannot be said to have lost his former knowledge of the facts of baseball, the hazards and perils usually incident to the game, as well as his past experience, his present intention and impression in that he knew he was sitting in an unscreened area where he might be struck

by a foul ball, but simply forgot or ignored the fact, neither of which is excused by his allegation. Citations omitted. He therefore voluntarily elected to
watch the game with full knowledge of the danger incident to it and of the
possibility of injury to himself, and his petition does not contain averments of
special circumstances which, if true, would entitle him to recover.

While the assumption of risk rule will preclude a spectator from recovering from many injuries suffered from foul balls and other common
hazards of the game, it does not always prevent recovery. Spectators are
presumed to only assume the ordinary and inherent risks of the game and
will not assume other risks.[43] Assumption of risk does not ban recovery
where the operators fail to maintain premises in a reasonably safe condition or to supervise the conduct of those on the premises to prevent injury.
Thus operators will be liable for hidden premises defects which cause injury to spectators. The duty of operators of sports facilities to protect
spectator-invitees from defective conditions has received judicial attention
in cases involving bleachers and seating arrangements. These cases trans-
late into a duty of the operator to (1) protect spectators against risks from
thrown or batted balls by providing some seats that are protected by
screens (usually behind plate and along the baselines) [44] and (2) periodically
inspect the seating facilities to insure that they are safe for occupancy.[45] Applying these general rules, courts have held operators liable for injuries
when the seating structure collapsed,[46] when seats were not properly attached to the floor,[47] when rotten wood was used in the construction of
bleachers,[48] and when needed repairs were not undertaken.[49]

When actions are brought against operators of ball diamonds and sta-
dia for injuries suffered by players and coaches, the legal issue will be
whether the operators have met their duty of care to participants invited to
use the facility. Thus operators will be liable for premises defects which injure participants if they know or should reasonably have discovered hidden
defects which pose unreasonable risks of harm which the participant will
not discover or protect against.[50] This translates into a duty to maintain the
premises in a safe condition, provide proper equipment, and supervise the
conduct of those on the premises.

Campgrounds

Camping is a big business in the United States with over a billion dollars spent each year on trailers, tents, camping equipment, entrance fees,
and other related expenses. There are over 7,600 private and 5,100 public
campgrounds in the United States providing more than one million individual campsites.[51] All offer at least a campsite with a firepit. More elaborate campgrounds have electrical, sewer and water hookups, hot showers,
swimming pools, playgrounds, and grocery stores. This section considers
the legal obligations and responsibilities that public and private camp-

ground operators have to their customers and guests. As with other recreation facilities, the injured party's status will be likely to determine the legal duty of care as will other factors such as the area in which the injury occurred and who had control of that area.

Generally, operators must exercise reasonable care to keep campgrounds in a safe and suitable condition and to take precautions to ameliorate unreasonable risks of harm. Concomitant with this duty is an obligation to make periodic inspections of the campgrounds and ancillary facilities to insure their proper working condition and to warn of hidden dangers. Although the duty of care is the same for public and private operators and for rustic and modern campground operators, the standard of conduct may differ depending on the degree of risk. As noted earlier, the operator has a duty to prevent unreasonable risks of harm to the user. A risk will be considered unreasonable when the probability of injury outweighs the burden of taking adequate precautions to prevent its occurrence. The degree of caution required by the campground operator will increase in proportion to the probability that its activities will cause serious injury to others.[52] For the operator of a modern campground in an urban environment with thirty times the users and a large swimming pool the risk of harm may be more unreasonable if the operator doesn't make daily inspections as contrasted with the operator of a rustic campground if only weekly inspections are conducted. The case of *Middaugh* v *United States* illustrates the problems associated with degree of control and preventing unreasonable risks of harm.

A related problem concerns the duty of operators to warn users of dangerous flora, fauna, and wildlife. As a general rule, the operator is under no duty to warn of known and obvious dangers, however, when the dangers are not obvious liability may arise. Correspondingly, when the degree of risk increases, the standard of conduct to prevent injury may require the removal of the dangerous plants and wildlife instead of merely warning of their existence. The case of *Rubenstein* v *United States* illustrates these principles.

MIDDAUGH v U.S.
U.S. District Court
293 F.Supp. 977 1968

Kerr, District Judge

The above entitled matter having come on regularly for hearing before the Court, and the Court having examined the evidence adduced for and on behalf of the plaintiff and the evidence adduced for and on behalf of the defendant, took said matter under advisement; and having examined the record on file herein, and having studied the authorities submitted by counsel on behalf of plaintiff and on behalf of the United States of America, and being fully advised in the premises, the Court does hereby make its Findings of Fact and Conclusions of Law:

Findings of Fact

1. This action is brought under authority of the wrongful death statutes of the State of Wyoming §1-1065 and §1-1066, W.S.1957, against the United States pursuant to the provisions of the Tort Claims Act, 28 U.S.C. §1346.

2. The plaintiff is a citizen and resident of Natrona County, Wyoming, and is the duly appointed, qualified, and acting Administrator of the Estate of Stephen Athan, Deceased.

3. The decedent, a resident of California, was killed by a falling lodge pole pine tree at a designated campsite in the Lewis Lake campground, Yellowstone National park, State of Wyoming, on July 2, 1966, at about 5:30 P.M.

4. Yellowstone National Park was opened to the public for the tourist season of 1966 on May 1, 1966. Lewis Lake Campground was opened to the public for the summer season on June 10, 1966.

5. The decedent, driving the personal family car and accompanied by his wife and three year old daughter, entered Yellowstone National Park through the south entrance in the late afternoon of July 2, 1966. He was required to and did pay a $7 fee for which he received a "golden pass" which permitted him to enter the Park and other Federal recreational areas.

6. The decedent, who desired to camp in the Park, was directed by a Park Service Ranger to the Lewis Lake Campground approximtely twenty-one miles north of the Park entrance. He drove via a main Park road to that campground where several vacant "walk-in" campsites were available. He chose site W-9 located sixty to seventy-five feet from the road leading into the campground, said site being one of the eighteen authorized campsites to which campers are confined. With the assistance of his wife and other campers, he carried his camping gear, food and other belongings to campsite W-9 where he erected his tent.

7. No camping is permitted in Yellowstone National Park outside designated campgrounds and the Lewis Lake Campground is equipped with water hydrants, outdoor toilet facilities, and fireplaces.

8. Within moments after the tent was erected and while decedent was standing therein, the tree collapsed and fell striking the tent and the decedent causing injuries to Stephen Athan from which he died within a few hours while enroute in a Park Service ambulance to the Yellowstone Local Hospital.

9. The tree which fell and killed the decedent collapsed approximately twenty feet from ground level, was approximately seventy feet in length and thirteen inches in diameter at the point where the collapse occurred. It was approximately three hundred years old and stood about fifty feet from the decedent's campsite. Prior to the time the tree fell, it was immediately adjoined by a smaller twin tree which was removed after the acci-

dent by person or persons unknown. A twin, or bifurcated, tree such as this one is suspect as being dangerous.

10. The Lewis Lake Campground is in the Snake River Subdistrict in Yellowstone National Park. The ranger in charge of the Snake River Subdistrict for the tourist seasons extending from 1964 through 1967 was Ranger Raymond L. Ives.

11. Subdistrict Ranger Raymond L. Ives, Park Service Ranger in charge of the Lewis Lake Campground, arrived at the scene of the accident ten to twenty minutes after it occurred. At a later time, he observed a "cat face" at the base of the tree which had fallen. A "cat face" is a wound or injury to a tree which can be caused by various sources resulting in an opening or depression in the tree. This condition was clearly visible to Ranger Ives when he inspected the scene of the accident.

12. Ranger Ives testified that if he observed the "cat face" on this tree prior to the accident, he would have investigated further into the condition of the tree, and that if he had discovered the tree's decayed condition, he would have caused it to be removed as a hazardous tree. Ranger Ives did not know whether any other government employee had inspected the tree.

13. Failure of this tree was a collapse as distinguished from a rupture. In the case of a collapse, the tree falls because of weakness and does not need the application of severe external forces which cause a rupture.

14. Examination of the tree June 23, 1967, which still lay as it had fallen with the exception that the crown portion of the tree had been removed, showed the occurrence of a rust canker affecting the same side of the tree and facing in the same direction in which it fell, the open part of the canker extending fifty feet above the ground. The canker, which appeared to have been present at least seventy-five years, resulted in a flattening of the affected portion. Beneath the canker was the opening, or "cat face," extending into the tree through what would normally have been the heartwood, which hole contained rot, insect chewings, and related material. Approximately seventy percent of the tree had rotted away. The hole at the base of the tree provided an entry court for diseases and forest insects and resulted in the advanced and incipient decay. At the point where the collapse occurred, the tree was in an advanced state of decay which had severely weakened it.

15. The basal hole in the tree had weakened it in the same manner as an undercut placed by a tree faller causing it to fall in the direction in which it fell.

16. The basal hole in the tree was clearly visible and should have been discovered by routine inspection of the Campground for hazardous trees leading to further inspection and investigation and removal thereof because of its hazardous condition.

17. It is the admitted policy of the National Park Service to inspect all campgronds for dead and diseased trees and to remove those which might constitute a hazard to campers.

18. Subdistrict Ranger Ives did not inspect the tree in question at any time prior to its collapse.

19. Seasonal Ranger Barton, who was stationed at Lewis Lake Campground in the summer of 1966 arrived at Lewis Lake Campground on July 1, 1966. He drove through the campground on the morning of July 2 in a motor vehicle. Ranger Barton did not inspect the tree which fell but examined it after the collapse and testified that he was surprised at the interior

condition of the tree at the point of collapse as opposed to its exterior. Ranger Barton is a mathematics teacher by profession and, including the summer of 1966, worked at Lewis Lake Campground for three summers. He stated, in referring to his background as a Ranger, "I haven't had much experience."

20. One of the Government witnesses, Ranger Lowell White, has been a Park Forester since September 1966. When his attention was directed to the decay shown in plaintiff's Exhibit 3, he described it as "pretty bad."

21. The tree was in fact hazardous to campers and other visitors at the time it fell and killed the decedent.

22. The weather in the vicinity of Lewis Lake Campground at the time the tree fell was normal for the season and the wind was moderate and blowing from the southwest, opposite to the direction in which the tree fell. No other trees fell on July 2, 1966, in the Lewis Lake Campground.

23. The United States of America failed to provide a safe place for the decedent to camp in that the opening near the base of the tree was clearly visible to the officials of the National Park Service had they looked, and a further examination of the tree would have disclosed that the trunk of the tree was in an advanced state of decay. The failure of the United States to provide a safe campsite was the sole and proximate cause of the death of the plaintiff's decedent, Stephen Athan.

Conclusions of Law

The Court has jurisdiction of the subject matter and the parties.

1. Plaintiff's intestate, the decedent Stephen Athan, was an invitee in Yellowstone National Park to whom the United States owed the duty to use ordinary and reasonable care to keep the premises reasonably safe for his visit and to warn him of any hidden danger.

2. The Government, as landowner, is required to have a superior knowledge of dangers which would not be obvious to the invitee if such dangers are discoverable in the exercise of due care.

3. A danger existed to the decedent and other invitees which should have been known to the Park employees. It was the Government's duty to have removed the hazard or to make an honest disclosure of the danger to the decedent so as to afford him an opportunity for an intelligent choice as to whether he wished to incur the risk incident to coming upon the land.

4. The collapse of the tree which killed the decedent was not due to an Act of God, which is an injury due directly and exclusively to natural causes without human intervention which could not have been prevented by exercise of reasonable care and foresight.

5. The Government, as owner and proprietor of Yellowstone National Park, was charged with the duty to inspect and to guard against injury to invitees drawn thereto since the tree was under the exclusive custody, control, and management of the proprietor.

6. The invitation extended to public invitees encourages visitors to enter upon the land with a sense of assurance that it has been prepared for their safety.

7. The decedent did not assume the risk of camping where he was directed to go and was not guilty of any contributory negligence.

8. The United States of America was negligent in the performance of its du-

ties and such negligence was the sole and proximate cause of the death of plaintiff's intestate, Stephen Athan.

9. The United States of America is liable to plaintiff and judgment should be entered in favor of the plaintiff and against the defendant in the sum of $43,750 which sum will reasonably compensate the survivors for the amount they failed and will fail to receive and for the loss they sustained and will sustain by reason of the death of decedent, together with death of the decedent.

Judgment for Plaintiff

RUBENSTEIN v UNITED STATES
United States District Court
388 F.Supp. 654 1968

Spencer, District Judge

Plaintiff Burrel Rubenstein brought this action against the United States under the Federal Tort Claims Act to recover for personal injuries suffered as a result of an attack by a bear while camping at Yellowstone National Park. The case was tried before the court without a jury and after careful review of the evidence and the law the court finds in favor of the defendant.

Findings of Fact

On the evening of September 9, 1965, Rubenstein, his son Loren, and his son's friend entered Yellowstone Park by automobile. The two boys had planned to sleep out that evening at Fishing Bridge Camp Ground and it was only after Rubenstein was unable to secure satisfactory lodgings for himself at the Lake Lodge that he decided to join them. The campers set up camp, purchased steaks and other supplies from the nearby store, prepared and ate dinner, and turned in sometime between 10 and 10:30 P.M. At about 11 P.M. the boys observed a black bear rummaging through trash cans close by. At approximately 1 A.M. the plaintiff was awakened in his tent by the pressure of a large bear paw on his chest. His understandably startled reflex apparently startled the bear, and in the tussle which ensued the bear severely mangled plaintiff's legs. The boys, who were in sleeping bags nearby, were awakened by the cries of plaintiff and were able to drive off the animal. Plaintiff was taken immediately by park officials to a nearby hospital for treatment.

The campground where the incident occurred was within one of the most populated areas in the Park. Located in close proximity were the fire station, gas station, store, ranger's office, and restrooms. Plaintiff's campsite was located only fifty feet from a lighted restroom. Electric lights were strung throughout the campground and were burning at the time of the incident. The campgrounds were filled almost to capacity the night in question.

While plaintiff was a novice camper, he had previously visited Yellowstone on several occasions. The party had been given the usual Park brochures upon entrance to the Park. These brochures generally admonish visitors about the dangers prevalent in a wildlife park and list suggestions as to how to conduct themselves with respect to the use of the campsites.

The following warnings are clearly printed in what the defendant refers to as the "special bear insert":

About Bears

Like all animals in our National Parks, bears are wild animals and fear man. While this may make them appear tame, actually in this state they are more dangerous.

Plaintiff testified that he read the brochures in detail and recalled they indicated the Park was populated by wild, dangerous, unpredictable animals. Plaintiff further testified that he complied with all camp rules, did not leave any food in the car or in the tent and completely cleaned the camp site after the meal.

The ranger stationed at the plaintiff's campground on the morning of the attack was not identified and was not available as a witness. Gary Hammond, the Park Ranger responsible for supervision of the region of the park which included Fishing Bridge, testified that it was the universal practice of rangers to advise visitors that all wild animals, including bears, are dangerous. He further stated that large signs are also posted throughout the park warning visitors that bears are dangerous.

There was uncorroborated testimony by Loren to the effect that at the time the Rubenstein party arrived at the campground he (Loren) made inquiry at the ranger station as to the possibility of trouble from animals and was assured by a ranger that they would have nothing to worry about.

Conclusions of Law

While reported cases dealing with facts similar to those presented here do not abound, two well-considered opinions have established useful guidelines.

In *Claypool v United States,* 98 F. Supp. 702 (S.D. CA 1951) the court found negligence on the part of the government and awarded the plaintiff damage.

It is essential to note that the danger to which Mr. Claypool was subjected was not of an uncertain nature relating to the general vicious propensities of bears. Rather, it was a very real, "new and extraordinary danger to persons camping out . . . shown to have been present in the Park by the raid of July 13th . . . "

In contrast, the danger of which plaintiff here contends he should have been warned was not specific and was certainly not known to, or even reasonably foreseeable by, the rangers. It is difficult, in fact, to envisage what additional measure the park authorities could have taken to ward off such an unexpected occurrence.

In Claypool it was found that the risk the government claimed plaintiff assumed was "a concealed one." In the instant case nothing was concealed by the park rangers. Absent a specific, undisclosed danger, plaintiff can be said to have assumed the generally known risks of camping in the park. Plaintiff testified he had been in the park on several previous occasions; that on each occasion he had read the brochures; and that he was at least familiar enough with bears to know the difference between a black bear and a grizzly bear.

Mr. Rubenstein maintains he was lulled into a "false sense of security" in that he was led to believe that if he obeyed all the rules and regulations he would not be attacked by a bear. The court holds that a reasonable man under circumstances similar to those described herein would have realized this type of danger exists in a wildlife park and that Mr. Rubenstein either knew or should have known of the risk of an unprovoked attack.

Both the legal and policy considerations involved in hte instant case are akin to those discussed in *Ashley* v *United States,* 215 F. Supp. 39 (D.NE 1963). There the plaintiff, a visitor to Yellowstone, was attacked by a bear in midafternoon while dozing in his automobile. While the court in that case may have been able to ultimately find contributory negligence on the part of the plaintiff, it expressly declined to reach that consideration, as it found the government had, by posting warning signs and issuing plaintiff the general park literature about bears, fulfilled the duty of care owed to him. Specifically, the court "did not find that the rangers in the area were aware prior to the plaintiff's injury that the bear which caused plaintiff's injuries . . . was dangerous to the safety of park visitors or employees, or more important that it would make an unprovoked attack on an automobile or on a passenger in it." And continuing, at page 47:

> The plaintiff . . . contends that defendant was negligent in failing to give the plaintiff a more adequate warning concerning bears than was given and that this negligence was a proximate cause of the injury. The court is of the opinion that no such failure on the part of the defendant caused plaintiff's injury. The plaintiff was told that bears were dangerous and that any attempt to feed or molest them was dangerous.

In the present case, the evidence indicates that the attack suffered by Mr. Rubenstein was even less predictable. The campground was bustling with campers, lights were on, and fires were blazing. Furthermore, Ranger Hammond described grizzly bears as "skittish and timid" animals that reside in the back-country regions of the Park and that he knew of no previous unprovoked grizzly attacks in the populated areas of the park. That a grizzly bear would embark on an unprovoked attack under these circumstances was totally outside the experience of the Park authorities.

It cannot be overemphasized that to a very great extent the value and attraction of national parks is their natural and untamed state. They offer vacationers a relief from the all too artificial and confining aspects of city life. As stated in the Ashley decision:

> The public interest in maintaining parks like Yellowstone, where the land is preserved in its undisturbed state and wild animals are found in their natural habitats, outweighs any interest plaintiff may have in holding the defendant as an insurer of the safety of visitors in bear country. The defendant made the choice to set aside the park land not for any selfish or personal reason . . . but for the good of the entire public, including the plaintiff.

With the increased public demand for opening wild areas for hiking and camping, the imposition of a standard of liability greater than that set forth in the Claypool case would create tremendous additional costs to the taxpayers and could conceivably inhibit the government's willingness to develop additional recreational areas. With the impending shorter work week and longer vacation periods, more and more persons will find additional time for this wholesome recreational activity. Warnings as to known physical dangers such as those in the various thermal areas are, of course, required. But warnings as to unanticipated earthquakes, lava flows, landslides should not be. So too, while reasonable control of animals such as that currently practiced, and warnings as to currently known presence of attack-minded animals are also required, the law imposes no duty on park authorities to warn about completely unforeseeable actions of wild animals such as indicated in this case.

The court concludes that actionable negligence is not shown on the part of the defendant and this order is hereby entered denying and dismissing plaintiff's claim.

Judgment for Defendant

SUMMARY

Owners and operators of recreation and sports areas and facilities are subject to the same liability rules imposed on possessors of land. Thus, when lawsuits are brought by participants and spectators against facility owners and operators the legal issue will generally be whether the operators have met their legal standard of care. The standard of care owed to a person who is using a recreation and sports facility is dependent upon whether the individual is regarded as an invitee, licensee, or trespasser.

An invitee is one who enters the premises in answer to an express or implied invitation by the owner. Operators have a duty to exercise reasonable care to protect invitees from injury caused, by either the condition of the facility and equipment located thereon, or by the conduct of third persons, provided that the injury could have been prevented by the exercise of reasonable care. As far as the invitee is concerned, the right to protection is a positive one in that the owner must inspect the facility to discover hidden or concealed defects, warn the invitee of these dangers, and promulgate and enforce rules of conduct. Generally, bona-fide participants and spectators are classified as invitees.

A person is a licensee if that person's entry upon or use of the facility is either expressly or impliedly permitted by the owner. Thus, a licensee differs from an invitee in that the former is using the facility only by the permission of the owner, while the latter is there at the invitation of the owner. The facility owner owes a licensee a duty to warn of hidden defects and to refrain from injuring him willfully or wantonly.

Lowest on the scale of legal protection is the adult trespasser, defined as a person who enters or remains upon the premises without permission to do so. A recreation and sports facility operator owes an adult trespasser no general duty of care except to avoid injury to the trespasser through intentional or reckless misconduct. There is no duty to make the facility reasonably safe or to discover and warn of dangerous conditions.

When the trespasser is a child at least forty-three states have adopted special liability rules (attractive nuisance doctrine) imposing on facility operators a greater duty of care. An operator is subject to liability caused by an artificial condition of the land if the operator knows children are likely to trespass, the condition involves an unreasonable risk of harm, and the children because of their "youth" do not discover or realize the danger. This doctrine applies to artificial or man-made conditions and not to natural conditions.

Many states have modified the facility owners' duty of care through the enactment of "recreational use" statutes. Although the statutes vary in their particulars all reduce the duty of care that landowners must give to nonpaying recreation visitors. This lower standard of care generally does not apply to enterprises that charge a fee to use a recreation facility.

Minimizing unreasonable risks of harm is best achieved when recreation and sports enterprises periodically inspect land, facilities, and equipment to discover obvious and hidden defects. Once discovered the defect must be quickly removed or repaired or the user made aware of its existence. In addition to an inspection, repair, and warning requirement, enterprises also have a duty to develop and enforce facility use rules and regulations to protect the invitee. While the frequency of inspections and the extent of operation rules will vary these general duties remain constant.

To fulfill the duty of care owed to invitees the recreation and sports enterprise should undertake the following actions if they manage these types of recreation facilities:

1. Beaches
   — Periodically check all swimming and diving areas for changes in water and for the presence of submerged objects.
   — Clear beach areas regularly of broken glass, cans and other sharp objects.
   — Install lifelines and flotation devices to divide shallow and deep water areas.
   — Provide functional and operating rescue equipment.
   — Continually check and maintain all warning signs.
   — Prohibiting boating in the beach area.
   — Provide lifeguards on beaches where the water currents, tides, bottom conformation and type of beach users presents unreasonable risks of harm to swimmers and bathers.

2. Pools
   — Train pool attendants in inspections and maintenance procedures.
   — Keep chemicals and pool equipment locked away from unauthorized children.
   — Test water daily and record chemical use.
   — Keep pool decks, stairs, walks, ladders, and platforms clear and clean of all algae and other substances.
   — Check pool furniture, floats, and other equipment for loose connections and other defects.
   — Prohibit the use of glass beverage containers in all pool areas.
   — Provide adequate numbers of lifeguards for pool use.
   — Insure that all guards meet your standards through independent and periodic testing.

3. Recreation Centers
   — Install safety glass in all doors and entrance areas.
   — Prevent rowdy activity and running in all halls, lobbies, and stairwells.
   — Slip and fall cases are bothersome so periodically check all floors for water and other slippery substances and remove promptly.
   — Check outside walks and lighting and promptly replace all burned out lights.

4. Playgrounds
   — Check equipment regularly for: protruding bolts, nails, or open ends of tubing; sharp edges; pinch, crush or shear points; tightness of joints and anchoring; and corrosion, wear, or missing parts.
   — Be aware that natural surfaces such as grass decrease the frequency of injuries.
   — Pick up broken glass, pop tabs, and other objects from play surface regularly.

5. Campgrounds
   — Clearly mark entrances and exits to camp.

— Clear away trees, brush and other obstructions to provide good view of traffic.
— Destroy poison ivy along high traffic areas and campsites.
— Search out and eliminate insect breeding areas.
— Post warning signs at hazards and around construction areas.
— Point out hazardous areas to guests at registration, particularly guests with small children.
— Check trees before the season begins and remove dangerous limbs.
— Properly grade and repair roads and pathways.
— Remove tree roots and holes from campsite areas.

These recommendations incorporate two types of hazard control measures—inspections and maintenance. They are based on the loss exposure facing enterprises and are reasonable measures to minimize risk.

DISCUSSION QUESTIONS

1. Define an invitee, licensee, and trespasser. Why are these categories important in recreation and sports injury cases?
2. What is an attractive nuisance and when does it apply to a park, recreation, or sports facility?
3. If a user remains in a recreation facility after closing hours how does this affect the facility owner's liability?
4. Under what circumstances would a warning sign not provide an adequate notice of danger to the user of a beach area?
5. Does the owner of a public swimming beach have a legal duty to provide lifeguards at the beach when it is open to the public?
6. Is a swimming pool owner liable for the failure to have specific types of rescue equipment available at poolside?
7. What is the predominate cause of injury in playground accidents?
8. Does a city or school have a duty to supervise a playground during the hours that it is open to the public?

NOTES

[1] See 72 A.L.R.3d 1269 (1976); 51 A.L.R.3d 711 (1973).
[2] *Tobin* v *Slutsky*, 506 F.2d 1097 (1974), *Peters* v *Holiday Inns, Inc.* 278 N.W. 2d 208 (WI, 1979).
[3] WILLIAM PROSSER, *Law of Torts* 4th Ed (St. Paul: West Publishing Co. 1971), p. 376.
[4] Restatement (Second) of Torts §329.
[5] Restatement (Second) of Torts §337.
[6] PROSSER, *Torts,* p. 365.
[7] Ibid. p. 367.
[8] Hawaii (1969), Colorado (1971), Minnesota (1972), Massachusetts (1973), Rhode Island (1975), Wisconsin (1975), New York (1976).

⁹*Yalowizer* v *Husky Oil Co.*, 629 P.2d 465 (WY 1981), *Payne* v *Greenberg Construction*, 636 P.2d 116 (AZ 1981), *Brett* v *Allen County Community Seminar College*, 638 P.2d 914 (KS 1982).
¹⁰Alaska, Mississippi, Rhode Island, and Utah have not enacted statutes.
¹¹Council of State Government, Suggested State Legislation (1965).
¹²*Copeland* v *Larson*, 46 Wisc.2d 337 (WI 1969).
¹³*Harrison* v *Middlesex Water Co.*, 403 A.2d 910 (NJ 1978).
¹⁴*Anderson* v *Brown Brothers, Inc.*, 65 Mich. App. 409 (MI 1975).
¹⁵*Gard* v *United States*, 594 F.2d 1230 (1979), See also *Good* v *United States*, 420 F. Supp. 300 (CA 1961), *Mongo* v *City of Vineland*, 371 A.2d 815 (NJ 1977), *Smith* v *United States*, 383 F. Supp. 1976 (WY 1974).
¹⁶RONALD KAISER and FREDERICK ROBINSON, *Injury Claims and Trial Court Litigation of Texas Park and Recreation Departments* (Austin: Texas Parks and Wildlife Department, Octber 1983), p. vii.
¹⁷Ibid. p. vii.
¹⁸See BETTY VAN DER SMISSEN, *Legal Liability of Cities and Schools for Injuries in Recreation and Parks* (Cincinnati: W.H. Anderson Co., 1968), p. 110 and Ronald Kaiser, *Tort Liability of Texas Park and Recreation Departments* (Austin: Texas Parks and Wildlife Department, 1982).
¹⁹*Dillashaw* v *Coogler*, 150 S.E.2d 161 (GA 1966), *McFarland* v *Grace*, 305 S.W.2d 91 (MO 1957), *Luck* v *Buffalo Lakes, Inc.*, 188 S.W.2d 672 (TX 1940), *Bolduc* v *Coffin*, 329 A.2d 655 (VT 1974).
²⁰*Caywood* v *Board of Co. Comm'rs.*, 599 P.2d 561 (KS 1965), *Ft. Worth* v *Barlow*, 313 S.W.2d 96 (TX 1958), *Rogers* v *Oconomowoc*, 128 N.W.2d 640 (WI 1964), *Macy* v *Chelan*, 369 P.2d 508 (WA 1962), *Dendy* v *Pascagoula*, 193 S.2d 559 (MS 1967), *McLaughlin* v *Rova Farms, Inc.*, 266 A.2d 284 (NJ 1970), *Herman* v *State*, 439 N.Y.S.2d 1018 (NY 1981), *Jacques* v *Village of Lake Placid*, 332 N.Y.S.2d 743 (NY 1972), *Fuller* v *State*, 125 Cal. Rptr. 586 (CA 1975), *Brightwell* v *Beem*, 90 So.2d 320 (FL 1956).
²¹*MacGillcuddy* v *New York*, 7 N.Y.S.2d 71 (NY 1938), contrast *Benton* v *Santa Monica*, 289 P. 203 (CA 1930).
²²*Beverly Beach Club, Inc.*, v *Marron*, 192 A. 278 (MD 1937), *Bristol* v *Ernst*, 27 N.Y.S.2d 119 (NY 1941), *Cheverie* v *Tatassit Bathing Beach, Inc.*, 116 N.E.2d 143 (MA 1953), contrast *Young* v *Gauthier*, 82 P.2d 959 (CA 1938).
²³*Caporossi* v *Atlantic City*, 220 F.Supp 508 (NJ 1963), *Davis* v *U.S.*, 716 F.2d 418 (IL 1983), *Surmanek* v *State*, 202 N.Y.S.2d 756 (NY 1960).
²⁴4 Am.Jur.2d Amusement and Exhibitions, §84., citing 11 cases.
²⁵See also *Longmont* v *Swearingen*, 254 P. 1000 (Col. 1927), *Nordgren* v *Strong*, 149 A.201 (CT 1930), *Larkin* v *Saltair Beach Co.*, 83 P. 686 (UT 1905), *Kreiner* v *Yezdbick*, 177 N.W.2d 629 (MI 1970), *Collins* v *Riverside Amusement Park Co.*, 145 P.2d 853 (AZ 1944).
²⁶*Gluckauf* v *Pine Lake Beach Club, Inc.*, 187 A.2d 357 (NJ 1963), *Nordgren* v *Strong*, 149 A.201 (CT 1970).
²⁷4 Am.Jur.2d, Amusement and Exhibitions, §84.
²⁸*Dillashaw* v *Coogler*, 150 S.E.2d 161 (GA 1966), *Swan* v *Riverside Bathing Co.*, 294 P. 902 (KS 1931), *Lyman* v *Hall*, 219 N.W. 902 (NE 1928), *Hahn* v *Perkins*, 46 S.E.2d 854 (NC 1948), *Justice* v *Prescott*, 129 S.E.2d 479 (NC 1963), *Wong* v *Waterloo*, 232 N.W.2d 865 (IA 1975).
²⁹*Tucker* v *Dixon*, 355 P.2d 79 (CA 1960), *Seligson* v *Victory Pool, Inc.*, 66 N.Y.S.2d 453 (NY 1946).
³⁰*Knowles* v *La Rue*, 116 S.E.2d 248 (GA 1960), *Weeks* v *Newark*, 162 A.2d 314 (NJ 1960), *Adam Dante Corp.* v *Sharpe*, 483 SW.2d 452 (TX 1972), *Campbell* v *Peru*, 198 N.E.2d 719 (IL 1964), *Tulsa* v *Goins*, 437 P.2d 257 (OK 1967), *Post* v *Camino Del Properties*, 343 P.2d 294 (CA 1959), *Marcus* v *Manhattan Beach Parks Corp.*, 284 N.Y.S. 952 (NY 1936).
³¹*Andrews* v *Narber*, 59 So.2d 869 (FL 1952), *Crystal Palace Co.* v *Lenox*, 299 S.W. 703 (TX 1927), *Sciarello* v *Coast Holding Co.*, 196 N.E. 591 (NY 1934).
³²*Schweitzer* v *Gilmore*, 251 F.2d 171 (CT 1958), *Pedone* v *Fountainbleau Corp.*, 322 So.2d 79 (FL 1975).
³³*Hammond* v *Balboa Bay Club*, 317 P.2d 658 (CA 1957), *Rosa* v *Breaker*, 49 A.2d 14 (NJ 1946), *Byron* v *St. George Swimming Club*, 28 N.E.2d 934 (NY 1940), *Keating* v *Jones Dev. of Missouri*, 398 F2d 1011 (FL 1968).

[34]*Benoit* v *Hartford Insurance Co.*, 169 So.2d (LA 1964), *Barrett* v *San Jose*, 325 P.2d 1026 (CA 1958), *Lincoln* v *Wilcox*, 141 S.E.2d 765 (GA 1965), *Bateman* v *Glenn*, 459 P.2d 854 (OK 1969).

[35]For example, see Mich. Comp. Laws Ann (M.C.L.A. 691-1401 to 1415) and Texas (V.A.T.S. § 6252-19).

[36]*Koder* v *Phoenix Ins. Co.*, 241 S.2d 257 (LA 1970), *Jones* v *Kansas City*, 27, P.2d 803 (KS 1958), *Lightner* v *Balow*, 370 P.2d 982 (WA 1962), *Cumberland College* v *Gaines*, 432 S.W.2d 650 (KY 1968).

[37]*Clary* v *Alexander County Bd. of Education*, 203 S.E.2d 820 (NC 1974).

[38]18 McQuillan Mun. Corp. §53.114 citing a long list of cases.

[39]See Mich. (M.C.L.A. §691.1406) and Texas (V.A.T.S. 6252-19).

[40]U.S. Consumer Product Safety Commission, *Handbook for Public Playground Safety, Vols. I and II* (Washington: U.S. Govt. Printing Office, 1980).

[41]U.S. National Bureau of Standards, Product Technology Div., *Impact Attentuation Performance of Surfaces Installed Playground Equipment.* Memo Report 1979.

[42]Restatement (Second) of Torts §496C, illustration 4 (1965).

[43]See *Bonetti* v *Double Play Tavern*, 274 P.2d 751 (CA 1954). (Player did not assume risk that a player when dropped a pop fly that lost his team the championship would throw the ball into the stands.)

[44]*Hummel* v *Columbus Baseball Club*, 49 NE2d 773 (OH 1943), *Grimes* v *American League Baseball Co.*, 78 S.W.2d S20 (MO 1935).

[45]*Miratsky* v *Beseda*, 297 N.W 94 (NE 1941), *Logan* v *Agricultural Society of Lenawee Co.*, 121 N.W. 485 (MI 1909).

[46]*Schweikert* v *Palm Beach Speedway*, 100 So.2d 804 (FL 1948).

[47]*Camp* v *Rex, Inc.*, 24 N.E.2d 4 (MA 1939).

[48]*Taylor* v *Hardee*, 102 S.E.2d 218 (SC 1958)

[49]*Sawaya* v *Tucson High School*, 281 P.2d 105 (AZ 1955).

[50]Restatement (Second) of Torts §343.

[51]_____ *Woodall's 1983 Campground Directory Statistics* (Highland Park, IL: Woodall Publishing Co., 1983).

[52]2 F. Harper and F. James, The Law of Torts §16.9 (1956).

seven

liability in recreation and sports activities

The preponderance of park, recreation, and sport accident cases are caused by poor facility maintenance, defective equipment, inadequate supervision, and improper instruction. The municipal cases are predominantly based on a failure to inspect and to properly maintain playgrounds, parks, pools, beaches, and athletic facilities. Case law involving school athletics and sports is often predicated on inadequate instruction and improper supervision. These case patterns reflect that municipal park and recreation services focus more on the provision of areas while schools offer more activity programs. To infer that municipalities have no duty to supervise activities and facilities or schools to adequately maintain facilities is a mistaken conclusion. Indeed the law is very clear that the public and private operator of recreation facilities and programs has a duty to exercise due care to prevent unreasonable risks of harm. Although the degree of maintenance and supervision varies depending on the user, the duty is unwavering. This duty of care has been addressed in several cases.

In *Diker* v *City of St. Louis Park*, 130 N.W.2d 113 (MN 1964), the question of the extent to which a municipality is bound to supervise activities at one of its recreation facilities was answered by the court. In this case, a ten year old was injured by a flying hockey puck while playing goalie in an unsupervised practice game. Although the city provided referees and coaches for regularly scheduled games, practice games were not supervised. The trial court concluded that a municipality is required to provide reasonable supervision of its recreational facilities and, on appeal, the Minnesota Supreme Court held that although a municipality must exercise due care under the circumstances this standard does not require supervision of those playing games on skating rinks made available to the public without charge. The court drew a narrow distinction regarding supervision. If a user fee is charged or the recreation facility is operated for a profit, the operator must provide reasonable supervision for the protection of its patrons. In other jurisdictions the due care requirement has been construed to include the duty of reasonable supervision.[1] A distinction has been drawn, however, between *general* and *specific* supervision. Thus the supervision of a particular activity need not always be direct but there must be a general superintendence over the recreation activities at each facility.[2] The number and location of supervisors will vary depending on the type of program and facility.

TYPE OF SUPERVISION

Supervision is a broad term implying a responsibility for the upkeep of a recreation area and for the activities that take place in that area. In a general sense, the operator has a supervisory responsibility to protect patrons from unreasonable risks of harm. This includes the responsibility for stopping or removing dangerous conditions or activities. Supervision encompasses all those things that should be done while instructing a program or providing general superintendence for a facility including such duties as

1. Inspecting the facility,
2. Planning for an activity,
3. Providing adequate and proper equipment,
4. Evaluating participants' abilities and skill,
5. Warning of inherent dangers in the activity,
6. Instructing in the proper techniques,
7. Closely controlling the conduct of the activity, and
8. Providing first-aid and access to medical treatment.

These duties are key elements in the concept of supervision. Depending on the facility and program the courts have recognized a duty to provide either *general* or *specific* supervision.

FAGAN v SUMMERS
Supreme Court of Wyoming
498 P.2d 1227 1972

McIntyre, Chief Justice

This case involves a suit for damages brought on behalf of seven year old George Fagan against a teacher's aid, Mrs. Lloyd Summers, and Park County School District No. 1.

During a noon recess a fellow student threw a small rock which hit a larger rock on the ground and then bounced up and struck George Fagan, causing him to lose the sight in his left eye. The trial court granted summary judgment for both Mrs. Summers and the school district.

Regarding defendant Summers, she has stated by affidavit that she walked past the plaintiff and five or six other boys twice prior to the accident while they were sitting on the ground near the school building. The boys were laughing and talking and she saw nothing out of the ordinary. After Mrs. Summers strolled by this group of youngsters, she had walked approximately twenty-five feet (taking about thirty seconds) when she heard an outcry from plaintiff. The accident happened in that interval.

There is no evidence or indication that Mrs. Summers' explanation is not true. Also, it is claimed on behalf of defendants that Mrs. Summers was reliable, conscientious, and capable in her work and a good playground supervisor. This does not appear to be challenged in the evidence.

There is no requirement for a teacher to have under constant and unremitting scrutiny all precise spots where every phase of play activities is being pursued; and there is no compulsion that general supervision be continuous and direct at all times and all places.

In *Butler* v *District of Columbia,* 417 F.2d 1150, the court considered it common knowledge, susceptible of judicial notice, that small boys may indulge in horseplay when a teacher's back is turned. And in *Ferreira* v *Sanchez,* 79 N.M. 768, 449 P.2d 784, 787, it was said:

"We must recognize the impossibility of a teacher supervising every minute detail of every activity."

A teacher cannot anticipate the varied and unexpected acts which occur daily in and about the school premises. Where the time between an act of a student and injury to a fellow student is so short that the teacher has no opportunity to prevent injury, it cannot be said that negligence of the teacher is a proximate cause of the injury.

As far as the instant case is concerned, counsel for appellant was asked during oral argument what should have been done by Mrs. Summers which was not done. His answer was to the effect that she could really not have done more than she did do and she could probably be dismissed from the suit. We consider counsel's answer frank and honest. In view of it and in view of what we have said about the absence of proximate cause on the part of Mrs. Summers, we hold summary judgment for her was proper.

Affirmed

SANTEE v ORLEANS PARISH SCHOOL BOARD
Court of Appeal of Louisiana
430 So.2d 254 1983

Williams, Judge

This is an appeal from a decision awarding plaintiff Francis Santee $5,000 for injuries suffered by her minor daughter Trina Hester.

Plaintiff's daughter was injured on February 16, 1977, while playing on the school grounds of an Orleans Parish public school. Plaintiff filed suit against the Orleans Parish School Board ("School Board") to recover for these injuries. After a trial before a judge, plaintiff was awarded $5,000. It is from this decision that defendant now appeals.

The following facts were presented by the plaintiff: Trina Hester was eight years old at the time of the accident. She was playing jacks in the schoolyard during her lunch recess at the same time several other children were rolling a stand used for volley ball nets or tether ball around the playground. These stands consisted of large tires filled with concrete in which poles were imbedded. The base of one of these stands was rolled over Trina's fingers by another student. The principal of the school, Junius Sanders, testified, however, that he observed Trina herself rolling a stand. He stated that students rolling a second stand ran away when they saw him and Trina's hand became caught between the stands.

The trial court found defendant to be liable regardless of how the accident occurred. The court below found the School Board negligent in allowing the student access to the stands for any purpose other than volley ball or tether ball. Furthermore, the trial court found that the school yard was inadequately supervised which provided an opportunity for the misuse of the stands.

Apparently there had been some problem before with the students having played with the stands in spite of warnings by the principal for them not to do so. Obviously, the principal was worried that an injury might occur through the misuse of the stands. He had told students that any one of them caught playing with the stands would receive a three day suspension. He testified that he had observed Trina Hester and the other students playing with the stands and was in the process of "sneaking up on them" when the accident occurred. He also testified that at one time the stands had been tied to a fence to prevent such incidents from occurring.

Although these stands have not been held to be inherently dangerous, misuse of them by students and the principal's knowledge of that continued misuse and possibility of injury required that measures be taken to
prevent access to the stands. The trial judge could have reasonably
inferred from Sanders's testimony that the stands presented a very real
possibility of injury to the students and that he was clearly aware of the risk
of danger.

The trial court also found that the playground was inadequately supervised at the time of the accident. We find that based on the evidence
presented at trial, it was not unreasonable for the trial judge to conclude
that the supervision was inadequate. Testimony at trial indicated that there
were about 200 children playing in the schoolyard at the time of the accident. There were only two teachers assigned to the school grounds and the
principal also patrolled the grounds during this time. The schoolyard was
divided into two parts, one on each side of the building. There was one
teacher in each portion of the schoolground, as well as the principal who
roamed around. Furthermore, as plaintiff points out in brief to the court, the
principal who should have been supervising was more concerned with trying to "sneak up" on the students playing with the stands than he was in
stopping them from engaging in a potentially dangerous activity as soon as
possible.

Affirmed

General Supervision

General supervision is epitomized by a playground leader, a chaper-
one at a dance, a community center director with general control over the
building or a teacher at recess. General supervision does not require constant and unremitting scrutiny of an activity or facility at all times when
open to the public. The concept of general superintendance is explained in
Caldwell v *Village of Long Island Park,* 107 N.E.2d 441 (NY 1952) where the
courts said

> Where a municipality undertakes to maintain an area for recreation in gen-
> eral some degree of supervision ought to be exercised to assure that the area
> is reasonably fit for that purpose. Under ordinary circumstances, the neces-
> sary degree of supervision of such an area may well be slight and may require
> no more than casual or periodic inspection.

Hence specific supervision has been held unnecessary for playground
equipment[4] and impromptu ballgames in public parks and ball diamonds.[5]
However, where an activity involves a high risk of serious injury, close supervision has been required.[6] In accordance with the principle that a recreation enterprise cannot be the insurer of the patron's safety, the courts
seem to be holding that only general supervision is required of park areas
and playground facilities.

The mere lack of supervision or inadequate supervision may not create liability but a determining factor is whether or not such lack or inadequacy of supervision was the proximate cause of the injury. The categories of issues dealt with in the supervision cases are the type of supervision, the location of the supervisor and the competency and number of supervisors.

Nature of supervision   The program sponsor has the responsibility to protect patrons from fighting, rowdy behavior, or the dangerous activities of others. This includes the responsibility to promulgate reasonable rules and regulations and to enforce those rules. Illustrative of this requirement is *Niles* v *San Rafael*, 116 Cal. Rptr. 733 (CA 1974), where the city park and recreation department was held liable for a failure to properly supervise a playground and prevent fighting. An eleven year old boy got into a fight with another boy over a turn at bat in a playground softball game and was hit in the head and suffered a skull fracture. The supervisor was in the school building at the time of the fight and his failure to properly supervise the game and prevent the fight resulted in liability to the city. For other cases dealing with the nature of supervision see: *Frank* v *Orleans Parish School Board*, 195 So.2d 341 (LA 1967), *Cirillo* v *Milwaukee*, 150 N.W.2d 460 (WI 1967), *Baum* v *Reed College Student Body, Inc.*, 401 P.2d 294 (OR 1965), *Viveiros* v *Hawaii*, 513 P.2d 487 (HI 1973), *Sly* v *Board of Education*, 516 P.2d 895 (KS 1973), and *Aaser* v *Charlotte*, 144 S.E.2d 610 (NC 1965).

Location of supervisor   When general supervision is required the supervisor must be on the premises and in reasonable proximity to the area or activity. The preponderance of cases imposed liability on the operator where the supervisor was absent when the injury occurred. In *Dailey* v *Los Angeles Unified School District*, 470 P.2d 360 (CA 1970), the school district was held liable for a death that occurred during the absence of a supervisor. During their lunch period two boys left the cafeteria and proceeded towards the north side of the gym, an area frequently used for slap-boxing. They had boxed for about five minutes when one boy fell backwards and hit his head on the asphalt surfacing. The boy died a few hours later from the skull fracture. There was no supervision in the immediate vicinity. The person on duty at the time was in his office eating lunch.

Several cases deal with the absence of lifeguards at swimming pools. One of the cases imposing liability on the operator for failure to have a guard present is *De Simone* v *Philadelphia*, 110 A.2d 431 (PA 1933). On a day when the pool was open to the public and about fifty girls were in the pool, the city had in attendance at the pool only an elderly lady whose job was to examine the feet of the patrons before they entered the pool. The court imposed liability on the city for the death of a fifteen year old girl because of a failure to have lifeguards on duty to prevent the drowning.

Number of supervisors   Other than the swimming pool cases where the adequacy of the number of lifeguards has been an issue, liability has not been imposed on the operator when at least one supervisor was present. For a discussion of the swimming pool cases see Chapter 6. In the three cases where the number of supervisors was alleged to be inadequate, the plaintiffs were not able to establish this insufficiency as a breach of legal duty.[7]

Specific Supervision

Specific supervision may also include program instruction and includes all the responsibilities of the sponsor and instructor in planning, directing, and evaluating a recreation activity. This level of supervision usually occurs as part of the instructional phase of an activity. Perhaps the best way to describe specific supervision is by comparing it with general supervision. For example, if a recreation center director stops an act of rowdyism while walking down the hallway, the supervisor has fulfilled a general supervisory duty. If that director inspects badminton equipment prior to its use in a class, the director has performed a specific supervisory duty. The following case example illustrates the responsibilities in general and specific supervision.

CATANIA v UNIVERSITY OF NEBRASKA
Supreme Court of Nebraska
329 N.W.2d 354 1983

Hastings, Justice

The action was brought by the plaintiff, Marcia Catania, under the State Tort Claims Act, Neb.Rev.Stat. 81-8, 209 et seq. against the University of Nebraska, a corporate governmental body, more accurately described as the Board of Regents of the University of Nebraska. From a judgment in favor of the university, and dismissing the plaintiff's petition, the plaintiff has appealed. She assigns as error, generally, that the court held that she had not proven negligence or proximate cause by a preponderance of the evidence.

The plaintiff was a student in a golf class offered by the University of Nebraska. At the time of her alleged accident and injury she was participating in an outdoor exercise wherein the students were hitting plastic golf balls. Although the defendant does not concede the fact, and the trial court made no findings in that regard, it may be assumed for the purpose of this appeal that the plaintiff was injured by being struck in the eye by one of these balls hit by a fellow student.

Because of inclement weather, the students were practicing indoors in a gymnasium which was approximately 96 to 102 feet in size. There were twenty-six students, using irons, who were arranged in an oval-circle formation approximately ten feet from the walls and eight feet apart. The balls used were made of plastic and simulated the look of real golf balls as compared to the perforated "whiffle" balls or cotton balls. The balls were hit toward the opposite wall or center of the oval. During the course of the practice session, the plaintiff looked up and saw a white mass and felt a pain in her eye, suggesting that she had been struck by one of these balls. Presumably as a result of that impact, she has sustained a near total loss of vision in that eye.

Several witnesses who qualified as experts in the field of physical education testified at this trial. John Schultz, who possessed a Ph.D. in education, gave as his opinion that the oval formation employed in this case, whereby the students are hitting the plastic-type ball toward each other, was inappropriate. He did concede that the most obvious danger to students was the risk of being struck by a swinging golf club. However, under the circumstances existing in this situation, he said that he would advocate a formation whereby the students would stand in two rows, back to back, approximately ten yards apart, facing the opposite wall, and hit the balls to that wall. He testified that he was not aware of any recognized textbook on physical education which mentioned any danger in the use of plastic golf balls. Janette Sayre, another expert in the field of physical education, who held a doctor's degree in physical education, stated that the principal danger in a golf class is the risk of being struck by a swinging club. In her thirty-seven years of teaching golf, she has used the oval formation and believed that it gave the instructor the best view of the class. She testified that the oval formation had certain safety advantages over other formations in that it kept the students away from each other and minimized the danger from being struck by a swinging golf club. It was her opinion that the formation being used by the university class instructor at the time of the plaintiff's injury conformed to the standards of golf instruction.

The instructor in charge of the university's class at the time in question, Doris O'Donnell, had been teaching golf at the college level for almost twenty-five years. She had a doctorate in physical education. She testified that she had used the oval formation for teaching golf for a number of years. In her opinion the primary danger in a golf class was from being struck by a swinging club. She believed that the oval formation being utilized at the time of the plaintiff's injury conformed to acceptable standards of physical education standards. It was her opinion that the double line formation suggested by the witness Schultz created a greater danger to students than the oval one employed in this case.

It would serve no useful purpose to set forth in greater detail the specifics of the various experts' testimony. It should be obvious from the above description that there was a direct conflict in their opinions as to whether or not the class was conducted with due regard for the safety of the students. Certainly there was believable evidence which would support a finding of no negligence on the part of the university. As such, we certainly cannot say that the judgment of the District Court was clearly wrong.

Affirmed

PROGRAM INSTRUCTION

Most of the case law establishing the legal duties of program sponsors comes from sports and athletic activities. Although park and recreation agencies offer a diversity of instructional programs from athletics to cultural pursuits, the legal principles from the sports cases also apply to these programs. While the discussion focuses on the liability of the program sponsor it should be noted that the instructor or coach may also be personally liable for acts of negligence.

Program Planning

This section is not intended to review the techniques regarding program planning but to reinforce the development of written program plans. Lawsuits alleging improper instruction, inadequate supervision, or other negligent acts are numerous, but only a few raise the issue of poor planning.[8] In these cases, lack of planning has been upheld as a basis for the lawsuit. Indicative of the importance of preparing an instructional plan and adhering to it is the *Keesee* case.

KEESEE v BOARD OF EDUCATION OF NEW YORK
Supreme Court
235 N.Y.S.2d 414 1962

Shapiro, Justice

On January 29, 1955, the plaintiff, then a student at Whitlow Reed Junior High School, Brooklyn, was injured in the course of a game of line soccer played on a gymnasium floor area of about sixty feet in length and fifty feet in width. The game was conducted and supervised by a regularly appointed teacher as part of a physical education program approved by the defendant. I accept and credit the uncontradicted testimony of plaintiff and another witness to the effect that they were given no choice in the matter and had to participate in the game. Defendant's own official syllabus provides that the game should be played by two teams of about ten to twenty players each, in a space of about thirty to forty feet, and that each team consists of guards and one forward. The guards line up along the goal lines, on opposite ends of the playing area and must remain there during the game. The object is to score by kicking the ball through the opposing guards and across the goal line. Toward that end, the forwards try to gain possession of the ball and advance it by dribbling and kicking it until in a position favoring a kick through the line of the opposing guards, who, in turn, try to block or trap the ball and kick it away from their goal line. Play is begun when the referee, on signal, rolls the ball slowly between the two forwards, who stand near the center of the play area as indicated by a diagram and contest for possession of the ball when it reaches them. A goal counts one point and after each score the referee puts the ball into play again, as at the beginning of the game. "After sufficient skill has been acquired, two or more forwards may be selected from each team." The syllabus cautions that care must be taken that the kicking is "not too severe" and provides that pushing, holding, or shoving an opponent is prohibited under penalty.

(T)he teacher, in the exercise of a discretion confirmed by defendant's director of physical education, did not adhere to the method prescribed by the syllabus. Instead, she divided a class of some forty to forty-five "prepared" students into two teams of twenty to twenty-two children on each team on each side and assigned them numbers one to five so that four children on each team had the same number. Each group then lined up on its own goal line without any forwards stationed at the middle area, and the teacher took her position on the side line, dead center, from which she rolled the ball along the center line, toward the midpoint and called out one of the assigned numbers at random. Thereupon, the students having that number ran out and converged on the ball to gain its possession, and if possible, kick it over the opposite goal line. It was during such a scrimmage that plaintiff was injured when she fell to the floor and two or three girls fell on top of her.

She has advanced two versions of that occurrence. On her examination of the claim (June 19, 1957), she testified, in substance, that while she and the other girls were trying to kick the ball, a member of the opposite team "kicked the ball and kicked me and I fell . . . on the slippery floor." On the trial, there was no claim that the condition of the floor caused the accident. Plaintiff, confronted with her prior inconsistent statement, explained that she had received a heavy kick before she fell, but that the fall itself was caused by a shove and not a kick. This happened on her "first time out" and about fifteen or twenty minutes after the game had started. Her trial version of the matter was supported by the testimony of a friend who had been her classmate and had witnessed the principal and background events. On the other hand, the teacher testified that plaintiff and two other girls fell as they were trying to kick the ball, but she could not say specifically just what happened before the fall. Plaintiff was thirteen years of age at the time, and weighed about 110 pounds, but there is no evidence of the relative sizes and weights of others involved in the scrimmage, and, therefore, no basis for any conclusion as to disparity in that area.

Plaintiff's theory of liability is that the teacher was negligent in directing such variances from the syllabus as made the game dangerous for novices and that the original negligence was compounded by her failure to intervene and enforce the rule against pushing and shoving when the violations occurred.

The first variance was in putting eight players into the field of play instead of two and the second was in sending them into action on the run rather than from standing positions. In short, plaintiff's position is based on the limits of defendant's syllabus to one forward on each side until "after sufficient skills have been acquired" and on its contention that the participants were novices without the skills to justify the variances. On the one hand, plaintiff and her classmate testified that the day of the accident was the first time that the game had been introduced to and played by them. On the other hand, the teacher testified that the children had played the game at least two or three times before then, but she had no actual recollection of the matter. . . But, in any case, excluding the date of the accident, the class could have had only two prior days of play that week, and there is no evidence detailing "the instructions . . . given on previous days," nor is there any evidence that the performance of one or more of the players was ever critiqued during or after a game, with a view to perfecting skills or avoiding danger of injury to themselves or others. All that appears is that the teacher would "go over the rules" and review them "every time" a game was played and that one variance employed by the teacher favored participation by eight students at a time, as "forwards."

[On] plaintiff's side of the case, an expert witness gave it as her opinion that the avoidance of danger of accidents from a youthful propensity to be thoughtless about restraints in bodily contact sports requires a restriction, in line soccer, to no more than two people "on the ball" at any one time. Based on her studies in the field, observation, and both personal and "exchanged" experiences (recounted by teachers at conventions, etc.) she testified that the accepted custom and usage is to give the members of respective teams consecutive numbers so that when a number is called only two children at a time run out and converge upon the ball. Elsewhere than in New York City, the limit to two contenders on the initial kick is invariable, without regard to whether the game is played in, or out of doors, and irrespective of the age of the players even in situations where, with coaching, no more than four advanced players are used, two as guards and two as forwards, to concentrate on passing and team work. She did not agree with the approval given by defendant's syllabus to the use of more than two forwards under any circumstances. It was her opinion that before children are put into this type of game at all, they should be given experience in kicking, dribbling, and passing, particularly at the Junior High School level.

On defendant's side of the case, its director of physical education testified, in substance, that the "sufficient skill" condition of the syllabus was "not a mandate"; that children are naturally skilled in running and kicking, and they do not have to be taught such things. But under cross examination, he changed his position. The skill referred to in the syllabus, he then said, was "skill in controls" such as controlling the ball, and the technique of managing "a small kick so as not to kick somebody else in the way and so on, those controls that the teacher must have to keep this a safe game" but, he grudgingly admitted, that "takes some time." In the course of her testimony, the teacher admitted devising her numbering system so that at least six girls would come out on each play. In her opinion the "sufficient skill" required by the syllabus could be acquired "in one session or fifteen minutes" if the instruction on dribbling were omitted, but what, if anything she did about the kicking, running, dodging, and changes of pace and direction that defendant's director of physical education regarded as "the whole game" or to better their "skill in controls" that "keep this a safe game" nowhere appears, although defendant was made aware of a claim for the consequences of its alleged negligence within ninety days after the accident and ordinary prudence should have impelled it to collect and preserve the teacher's plan book and other evidence by which the length and nature of the instruction actually given could be proved. Admittedly, the teacher kept a plan book but apparently it was not preserved for use as evidence. The shortcomings of the defendant's case do not, of course, entitle plaintiff to a recovery, but their reflection on the credibility of professional people who are supposed to exemplify the basic virtues cannot be avoided. The consequence is a persuasion that neither they nor the plaintiff were completely candid at the trial.

The teacher's testimony that the necessary skill to play the game can be developed in one session is reject conclusion that they were actually promoted or, for that matter, that there was any effort at all to improve them before the occurrence that resulted in plaintiff's injury. To the contrary, the evidence requires a conclusion that, by direction of the teacher, from six to eight novices, including plaintiff, converged on the ball, at a run, in two numerically equal—or nearly equal—groups and, on meeting, kicked away, inexpertly and without either self-imposed or externally visited restraint, in a lively effort to gain its possession and that during the action plaintiff was kicked by another player and was injured as a direct or indirect result of the kick.

That an injury would result to someone from the melee ensuing on such occasions was, if not inevitably, at least reasonably foreseeable. To permit such a large aggregation of novices to engage in such a dangerous sport evidenced a complete disregard by the teacher for the safety of her pupils—although her motive, thus to enable more girls to participate in the game, is understood and appreciated.

In discussing the provisions of the defendant's syllabus, I have not made mention of the fact that this so-called sport of line soccer was by the syllabus designated as an activity for boys only. If the game, improperly supervised, controlled, and directed, is dangerous to boys, how much more is it when the evident rules of safety are disregarded and violated with girls as the participants.

As the foregoing makes evident, I find that the defendant was negligent in permitting the game to be played under the circumstances portrayed in this record; that the infant plaintiff was injured as a direct consequence of such negligence, and that she—as an involuntary participant in the game—was free from contributory negligence.

The infant plaintiff sustained an incomplete greenstick fracture of the right tibia, with no displacement of fractured fragments. The hospital records make no mention of any bowing of the right leg, but assuming the testimony of plaintiff's expert to be correct in this regard he admitted that the bowing had "no functional effect," was "not discernible to the naked eye," and "doesn't affect the appearance of her leg." The hospital bill for five days' treatment was $91.80, and no other special damages were claimed. Under the circumstances an award to the infant plaintiff of $4,000 and to the other plaintiff of $100 would seem both fair and adequate.

The clerk is directed to enter judgment accordingly.

Affirmed

Equipment Inspections

When a participant is injured as a result of inadequate or defective equipment, the injured person frequently sues the program sponsor, instructor, equipment supplier, and the manufacturer. This section focuses on the liability of all of these parties except the manufacturer.

A report on equipment safety published by the National Injury Report Clearinghouse notes that three of the top four categories of equipment that produce injuries are recreation and sports related. The report is based on an index derived from injuries reported to hospital emergency rooms plus the severity of the injury.[9] While the pattern of defective equipment litigation is predominantly sports related, it is not limited to contact sports. In Florida, for example, there is an average of three lawsuits a week involving three-wheeled golf carts which easily tip over.[10] It is apparent from the cases that program sponsors and instructors have a legal duty to inform participants of needed protective and safety equipment, to recommend the proper equipment and, when furnishing equipment, to exercise reasonable care in supplying equipment that is suitable for the purpose for which it is provided.[11]

Protective equipment   Indicative of the necessity to recommend equipment and to ascertain that it is being used is *Brackman* v *Adrian*, 472 S.W.2d 735 (TN 1971). In this case, the plaintiff, an eighth grade girl, was participating in a physical education softball game as a catcher. After a batter hit the ball and began running to first she threw the bat in such a way that it flew back and struck the plaintiff in the face. The school furnished catcher's masks but students were not required to use them and the plaintiff was not wearing one at the time of the injury. The plaintiff filed an action against the school claiming that the failure to require the mask was an act of negligence. In discussing the equipment requirement the court said

> As to the matter of requiring the catcher in a softball game to wear a mask, again we think it is common knowledge that the very nature of the game in question calls for the use of a soft ball as opposed to the regulation hard baseball and we also know that this game, which is played by many thousands of youngsters throughout the country, contemplates the pitching of a slow ball rather than the fast curve ball such as is thrown by baseball pitchers in the regular game of baseball.
> The evidence in the record before us indicates that plaintiff had played softball at home and at school many times, was a skilled player, and knew what she was doing. She testified that she had seen other batters sling the bat after striking the ball. There can be no question but that she was familiar with the risk she was taking when she got behind the bat to catch the ball . . . Thus we find no satisfactory evidence of actionable negligence on the part of the school or its representatives in the failure to require the wearing of a mask by the plaintiff. . . .

Although the school was not liable because the plaintiff assumed the risk, the message of this case is clear—where protective and safety equipment is standard, advise the participants of this requirement and insure that they use it.

Defective equipment   A sponsor has a legal duty when furnishing equipment to provide adequate and proper equipment. There is an obligation to provide the proper equipment, inspect and test the equipment to insure that it functions properly and remove from distribution any malfunctioning equipment. Supplying a participant with defective or improper equipment creates a substantial risk of injury and is an open invitation to a lawsuit.

The following cases illustrate the importance of advising about and providing safety equipment and when providing nonprotective equipment to ascertain that it functions properly.

MEESE v BRIGHAM YOUNG UNIVERSITY
Supreme Court of Utah
639 P.2d 720 1981

Croft, Justice

This case is on appeal by Brigham Young University, defendant below, (hereinafter BYU) from a judgment entered against it in the district court following a trial by the court sitting without a jury.

The plaintiff was a student duly enrolled at BYU, having preregistered on December 12, 1977. Included among her classes was a beginner's ski class. Prior to her attendance at BYU plaintiff had lived in Tuscon, Arizona, an area of our country not known as a winter time ski haven. Plaintiff, without prior skiing experience, attended her first ski class on January 5, 1978, consisting of a film and oral ski instruction in the BYU fieldhouse. Pursuant to a suggestion of her instructor, she rented skis and equipment from the BYU bookstore where a part time employee, a student, made a brief adjustment on the tension of the bindings. During her second day on the ski slopes, she was skiing during "free time" and attempted a "snowplow turn." The inside edge of the left ski caught in the snow, she felt pain, and fell. The resulting injury required surgery and she commenced this action on September 21, 1978.

After trial in the spring of 1980, the trial court issued a brief memorandum decision stating the court concluded BYU's agent was negligent in adjusting the bindings and that such negligence was a proximate cause of the injuries to the plaintiff. The court further concluded the plaintiff was also negligent because of her inattentiveness in class concerning instructions given by the teacher and that such negligence was also a proximate cause of her injuries. The trial court apportioned the negligence 25 percent to plaintiff and 75 percent to BYU and found special damages of $1,796.70 and general damages of $17,500. Findings of Fact and Conclusions of Law were filed, and based thereon judgment was entered in the amount of $14,715.08 on May 15, 1980. BYU appealed therefrom. No challenge is made in this appeal to the finding that plaintiff was 25 percent negligent.

The relief sought on appeal is to have the judgment of the trial court reversed, based upon a determination by this Court that, as a matter of law, BYU is not liable to plaintiff for her injuries. In the alternative, BYU seeks to have the decision of the lower court reversed and the case remanded for a clarification of the Findings of Fact and Conclusions of Law, or for a new trial.

A review of the transcript of the testimony given at the trial discloses that in the skiing world the adjustment of the bindings to a skier's needs and boots is the responsibility of the agency from which boots and skis are acquired, whether it be by rental or purchase, which in this case was the bookstore of the BYU. Appellant does not suggest otherwise. This responsibility imposes upon such rental agency the duty to use ordinary care commensurate with the standards of the industry in installing and adjusting the bindings, giving due regard to the factors that are relevant thereto. Such factors would include the weight and experience of the person renting the skis; the proper placement and adjustment of the bindings to the person's needs; an explanation of how to adjust the bindings to tighten or loosen them; and to employ competent persons knowledgable about the matters involved. Any breach of that duty would constitute negligence.

A review of the testimony of the plaintiff and that of Ronald Earl Beck, the bookstore employee who rented the skis to plaintiff, discloses a substantial conflict in the testimony between them as to what Beck did or did not do. The encounter between them was brief and Beck had no recollection of the transaction but did identify his handwriting on the rental agreement. One fact seems clear. That is that after Beck affixed the bindings to the skis and had plaintiff step into them, he did not have her twist or turn to see if the bindings would release under such movement. Given the circumstances that plaintiff had never been on skis before in her lifetime and so advised Beck, we believe that ordinary care would require Beck to do more than to merely fix the tension on the bindings from a chart and that he should have directed plaintiff to at least go through the necessary motions to test the release mechanism of the bindings.

Affirmed

SUTPHEN v BENTHIAN
New Jersey Supreme Court
397 A.2d 709 1979

Per Curiam

Plaintiffs appeal from a summary judgment entered against them dismissing their complaint in this personal injury action.

The essential facts are not in dispute. On March 4, 1975, the infant plaintiff, Thomas Sutphen, then a tenth grade student at the Loundsberry Hollow Middle School in the Vernon Township school system, was struck in the right eye by a flying hockey puck causing retinal detachment and eventual removal of the eye. At the time, he was engaged in a game of floor hockey in the school gym, an activity in which he was required to participate as a member of a physical education class. He sued defendants Robert Bethian, the physical education instructor at the time, and the township board of education, seeking damages for the injuries which he sustained. The thrust of his claim is that his injuries resulted from defendants' negligence in requiring him to participate in the hockey game, with an excess number of players on each team, in a playing area that was too small for the purpose and without providing him with, and requiring him to use, proper protective equipment during the contest. Plaintiff William Sutphen, the infant's father, sued per quod.

It is undisputed that the school authorities were aware from the time the infant plaintiff was registered for kindergarten that he had a sight deficiency in his right eye. His mother had supplied the information that when he was about two years old he was "injured by . . . a stick." It is also undisputed that at the time of the accident the school gym "was split in half by a wooden partition," and the "playing area" for the hockey game "was thirty yards long and maybe fifteen yards wide"; that the school did not provide the players with protective equipment "for the facial areas and the eyes," and that while safety glasses were available if requested by a student, the infant plaintiff made no such request.

Some of the more obvious issues requiring resolution are:

Whether the floor hockey game sponsored by defendants was an activity having "more than the basic elements of risk, due to the nature of the game?"

Whether participation in this activity required the wearing of protective equipment?

Whether, in the circumstances, the supervision provided was adequate?

Whether the defendants were negligent in leaving to the infant plaintiff the decision to wear or not to wear a face mask and safety glasses?

Whether defendants were negligent in allowing the infant plaintiff, who they knew had defective vision in his right eye, to participate in a potentially dangerous activity without protective equipment?

Whether defendants had given the infant plaintiff adequate prior instruction in the skills and dangers of floor hockey?

Whether defendants were negligent in organizing and sponsoring the floor hockey game to be played in a small area of the gym and with an excess number of players on each team?

Defendant's suggestion that they had no duty properly to supervise the floor hockey game is without merit. Beyond this, their claim that the negligence alleged against them was not a proximate cause of the infant plaintiff's injury, is clearly a matter to be determined at trial. Finally, their suggestion that the accident may have been caused by a "condition of property" is, in the circumstances, without substance.

Reversed and Remanded

LYNCH v BOARD OF EDUCATION OF COLLINSVILLE
Supreme Court of Illinois
412 N.E.2d 447 1980

Clark, J.

The plaintiff, Cynthia Lynch, filed a two-count complaint in the circuit court of Madison County on September 12, 1975. In count I, Cynthia alleged that the defendant was negligent in failing to provide her with protective equipment. At the conclusion of the trial, a jury returned a general verdict for Cynthia in the amount of $60,000. The defendant appealed to the Appellate Court for the Fifth District. The appellate court affirmed the judgment of the circuit court.

The plaintiff, Cynthia Lynch, was playing quarterback on the junior girls' football team on October 27, 1974. She had thrown a pass to a teammate when she was struck in the face by an opposing player and knocked down. The back of her head struck the ground with considerable force.

Cynthia was taken to the hospital by her parents, who had been at the game as spectators. The hospital records admitted into evidence at the trial reveal that Cynthia suffered a small linear fracture of the nasal bone.

From the voluminous testimony adduced at trial it appears that the junior-senior "powderpuff" football game had been played each year as a half-time event of the homecoming varsity football game from 1970 to 1973. In 1974, when Rodney Woods became the principal of Collinsville High School, he ordered that the game not be held during half time of the homecoming game. Nevertheless, several students approached some of the teaching faculty and requested them to coach the girls' teams. Three teachers agreed to do so. None of the three teachers had been hired by the district to be coaches. It is not entirely clear from the record, but between four and six practice sessions were held in preparation for the football game. These sessions were held after school on school grounds. The girls changed their clothes in the school locker room prior to the practices. It is unclear whether a school football was used in either the practice sessions or during the game. There was testimony that one of the footballs was supplied by a student while no one knew the owner of a second football which was used. The game was played on Sunday of homecoming weekend, October 27, 1974, but not during half time of the varsity football game.

The testimony is undisputed that little instruction in the rules of football was given during the practice sessions. Two witnesses who had played in the game, in addition to the plaintiff, testified that these sessions consisted primarily of passing and hiking the ball and blocking each other in order to get an idea as to which girl was best suited for each position. It was suggested by one of the teachers that the girls purchase mouth guards since tackle football could be "rough" at times. Most of the girls, including the plaintiff, did purchase and wear mouth guards for the game.

Donald Eugene Arnold, an instructor in football officiating and football coaching at the University of Illinois, also testified. Professor Arnold testified concerning the rules governing high school football in Illinois. He stated that the object is to promote the safety of the players. He further testified that he knew of no organized tackle football games where equipment such as helmets, shoulder pads, and the like are not used; that such equipment is required by the rules promulgated by the Illinois High School Association. Professor Arnold further stated that he had coached a powderpuff tackle football game while he was an undergraduate in college. He testified that, in that game, attendance at two weeks' practice prior to the game was mandatory, and that helmets and full football gear were worn by the participants. Professor Arnold also stated that since head injuries are usually severe, it is mandatory that football players wear helmets for all practices and at all times when they are playing football. Finally, Professor Arnold testified that the Illinois High School Association rules provide that a major penalty for roughing the passer after the ball has been released.

Based primarily upon the foregoing facts, the jury returned a general verdict in favor of the plaintiff. It is the jury's function to determine the preponderance of the evidence, and a reviewing court will reverse only if that determination is against the manifest weight of the evidence.

The inquiry on appeal is whether the result reached below was one which is reasonable on the facts in evidence, not whether other conclusions might also have been reached. Mindful of all of the evidence in this case, we will not substitute our judgment for that of the jury which heard the testimony and observed the witnesses; "the verdict is not palpably erroneous or wholly unwarranted from the manifest weight of the evidence."

Affirmed

Participant Evaluations

Unquestionably the preponderance of litigation involving improper or incorrect evaluations of a participant's physical and mental ability occurs in sports and athletic programs. Before undertaking an inquiry into the cases and outlining rules of law, it is useful to state factors which bear upon those involved with these activities. The first is that injuries in sports related activities are inevitable even when those in charge of programs exercise due care in conducting the activity. A second consideration relates to the severity of the injury. Given the competitive nature of sports and athletics and the propensity for physical contact, the potential for severe physical injury is high.

The pattern of litigation under this category involves allegations that sponsors, instructors, or coaches failed to match participants by physical ability in contact sports, evaluate participant skills prior to engaging in the activity, and evaluate participants for injury or incapacity. These cases reiterate that liability will be denied for injuries that no amount of precaution or evaluation could have prevented.

Matching of participants   Youthful participants in contact sports should be paired according to age, maturity, weight, height, and motor skill. Several lawsuits have alleged that the uneven pairings of athletes based on these factors presented an unreasonable risk of harm and was an act of negligence.[12] As a result, many of the traditional methods of dividing students into teams should be used with caution, particularly where the activity involves physical contact. Illustrative is *Brooks* v *Board of Education*, 205 N.Y.S.2d 777 (NY 1980), where a twelve year old was injured in a game of kickball, conducted as part of the physical education class. In this game twenty boys were lined up on each side in the gym and were assigned numbers. When the instructor called out a number a boy from each side ran at full speed to the center of the gym and attempted to kick the ball over the opponents' goal line. The injured boy, matched against a six foot, 180 pound boy, was kicked by the opponent and suffered a concussion. The court found for the injured boy on the basis of a hazardous contact game with unmatched opponents. A contrasting result was found in *Pirkle* v *Oakdale Union Grammer School District,* 253 P.2d 1 (CA 1953), where a class division (eighth v seventh grade) was sustained as a logical method of organizing noon free play. An eighth grader, thirteen years old, five feet four inches tall, weighing ninety-seven pounds, blocked a seventh grader, fourteen years old, five feet ten inches tall, weighing 145 pounds and was stuck in the abdomen by the opponent's knee. This blow injured the plaintiff's spleen and kidney resulting in their removal through emergency surgery five hours later. The court held that touch football was not inherently dangerous and the grade selection classification was reasonable.

The following caveat is offered to the program instructor or coach. *Where the activity involves physical collision and not merely incidental contact, participant pairing must not ignore age, maturity, weight, height, skill and experience.* This collision/contact dicotomy is best illustrated by the comment attributed to Hugh "Duffy" Daugherty, former football coach at Michigan State University—ballroom dancing is a contact sport and football is a collision sport. Thus in *Underhill* v *Alameda Elementary School District,* 24 P.2d 849 (CA 1933), the court stated that

> baseball, basketball, volleyball, and handball contribute to the physical development of the pupils participating, and there is nothing inherently dangerous about any of them. They seldom result in injury to either the participants or spectators and are ordinarily played by school children of all ages without adult supervision.

Skill evaluation A competent instructor must consider not only physical attributes but also the skill and maturity of the participant when conducting sports and nonsports programs. When a participant possesses neither the physical skills nor the mental attitude critical to his or her safety, the instructor should not allow the participants to continue. In addition, the instructor may have an affirmative duty to test the participant for these skills prior to the program.

These requirements are critical in those activities where the failure to perform a physical task could result in serious physical injury or death. So called high risk or adventure type recreation activities fall within this category. This conclusion is supported by the holding in *Bellman* v *San Francisco High School District*, 81 P.2d 894 (CA 1938), upholding liability of the school district. In this case a high school girl was injured while attempting to perform a tumbling exercise. At the time she attempted the exercise, she was suffering from a knee injury and was taking part in the class against her wishes. The record indicated that the instructor knew that she had failed in prior attempts to perform the trick. The court found from the evidence that the exercise was inherently dangerous and that its performance required, in addition to physical strength and agility, a proper mental attitude.

Evaluation of participants' physical condition   A medical examination of athletes, as a condition to their participation in competitive sports, is the standard of practice for most school programs. If, in the judgment of the examining physician, participation in the activity presents a health hazard, the instructor or coach is justified in refusing to play the athlete.[13] When the exam indicates no physical infirmity or the instructor has no actual or constructive notice of impaired ability, there is no liability for resulting injury from the unmanifested disability. This principle was affirmed in *Kerby* v *Elk Grove Union High School District*, 36 P.2d 431 (CA 1934), where the court considered the duty of determining incapacities in supervising free play activities. In that case, a student was playing basketball during a supervised free play period in class. The student had been advised of the rules of the free play basketball game and understood the game. He was described as a "vigorous robust boy" sixteen years of age and was considered a good player. During the course of the game he was hit on the head by the basketball and was seen to stoop over and rub his head. He then left the game and was later found unconscious in the locker room. The boy was taken to the hospital but later died. An autopsy revealed a preexisting cerebral aneurism as the cause of death. In refusing to hold the instructor or school liable for his death, the court held that no one knew or could have been expected to know that the student had an aneurism.[14]

A more difficult problem arises when a participant has a known physical injury and the considerations are how soon, how much, and what type of activity can be engaged in. Liability has been found when an instructor or coach requires a player to compete when he or she knows, or in the exercise of ordinary care should have known, that the player was suffering or had not fully recovered from an injury.[15] While the cases do not precisely answer the questions of how soon can the athlete begin playing and how much activity is reasonable, the coach or instructor should require a followup medical exam prior to playing the athlete.

SUMMERS v MILWAUKEE
UNION HIGH SCHOOL DISTRICT
Court of Appeals of Oregon
481 P.2d 369 1971

Foley, J.

Plaintiff was injured while performing an exercise in a physical education class conducted by defendant school district. She claims defendant was negligent in requiring her to perform the exercise. The jury verdict awarded plaintiff damages and defendant appeals.

The exercise consisted of jumping from an elevated board fourteen inches high which rested on a coiled spring, touching the toes in the air and landing on the feet. When plaintiff attempted the exercise she landed on her feet, lost her balance, and fell backward. She suffered a compression fracture of two vertebrae.

Defendant school district required all students to earn a certain number of physical education credits as a requisite to graduation unless excused by a doctor. When plaintiff was a freshman in high school, 1965 to 1966, she was excused pursuant to a doctor's excuse dated November 25, 1966, from doing situps in physical education classes because of a back disability. These doctor's excuses were part of the permanent records of plaintiff maintained by the defendant school district.

Plaintiff's mother testified that her daughter complained of back pain in November and December of 1967 and plaintiff's mother requested a list of the exercises and type of gymnastics plaintiff was required to perform at school. Plaintiff's mother relayed that request to plaintiff's counselor at school. This request was made at least four different times, the last being about one week prior to the accident. The list was never provided. Plaintiff's doctor testified that plaintiff should not have been doing the springboard exercise because she was not coordinated enough to do it correctly and he would have recommended that she not participate in that exercise had he known she was doing so.

Defendant concedes that there was sufficient evidence to enable the jury to find that defendant required the performance of the exercise in question and the plaintiff had a previous infirm back condition. Defendant contends there is no evidence that defendant knew or should have known that such previous infirm back condition created a hazard of injury to plaintiff. Had it not been for defendant's failure to furnish the requested list of exercise, the defendant, presumably, would have been advised of the hazard by an excuse from the doctor. A person is bound not only by what he knows but also by what he might have known had he exercised ordinary diligence.

A physical education instructor is required to exercise reasonable care for the protection of the students under his supervision. It is the foreseeability of harm which in turn gives rise to a duty to take reasonable care to avoid the harm.

This court has said: " . . . Foreseeabilty of harm gives rise to a duty to take reasonable care to avoid the harm. Whether or not those supervising schoolchildren exercise reasonable care for their protection is likewise a fact question. . . ."

Under the circumstances in this case, we think that whether the kind of harm which resulted from requiring plaintiff to attempt the springboard exercise was reasonably foreseeable was a question of fact.

Affirmed

Proper Instruction

It is beyond dispute that instructors and coaches have a duty to teach the correct techniques. The cases suggest that proper instruction involves more than just teaching the best techniques, but also includes teaching fundamental techniques, warnings of risk, explaining safety rules, avoiding coercion of participants, and outlining emergency procedures. Although the law on this topic is derived primarily from football, wrestling, tumbling, and gymnastics activities, the rules are applicable to all types of program instruction. Thus the downhill ski instructor must outline not only the techniques of skiing but also the rudiments on how to fall, conditions of terrain and snow, and risks of the sport.

Proper techniques   Proper instruction has been held to be essential in contact sports such as football[16] and soccer[17] and can be a crucial factor in such noncontact sports as gymnastics[18] and golf.[19] At least eight cases are cited alleging improper instruction as the cause of an injury.[20] These principles also apply to the diverse range of other recreation activities such as canoeing, caving, climbing, diving, hiking, skiing, and aerobic dancing.

Safety warnings   Instructors and coaches have a duty to warn participants of the dangers present in an activity. The better practice is to go beyond simply warning of risks to one of ensuring that specific risks are understood by the participant. This practice is tied to *assumption of risk* (Chapter 5) and places responsibility on the instructor for informing participants of specific dangers. It is clear that a standard warning message will not suffice for all programs but should be of the type to inform the participant of the dangers. The ability of the participant to understand and appreciate the risk is influenced by their mentality and experience and the obviousness of the danger. It is safe to suggest that a one-time verbal warning is the lowest standard and may not be adequate for many activities. When substantial danger is involved, instructors should constantly remind participants about safety procedures and discipline participants who violate such procedures.

An interesting example of the importance of warnings was presented at a conference on Sports Injury Litigation.[21] In the described case, a school baseball player was injured while attempting to score on a suicide squeeze play. The batter missed the ball and the catcher caught the pitch and moved out to block the plate from the charging baserunner. Instead of sliding feet first, the runner dove head first into the catcher and was injured. In his lawsuit, the injured ballplayer claimed that the school board failed to provide adequate coaching and that the coach negligently trained, supervised, and coached the student in the rudiments of the game. Further, the injured player alleged that the risk of injury was enhanced by the omission of the coach to give explicit warnings against charging into other players head first. Evidence was presented that the coach taught feet first sliding but didn't stress that this was the only way to slide. Further, in an earlier game, the injured player had used his shoulder to knock over a catcher and score a run after which the coach praised him for his play. Despite the player's experience, because he had never been taught the head first slide but only the feet first slide, the jury awarded him $1,800,000.

Most sports involve at least some risk of injury which cannot be eliminated. In order to encourage participants to overcome fear and accept challenges, instructors must motivate students in a variety of ways. One technique of motivation that should be eliminated is coercion. Where undue pressure is applied to the student so that participation is involuntary, the defenses of assumption of risk and contributory negligence are not available to the defendant. Avoidance of coercion is illustrated by *Morris* v *Union High School District 294*, p. 988 (WA 1931), where it was alleged that the player had been induced and coerced into playing football without the knowledge and consent of his father. The boy was injured while playing before he was physically ready to play and as a result suffered serious injury. The boy's father contended and the court concurred that the coach knew or should have known of the boy's physical condition and that the boy had been injured because of coercion.

Medical Considerations

Accidents and injuries in recreation and sports programs can be minimized but not eliminated. When an injury occurs, it may frequently require prompt and proper medical treatment.[22] Program sponsors, instructors, and coaches have a duty to provide reasonable medical assistance to participants as soon as possible.[23] Program sponsors have a duty to administer first aid or medical assistance promptly and properly and, if assistance is not available, to transport the participant to a medical facility. Whether the duty has been fulfilled depends on the quality of the treatment and the speed at which it is rendered.

When a participant is injured and the sponsor or staff fails to provide medical assistance, the injured party will single out this failure as a cause in complicating the injury or death. Correspondingly, if medical assistance is improperly rendered or delayed, the plaintiff's attorney will usually claim that such misfeasance further complicates the injury. In either instance the burden of proof is on the plaintiff to prove that this failure was the proximate cause of further injury. Those in charge of recreation and sports programs are not the insurers of the medical safety of participants and there will be no liability if there is no proof that the failure to render proper medical assistance exacerbated the injury.

Duty to provide medical assistance   Program sponsors, instructors, teachers, and coaches have a legal duty to render appropriate medical assistance in case of an injury. A leading case on this point is *Clark* v *State*, 99 N.E.2d 300 (NY 1951), where a bobsledder was injured when the sled missed a turn, hurtled off the course, and rammed into the mountainside. The plaintiff suffered a fractured left leg, collapsed lung, and numerous cut and contusions. Immediately after the accident, employees of the state-operated bobsled run carried Clark by stretcher to a truck for transportation to a hospital. A total of forty-three minutes elapsed from the time of the accident until admission into the hospital. A cast was applied to the fractured leg and when normal circulation did not return, gangrene set in and the leg had to be amputated. Clark alleged among other things that the operator of the bobsled facility failed to provide appropriate medical assistance. The court rejected this claim, finding that the state had promptly and properly discharged its duties to Clark after the accident, inasmuch as it had produced stretchers, blankets, a doctor, and prompt transportation to the hospital.

Duty to render proper medical assistance   The *Clark* v *State* case illustrates that reasonable medical assistance encompasses the provision of reasonable facilities and persons with necessary skill and first aid experience. There is also a duty to ensure that an injured party be properly attended until appropriate medical assistance can be obtained. A number of cases deal with the liability of the sponsor or staff for the failure to provide prompt and proper attention.[24] Six cases involved allegations of misfeasance in the treatment of football injuries. The case of *Welch* v *Dunismur Joint Union High School Dist.*, 326 P.2d 633 (CA 1958), is often cited in discussions of the misfeasance of coaches in treating injuries. The plaintiff was injured when tackled and the coach, suspecting a neck injury, asked the boy to move his fingers and to grip the coach's hand. The boy was able to do so before being moved to the sidelines. Eight boys picked up the plaintiff and carried him to the sidelines, thereafter the plaintiff was unable to move his hand and feet. Undisputed medical testimony indicated among other things that the plaintiff was now quadriplegic and that moving the boy to the sidelines without the use of a stretcher was improper medical assistance in view of the symptoms. In this case, the diagnosing and treatment of the injury was the prerogative of medical personnel. In light of the gravity of the injury and the potential for catastrophic injury, the coach should have waited for the team doctor.

Another leading football injury case applying these principles is *Mogabad* v *Orleans Parish School Bd.,* 239 S.2d 456 (LA 1970), where the coach's delay of two hours in providing medical aid for heat exhaustion was the proximate cause of death. The plaintiff, in the course of football practice on a hot and humid day, staggered to the sidelines and became faint. The coach sent him to the bus, and about twenty minutes later when the bus arrived at school, the deceased was assisted into the locker room. He was undressed and immediately given a warm water shower and then covered with a blanket. About two and one half hours after showing symptoms of heat exhaustion the boy's mother was summoned and about one-half hour after the physician arrived the boy was rushed to a hospital and died the next morning. The court held that the coach rendered improper first aid by covering the victim of heat stroke with a blanket and failed to promptly notify a physician.

Just as these cases imposed liability on the sponsor and coaches for failing to provide prompt and proper medical assistance, liability may also be imposed for providing unnecessary medical assistance. In the absence of an emergency situation, if a person in charge of the activity is not possessed of medical training and renders assistance that is unnecessary and detrimental there may be liability.[25] Further, if the injured party protests the proffered medical assistance liability may also result.[26]

Transportation to medical facilities   When proper medical assistance is not available to treat the injury, the sponsor and staff has a duty to see that the injured is transported as quickly as possible to a facility where assistance can be provided. In *State* v *Clark,* the court concluded that the State acted expeditiously in treating the injured bobsledder and stated that

> [W]e do not find any breach of this duty by the state in the present case. It promptly produced stretchers and blankets, and under the supervision of a physician . . . placed claimant and his teammates thereon, covered them, removed them with reasonable expedition to vehicle and transported them to a hospital without unreasonable delay.

In *Sayers* v *Ranger,* 83 A.2d 775 (NJ 1951), the court reviewed a school's emergency medical procedure. In this case, a student received a broken arm during a school activity program and was given first aid at the school. After receiving the first aid, the student was transported to the hospital for further treatment. The court approved this procedure, viewing the transportation to a hospital as being better under the circumstances than waiting for a physician to come to the scene of the injury.

Good samaritan statutes   In response to citizen fears of liability for improperly rendereing emergency aid at the scene of an automobile accident, all states have enacted statutes to encourage prompt treatment to accident victims. The majority of states have enacted these statutes to encourage physicians to render prompt treatment for accident victims by excusing physicians from civil liability in rendering care in an emergency.[27] Some jurisdictions extend immunity to all licensed medical persons, while a few states provide immunity to any person who administers emergency care at or near the scene of an emergency.[28]

Since the majority of the statutes apply to only licensed physicians, those statutes do not protect the park and recreation employee who negligently renders first aid at the scene of an accident. Nor do team physicians or trainers receive this protection in most jurisdictions. This concern prompted the California legislature to specifically extend this protection to volunteer team physicians.[29] The advice of a local attorney should be sought in this matter when questions arise regarding parks, recreation, and sports activities.

STINEMAN v FONTBONNE COLLEGE
U.S. Court of Appeals
664 F.2d 1082 1981

Heaney, Circuit Judge

Defendant Fontbonne College appeals from a jury verdict finding it negligent in failing to provide medical assistance to plaintiff Patricia Stineman. The trial jury awarded Stineman damages of $800,000 for loss of vision in one eye. We affirm the judgment below with respect to Fontbonne's liability, but find that the damage award is excessive and not supported by the evidence.

Stineman has been deaf since infancy and must rely upon lipreading to communicate. At the time of her injury in 1976, she was a freshman at Fontbonne College where she played on the school's intercollegiate softball team. Fontbonne was aware of her deafness and, as with all of its students, required Stineman and her parents to sign authorizations for emergency medical treatment. The three softball coaches were also aware of Stineman's deafness: Shirley Greenspan, the Athletic Director, Jim Johnson, a paid student coach, and Everett Brake, the College's Director of Buildings.

Stineman was injured during softball practice when a ball, thrown by defendant Mary Jo Lopiccolo, struck her in the right eye. The impact of the ball striking Stineman could be heard eighty to 100 yards away, according to the testimony of other players in the outfield. Coach Johnson heard Stineman cry out from the impact. Ice was applied to the area of the eye, and Coach Brake told Stineman to go to her dormitory room and rest, and that she would be all right. Neither coach directed or suggested that Stineman should see a doctor, although both were aware that the ball's impact was quite hard and that Stineman was especially dependent upon her eyesight.

Athletic Director Greenspan was not present during the practice but was told of the injury later the same day. She did not attempt to contact Stineman, examine the injury, or suggest that Stineman visit a doctor. Greenspan testified, however, that she was certified to teach first aid, that she knew loss of vision can result from a blunt injury to the eye, and that if she had observed someone being hit in the eye with a softball, she would take the person to a doctor.

Following the injury, Stineman returned to her dormitory room where she remained that evening and the next day. She testified that she was under the impression she would be all right because none of the coaches said anything to indicate something could be wrong. The next evening, she went to a dance, and on the following day, she began experiencing dizziness and severe blurring and coloring of her vision. She returned to the home of a friend and arranged to have her parents telephoned. Her parents directed her to an internist who observed blood in the anterior chamber of the eye. Realizing that Stineman had a serious injury, the internist immediately referred her to an opthalmologist, Dr. Thomas Eggleston.

Dr. Eggleston's examination revealed a dilated, irregular pupil which he testified occurred at the time of the injury. He also saw blood in the anterior chamber of the eye, a condition called hyphema. Traumatic hyphema is a relatively common injury. Treatment for it consists of prompt immobilization of the eye and absolute bed rest, the aim of which is to reduce the chance of secondary hemorrhage. According to the expert testimony, when such treatment is given before rebleeding, there is a ninety percent or greater success rate. It was a secondary hemorrhage, or rebleeding, that Stineman experienced two days after she was struck by the ball.

Dr. Eggleston hospitalized Stineman and attempted to drain the eye. This proved temporarily successful, but two days later, the eye again began to bleed, an infection developed and Stineman completely lost the vision in the eye. The eye began to shrink in the socket and she was fitted with a prosthesis.

Fontbonne contends that, as a matter of law it owed no duty to provide medical assistance and, therefore, should have been granted a directed verdict or judgment N.O.V. We note that courts have generally found such a duty in similar circumstances. Fontbonne contends, however, that it owed no duty to render medical assistance in this particular case, relying principally on *Kersey* v *Harbin* 531 S.W.2d 76 (MO App 1975), a Missouri state court decision setting forth certain elements necessary to imposing such a duty. Although it is arguable whether Kersey controls the present case, we need not reach that issue because we find that the elements in Kersey are satisfied here. To find a duty to render medical assistance, the first element under Kersey requires that the defendant must have been able to appreciate the severity of plaintiff's injury. Here, both coaches who were present knew that the ball made a tremendous impact when it struck Stineman, that it struck her in the area of the eye and that she was dependent upon her eyesight to communicate. Further, Coach Greenspan was made aware of the injury the same day, knew of the risks associated with such injuries and knew of Stineman's special dependence on her eyes. Based on these facts, Fontbonne should have appreciated the severity of Stineman's injury.

The second element of Kersey requires a determination that one or more of the defendants had the skill to provide adequate medical treatment. The only treatment required here was to get the injured person to a doctor. All of the coaches knew that the school's medical clinic was across the street from the softball field. The defendants certainly had the skill to provide this much treatment.

The third element of Kersey addresses whether providing medical attention would have avoided the injury's ultimate harm. Kersey involved avoiding death, but the question here is avoiding loss of vision. The record establishes that if Stineman had received prompt medical attention, there was a substantial likelihood the eye would have healed with no loss of vision. The expert testimony established that when treatment is obtained before rebleeding, successful healing occurs in ninety to ninety-eight percent of the cases.

We thus find that Fontbonne had a duty to provide medical assistance and that here was sufficient evidence to submit to the jury questions of whether Fontbonne breached this duty and whether such breach caused the loss of vision.

Fontbonne also contends that the jury's award of $800,000 was excessive and not supported by the evidence. We recognize that the determination of excessiveness is, in the first instance, a matter for the trial court and that an appellate court should be hesitant to overturn jury verdicts which include damages for pain and suffering. In the present action, however, the jury award so grossly exceeds the damages proven at trial that it cannot be affirmed.

It might be possible to affirm the $800,000 award if there was evidence of substantial medical bills or loss of earnings. The record indicates, however, that the total medical bills do not exceed $5,000. The evidence on loss of earnings is difficult to assess. The plaintiff was twenty-three years old at the time of trial and, hence, has forty-two years of projected earnings.

She has a college degree and earns $4 per hour as a teacher's aid. Plaintiff's vocational expert testified that the starting salary of elementary school teachers ranges between $9,500 and $14,000, and that the plaintiff, with her multiple handicaps, will have a difficult time finding employment other than her present position. There was no specific estimate, however, of the likely earnings of someone with the plaintiff's skills, education, and handicaps. No attempt was made to provide the jury with methods of calculating the present value of an award for loss of earnings, nor for estimating the possible effects of inflation.

Viewing the evidence on economic loss in the light most favorable to the plaintiff and allowing for substantial pain and suffering damages because of the multiple handicaps here, a total award of $600,000 could be sustained on this record. The award of $800,000, however, seems clearly excessive. It may be due to understandable sympathy for plaintiff's circumstances and to emotional reaction to her testimony at trial, but these are not grounds on which we can affirm an award.

Remanded to trial court

GILLESPIE v SOUTHERN UTAH STATE COLLEGE
Supreme Court of Utah
669 P.2d 861 1983

Durham, Justice

This is an action to recover damages for personal injuries to the plaintiff Rickey Gillespie and emotional injuries to, and loss of educational and employment opportunities by, the plaintiff Ghislaine Gillespie, Rickey's wife. At the conclusion of the plaintiff's case, the trial court dismissed Ghislaine's cause of action. In addition, after the entry of the jury's special verdict finding that the defendant Southern Utah State College (hereafter "College") was not negligent, the trial court also dismissed Rickey's cause of action. We affirm.

Rickey was attending the College on a basketball scholarship for the 1977 to 1978 school year. On January 4, 1978, Rickey sprained his ankle in a practice scrimmage. The basketball coach turned the treatment of Rickey's injury over to David Slack, a student trainer for the College. The treatment applied by Mr. Slack consisted of spraying the ankle with a tape adherent, applying a prewrap to prevent the tape from coming into contact with the skin, and then taping it.

After taping the ankle, Mr. Slack instructed Rickey to immerse his ankle in a bucket of ice water for ten to fifteen minutes, then to remove it and walk on it for three to five minutes, and to repeat this cycle two to three more times. Rickey followed this procedure for the remainder of the practice scrimmage and then continued it for two hours at home. Later that evening, Mr. Slack brought a bag of ice to Rickey's apartment, helped Rickey into bed, elevated his foot, and put the bag of ice on his ankle. The ice lasted approximately two hours.

On January 5, 1978, the morning after the injury, Mr. Slack made arrangements for Rickey to see the third-party defendant Dr. Scott L. Brown that afternoon. Dr. Brown noted in passing that due to the swelling the tape was difficult to remove. Dr. Brown took an X-ray of Rickey's ankle which revealed that it was not fractured, only sprained. Upon inquiry regarding the treatment that Mr. Slack had prescribed for Rickey's ankle, Mr. Slack replied that he had been "icing" it. Dr. Brown assumed that "icing" meant applying ice packs. Dr. Brown instructed Rickey and Mr. Slack to continue wrapping and "icing" Rickey's ankle for a period not to exceed seventy-two hours from the time of injury and prescribed codeine for pain.

After leaving Dr. Brown's office, Rickey and Mr. Slack went to the training room, where Rickey's ankle was retaped with a pressure bandage to allow for swelling and the ice water immersion treatments were continued. That evening, Mr. Slack brought a bag of ice to Rickey's apartment and told Rickey to continue the ice water immersion treatments. There was testimony indicating that Rickey slept that night with his ankle submerged in a bucket of ice water.

On the evening of January 6, 1978, two days after the injury, Rickey sat on the bench and periodically immersed his foot in ice water during the first and second halves of the basketball game. After the game, he continued the ice water immersion treatments at home. On the evening of January 7, 1978, Rickey again periodically immersed his foot in ice water during the first and second halves of the basketball game. Rickey did not recall any treatment after the game. On January 8, 1978, Rickey may have used the ice treatments during the day.

Late in the afternoon on January 9, 1978, the basketball coach and/or Mr. Slack started Rickey on warm whirlpool treatments. That evening, Mr. Slack visited Rickey at his home and found him using the ice water immersion treatment because Rickey said it made his foot feel better. Mr. Slack immediately called Dr. Brown, who instructed Mr. Slack to stop the ice water treatment, to wrap Rickey's foot with Atomic Balm, which created heat, and to have Rickey sleep with his foot elevated.

On the morning of January 10, 1978, six days after the injury, Rickey visited Dr. Brown, who sent Rickey to the Valley View Hospital to be admitted and treated for the injury to his foot. Rickey was diagnosed as suffering from thrombo phlebitis and as having apparent frostbite of the fourth and fifth toes along with smaller areas on the bottom of his foot and heel. On

January 23, 1978, Rickey was discharged from the Valley View Hospital for further treatment at a hospital nearer his home in Milwaukee, Wisconsin. Dr. Rydlewicz, who treated Rickey in Milwaukee, rated Rickey's right lower extremity as being ninety percent disabled due to amputation of a gangrenous toe, removal of some tissue and muscle of the right foot, and osteomyelitis of the right foot. During his testimony at the trial, Dr. Rydlewicz also expressed his concern as to whether Rickey's foot could be saved because of the osteomyelitis, and said that a below the knee amputation may be necessary at some future time.

On March 2, 1979, Rickey and Ghislaine filed suit against the College, claiming that the basketball coach and Mr. Slack were negligent in their treatment of Rickey's injury. On August 14, 1979, the College filed a third-party complaint against Dr. Brown. At trial, at the conclusion of the plaintiff's case, the trial court dismissed Ghislaine's cause of action. The jury subsequently returned a special verdict in which it found that Rickey was 100 percent negligent and such negligence was the proximate cause of his injuries, and the College and Dr. Brown were not negligent. Based on the jury's special verdict, the trial court also dismissed Rickey's cause of action.

Rickey contends that the jury's verdict that the College was not negligent is contrary to the uncontroverted evidence and therefore should be set aside. Rickey claims that the evidence is uncontroverted and Mr. Slack's taping of Rickey's ankle on January 4, 1978, which did not allow for swelling, was negligent. If the evidence were uncontroverted, Rickey's assertion would merit consideration. However, the evidence was not uncontroverted. While some of the physicians and trainers that testified at trial stated that Mr. Slack's tight taping of Rickey's ankle might, in conjunction with the ice immersion treatments and the failure to elevate the ankle, have contributed to Rickey's injuries, there was other testimony to the contrary. Although Dr. Brown agreed with the above general statements by the other physicians and trainers, he testified on redirect examination that Mr. Slack's tight taping did not play any part in Rickey's injury.

The testimony of the other physicians and trainers was based on hypothetical questions. They did not personally examine the tightness of the taping of Rickey's ankle. Dr. Brown, on the other hand, personally examined and removed the taping. We acknowledge the personal tragedy suffered by the plaintiffs, but we are constrained to recognize that the jury was free to find Dr. Brown's testimony more credible and base its findings thereon. Thus, viewing the evidence in a light most favorable to the jury verdict because the evidence does not so clearly preponderate in Rickey's favor that reasonable persons could not differ on the outcome of the case.

Affirmed

TRANSPORTATION

Transportation of participants is a potential liability trap for the program sponsor and staff. Whether transporting children a short distance to another park for a summer playground program or transporting backcountry hikers to a national park, safe travel is the duty of the program sponsor and staff. The sponsor may be liable, under the *doctrine of respondeat supervisor,* for the negligent operation of a vehicle by its employees or for the use of a defective vehicle. Program staff may also be individually liable for their own acts of negligence in the operation of a motor vehicle.

A number of options are available to the sponsor, including transportation via public carrier, sponsor vehicles, employee vehicles, or volunteer drivers. From the standpoint of reducing sponsor and staff liability, the best option is transportation by public carrier. Public carriers are independent contractors, and when injury results from operator negligence or equipment failure, the carrier assumes the risk of loss. This principle is illustrated in *Lofy* v *Joint School Dist.,* 166 N.W.2d 809 (WI 1969), when a private transportation company was used to transport students and chaperones to a baseball tournament. In a multiple car and bus accident in which one passenger was killed and several injured, the school was not liable inasmuch as the bus company was an independent contractor.

Sponsor liability   The most common means of transporting participants is through the use of the sponsor's or staff's vehicles. Where the sponsor is a nongovernmental entity, liability risk is generally handled though sponsor or staff auto insurance. However, where the sponsor is a public agency, affixing liability to the agency is often controlled by statute. Without abrogation of governmental immunity, a city or school is not liable for an injury or damage resulting from use of a city- or school-owned vehicle operated by an employee engaged in a governmental function. Conversely, a city or school is liable for injuries caused by the negligent operation of a motor vehicle while engaged in a corporate or ministerial function.[30] The trend is to impose liability on cities and schools for the negligence of their officers and employees in the operation of motor vehicles. For example, under the Texas Tort Claims Act, cities and school districts are liable

> [F]or money damages for property damage or personal injuries or death when proximately caused by the negligence or wrongful act or omission of any officer or employee activity within the scope of his employment or office arising from the operation or use of a motor driver vehicle. . . .[31]

When private cars are used for transporting participants, especially if the owner is reimbursed, the same rules of law apply as to the public agency.

Staff liability Employees may be personally liable for the negligent operation of motor vehicles regardless of whether the vehicle is the sponsor's vehicle or a private auto. When the employee acts within the scope of employment, a public agency may indemnify the employee for any court awarded judgment. Under most state statutes this is optional and not mandatory. Therefore an instructor or coach should ascertain the indemnification policy of his or her employer prior to driving participants to activities. When the employee uses a personal vehicle for transporting participants without the consent of the sponsor, the employee will be personally liable for any negligence that causes injury to others.

Guest passenger statutes Liability of the defendant in a transportation injury case may depend upon whether or not the injured passenger was a guest as defined by the statute. Usually guests are described as passengers who ride in an auto without paying a fee or sharing part of the cost of the trip with the driver. The standard of care required of the driver is lower when the passenger is a guest. If passengers are guests, the driver will only be liable for willful and wanton misconduct or gross negligence, but if the passengers are not guests, the driver will be liable under ordinary negligence standards. In *Fessendess* v *Smith*, 124 N.W.2d 554 (IA 1964), a cheerleader who was injured in an auto accident was found to be a guest. Therefore, the defendant was not liable because the cheerleader could not prove willful and wanton misconduct or gross negligence. A contrary finding was reached in *Kitzel* v *Atkison*, 245 P.2d 170 (KS 1952), where a softball player was found not to be a guest and the driver was held to an ordinary negligence standard.

Guest passenger statutes have filled the courts with many knotty problems. There is first the question of who is a guest and what is the status of a passenger who shares expenses for the trip or buys a tank of gas. A local attorney should be consulted for applicability of these statutes to recreation and sports activities.

SUMMARY

Without a doubt the forum for organized recreation and sports activities is on the fields, courts, and the gyms of municipal park and recreation agencies, public and private educational institutions, and other profit and nonprofit sports and health organizations. It is also within this context that the majority of recreation and sports related injuries occur. Although the sponsorship of and types of activities vary, the basic legal principles governing liability do not materially differ.

With respect to the recreation and sports programs conducted under their auspices, sponsors have a duty to exercise reasonable care to prevent unreasonable risks of harm to participants and spectators in their programs. This general duty of care translates into an obligation to (1) provide adequate supervision and instruction for the activities held under their auspices, (2) exercise due care in the selection of supervisors and instructors, (3) establish and enforce rules for the maintenance of safety and discipline in activities, (4) provide suitable equipment and facilities for the conduct of activities, and (5) provide first aid and accesss to medical treatment for participants and spectators. These specific obligations apply to activities sponsored by schools as well as to municipalities. They apply to the regular school curriculum and to extracurricular activities.

This chapter has synthesized from case law the legal obligations of cities, schools, and other public and private recreation program sponsors in the supervision and conduct of recreation programs. These judicial perceptions regarding the operation of recreation programs can be translated into guidelines for minimizing avoidable accidents and legal risks. The following statements reflect reasonable diligence for sponsors, supervisors, instructors, and other staff in carrying out general supervisory obligations:

1. Supervision is a general term implying a responsibility for an area and for the programs that take place in an area.
2. The degree of supervision is proportional to the risk of harm that is known or can reasonably be expectd. Thus is has been held tha specific supervision is not required for playground areas, ball diamonds, and extensive recreation areas. Where an activity or area involves a high risk of serious injury, specific supervision is required.
3. Safety and operational rules for areas and programs must be developed and enforced consistently and regularly.
4. Users must be protected from the acts of rowdyism, boisterous conduct, fighting, and dangerous activity of others.
5. Supervisors should remain at their supervisory posts and leave only in emergency circumstances.
6. Warn participants of hidden dangers in the conduct of programs or in the maintenance of areas.
7. Keep those facilities that present a high risk of injury when not supervised locked and render equipment inaccessible where unsupervised use could reasonably be expected to cause injury.
8. periodically inspect facilities and equipment for hidden defects and then remove those defects or warn users of their existence.

The following guidelines address the obligations of sponsors and staff in the conduct of programs of activity instruction:

1. Prepare instructional plans indicating program goals, performance measures, and testing procedures and adhere to this plan in conducting the program.

2. Provide appropriate protective and safety equipment that is properly designed and maintained.
3. Inspect all program equipment for defects and remove defective equipment from use. Maintain equipment and inspection records to establish sound management practices.
4. When conducting contact sport programs, group participants according to age, maturity, weight, height, and motor skill.
5. Evaluate participant's physical condition and skill level prior to undertaking high risk recreational activities.
6. Warn particiapants of the unique and particular risks of a given activity. While some element of risk is inherent in nearly all activities, never assume that participants know and understand all of the risks of an activity.
7. Develop procedures to provide proper medical assistance for injuries.
8. Institute, practice, and follow emergency procedures for transporting injured persons to appropriate medical facilities.

DISCUSSION QUESTIONS

1. What is the difference between general and specific supervision?
2. What type of supervision is required at a playground, swimming pool, and baseball game?
3. Under what circumstances is it advisable to conduct physical examinations for participants?
4. List the requirements for proper program instructions.
5. What type of first aid does a program sponsor have to provide for participants?
6. Does a program sponsor have a legal obligation to transport an injured participant to a medical facility?
7. How do "Good Samaritan Statutes" affect recreation and sports personnel?
8. What is an employee's liability for passenger injuries while transporting students to or from a sports event?

NOTES

[1]*Longmont* v *Swearingen*, 254 P. 1000 (CO 1927), *Clark* v *City of Buffalo*, 41 N.E.2d 459 (NY 1944), *Monell* v *City of New York*, 160 N.Y.S.2d 321 (NY 1957), *Styer* v *City of Reading*, 61 A.2d 382 (PA 1948).
[2]*Pickett* v *City of Jacksonville*, 20 So.2d 484 (FL 1945).
[3]*Aaser* v *Charlotte*, 144 S.E.2d 610 (NC 1965), *Williams* v *Longmont*, 129 P.2d 110 (CO 1942).
[4]*Lopez* v *City of New York*, 152 N.Y.S. 2d 700 (NY 1956).
[5]*Turano* v *City of New York*, 233. N.Y.S.2d 330 (NY 1962).
[6]*De Simone* v *City of Philadelphia*, 110 A.2d 431 (PA 1955).
[7]*Cooper* v *Pittsburgh*, 136 A.2d 463 (PA 1957), *Carr* v *San Francisco*, 338 P.2d 509 (CA 1959), *Rodriguez* v *San Jose*, 322 P.2d 70 (CA 1958).
[8]*Dailey* v *Los Angeles School District*, 470 P.2d 360 (CA 1970), *Bellman* v *San Francisco School District*, 81 P.2d 326 (CA 1938), *Keesee* v *Board of Education of New York*, 235 N.Y.S.2D 300 (NY 1962), *Brakatcek* v *Millard School District*, 273 N.W.2d 680 (NE 1978).

[9]Cited from Herb Appenzeller, *Sports and the Courts* (Charlottesville: The Michie Co., 1980), p. 299.

[10]"Sports Injury Litigation" (Practicing Law Institute Seminar, St. Francis Hotel, San Francisco, Ca., September 13–15, 1979). (New York: Practicing Law Institute, 1979).

[11]*Diker* v *City of St. Louis Park*, 130 N.W.2d 113 (MN 1964), *Hanna* v *State*, 258 N.Y.S.2d 694 (NY 1965), *Fein* v *Board of Education*, 111 N.E.2d 732 (NY 1953), Restatement (Second) of Torts §388 (1965).

[12]*Chimerofsky* v *School District*, 257 N.E.2d 490 (IL 1970), *Vendrill* v *School District No. 26*, 360 P.2d 282 (OR 1962), *Pirkle* v *Oakdale*, 253 P.2d, (CO 1953), *Brooks* v *Bd. of Education of City of New York*, 189 N.E.2d 497 (NY 1963).

[13]*Colombo* v *Sewanhaka Central High District*, 383 N.Y.S.2d 518 (NY 1976), Contrast. *Mancini* v *Bd. of Education*, 23 N.Y.S.2d 130 (NY 1940), *Rodriquez* v *San Jose Unified School District*, 322 P.2d 70 (CO 1958).

[14]Contrast *Brevard County* v *Jacks*, 238 S.2d. 156 (FL 1970).

[15]*Morris* v *Union High School District*, 284 P.998 (WA 1931), *Hall* v *Davis*, 70. S.E.2d 923 (GA 1952), *Cherney* v *Bd. of Ed.*, 297 N.Y.S.2d 668 (NY 1968), *Summers* v *Milwaukee School Dist.*,481 P.2d 369 (OR 1971).

[16]*Vendrill* v *School District No. 26C Malheur County*, 376 P.2d 406 (OR 1962).

[17]*Darrow* v *West Genessee School Dist.*, 42 N.Y.S.2d 611 (NY 1973).

[18]*Gardner* v *State*, 22 N.E.2d 344 (NY 1939), *Lveck* v *Janesville*, 204 N.W.2d (WI 1973).

[19]*Lanson* v *Independent School Dist.*, 289 N.W.2d 112 (MN 1980).

[20]*Iacoma* v *Bd. of Ed.*, 140 N.Y.S2d 539 (NY 1955), *La Valley* v *Stanford*, 70 N.Y.S.2d 460 (NY 1947), *Petrick* v *New Orleans City Parks Improvement Assoc.*, 188 So. 199 (LA 1939); *Bellman* v *San Francisco High School Dist.*, 81 P.2d 894 (CA 1938); *Stehn* v *Bermann MacFadden Foundation, Inc.*, 434 F.2d 81 (TN 1980), *Grant* v *Lake Oswego School Dist.*, 515 P.2d 947 (OR 1973); *Green* v *Orleans Parish School Bd.*, 365 So.2d 834 (LA 1924), *Reynolds* v *State*, 141 N.Y.S.2d 615 (NY 1955).

[21]"Sports Injury Litigation" (Practicing Law Institute Seminar, St. Francis Hotel, San Francisco, Ca., Sect. 13–15, 1979) (New York: Practicing Law).

[22]See generally, Joseph Kings, "Duty and Standard of Care of Team Physicians," *Houston Law Review, 18:* 657 (1981); Allen Ryan, "Medical Practices in Sports," *Law and Contemporary Problems, 38:* 99 (1973); Nathaniel Shafer, "Sports Medicine," *Lawyers Medical Journal 9:* 31 (1980).

[23]*Clark* v *State*, 99 N.E.2d 300 (NY 1951), *Welch* v *Dunismur Joint Union School Dist.*, 326 P.2d 633 (CA 1958), *Sayers* v *Ranger*, 83 A.2d 775 (NJ 1951), *Mogabgad* v *Orleans Parish School Bd.*, 239 So.2d 456 (La 1970).

[24]*Mogabgad* v *Orleans Parish School Bd.*, 239 So.2d 456 (LA 1970), *Cramer* v *Hoffman*, 390 F.2d 19 (1968), *Welch* v *Dunismur Joint Union High School Dist.*, 326 P.2d (CA 1958), *Pirkle* v *Oakdale Union Grammar School Dist.*, 253 P.2d 1 (CA 1953), *Duda* v *Gaines*, 79 A.2d 695 (NJ 1951), *Briscoe* v *School Dist.*, 201 P.2d 697 (WA 1948).

[25]*Guerrieri* v *Tyson*, 24 A.2d 468 (PA 1942).

[26]*Clayton* v *New Dream Land Roller Skating Rink*, 82 A.2d 458 (NJ 1951).

[27]*Dahl* v *Turner*, 458 P.2d 860 (NM 1969).

[28]*Wallace* v *Hall*, 244 S.E.2d 129 (GA 1978).

[29]Chapter 347, California Education Code, §49409.

[30]See Tort Liability of Public Schools for Accidents Associated with Transportation of Students, 34 A.L.R.3d 1210.

[31]V.A.T.S., Art. 6252, §19.

eight

intentional torts in recreation and sports

The traditional analysis of recreation and sports injury litigation focuses on principles of negligence and the defenses of assumption of risk, governmental immunity, and contributory negligence. A growing incidence of intentional violence in professional sports, however, has prompted the use of the lawsuit in areas of recreation and sports activity heretofore free of litigation. Two recent cases, *Hackbart v Cincinnati Bengals, Inc.,* 601 F.2d 516 (1979) and *Tomjanovich v California Sports, Inc.,* No 78-243 (D. TX 1981) suggest the possibility of recovery for injuries resulting from intentional torts. The Hackbart decision made it clear that athletes who are intentionally injured by opposing player's reckless disregard of the rules may have legal redress against that player. Although these two cases arose in the context of professional sports the basic legal principles which govern the rights in these cases do not materially differ from those in the recreation and sports context as described in this book.

An involuntary tort can be described as an accident caused by an act of negligence, whereas a voluntary tort, such as assault and battery, occurs through a deliberate and intentional act. The premise of this area of tort law is the concept of intent. Intent is a state of mind wherein a person knows and desires the consequences of the act or desires to bring about a result that invades a legally protected interest of another. The law presumes that a person's voluntary act, manifested as intent, extends not only to those consequences which are desired but also to those where a reasonable man would believe that a particular result was substantially certain to follow. For example, a prankster who yells "fire" at a crowded rock concert or in a nightclub may actually only wish to disrupt the show, but a reasonable person would know that a mass exodus is also possible with attendant injury and death. Therefore the law presumes the person intended all the reasonable consequences.

A unique provision of intentional tort law is the assessment of punitive damages. Such damages are awarded to an injured party over and above compensating damages to punish a tortfeasor and to deter others from similar conduct. Punitive damages may be awarded where the person's conduct was especially flagrant, that is, intentional and deliberate or willful and wanton.

The doctrine of *respondeat superior* does not apply to intentional torts committed by an employee. Thus, the employee and not the enterprise will be liable for injuries and damages caused by the employee's intentional torts. This rule is recognized in case law and is applicable to public and private sector employees. Many states have adopted this concept in tort claim acts. The Texas Tort Claims Act is illustrative. The act abolishes the doctrine of governmental immunity and allows injured users to recover damages from state and local park and recreation departments but prohibits recovery for claims

> arising out of assault, battery, false imprisonment, or any other intentional tort including, but not limited to disciplinary action by school officials.[1]

This rule may not preclude a person from recovering from the employer-agency under a ratification theory or a negligent supervision theory. Both are recognized exceptions to the doctrine of *respondeat superior*. The ratification theory provides that when an employer-agency endorses, ratifies, and supports the intentional conduct of its employees-players it thus accepts liability for the commission of the tort. Under the negligent supervision theory, upheld in the Tomjanovich case, the employer-agency is liable for the torts of its employee-player's torts where the act is committed in conformance with the employers expressed or implied directives. These exceptions provide excellent rationale for reprimanding or dismissing employees when they commit intentional torts that could subject the employer-agency to liability.

Unless the enterprise agrees to indemnify its staff, the employees may have to pay for user injuries caused by their intentional torts. With this in mind, the remaining section of this chapter discusses the intentional torts most likely to occur in parks, recreation, sports, and leisure enterprises.

Assault/Battery

An act which intentionally places a person in fear of an immediate and offensive contact without the person's consent is an assault. The key elements of this tort are intention, apprehension of contact, and without consent. No actual contact is needed, only a fear of contact, and any act causing this fear may constitute an assault. Thus it has been held that to shake a fist under another's nose[2], to aim a weapon at another,[3] or to chase a person in a hostile manner [4] is an assault. Mere words, no matter how threatening or abusive, do not constitute an assault. This tort is often termed the "fear of touch tort."

An intentional, unpermitted, unprivileged contact with another in an offensive and harmful manner is a battery. The interest protected by this tort is freedom from unpermitted contacts and it is often called a "touch tort." The wrongful action must be a voluntary act intended to cause unpermitted contact. Assault and battery may occur independent of each other but usually they result from the same action. A defendant may be exposed to civil and criminal liability for an assault and battery since the plaintiff is not precluded from seeking independent relief. The results of a criminal prosecution do not determine the results of a civil action.

Employees of recreation and sports enterprises are liable if they commit an assault and battery either on a user or a fellow employee. The range of factual situations in which an assault and battery may arise is limitless. The lifeguard at the swimming pool who physically removes an obnoxious user from the pool may be guilty of assault and battery and would be well advised to call the local police to remove the user. In addition to employee liability, participants in athletic contests may be liable for assaulting and battering fellow athletes. The sizable number of recent lawsuits between athletes, participants, or coaches in recreation and sports events is indicative of this trend.[5] While most physical contact is considered just part of the game, many violent acts may result in either criminal prosecution or civil action. More frequently than is realized, a player who inflicts injury on another player is drawn into litigation. The injured player may sue in tort, based on either intentional assault and battery or negligence. Though tort law may not be an effective deterrent to violence in sports, it has been used by players to recover monetary damages for an injury.[6]

HOGENSON v WILLIAMS
Texas Court of Appeals
542 S.W.2d 456 1976

Cornelius, Justice

Appellants brought suit to recover damages for an assault they alleged appellee committed upon Rory Melvin Hogenson. Appellee was

Rory's football coach at Terrell Middle School in Denison, Texas. During a practice session of the seventh grade football team, appellee became displeased with Rory's performance of blocking assignments, and as a result started yelling at Rory, then struck the boy's helmet with force sufficient to cause him to stumble and fall to the ground, and then grabbed his face mask. Shortly thereafter Rory was admitted to the hospital complaining of weakness of his left hand, left forearm, and elbow region and spasms of the left neck muscles. His condition was diagnosed as a severe cervical sprain and bruising of the brachial plexus. He was discharged from the hospital after eight days and completely recovered within several months. Appellee was twenty-eight years old, was five feet eleven inches tall and weighed 195 pounds. Rory was twelve years of age and weighed 115 pounds. In response to special issues and instructions the jury found that appellee did not commit an assault upon Rory and that appellee's contact with Rory was done for instruction and encouragement without any intent to injure him. Based upon such answers, the trial court rendered judgment that appellants recover nothing.

The appeal first contends that the trial court erred in instructing the jury, in connection with Special Issue No. 1, that intent to injure is the gist of an assault. The issue and the instruction were as follows:

SPECIAL ISSUE NO. 1

Do you find from a preponderance of the evidence that at the time and on the occasion in question Gary L. Williams committed an assault upon Rory Hogenson?

ANSWER: *We do not.*

In this connection you are instructed that a person commits an assault if he intentionally, knowingly, or recklessly causes bodily injury to another; or intentionally or knowingly causes physical contact with another when he knows or should reasonably believe that the other will regard the contact as offensive or provocative. An intent to injure is the gist of an assault.

An assault is an offense against the peace and dignity of the state, and the conduct constituting an assault is that which is described in the Penal Code. That conduct is also an invasion of private rights constituting a civil tort, but the definition of an assault is the same whether it is the subject of a criminal prosecution or a civil suit for damages.

But the new Penal Code, which was enacted prior to the event in question here, included additional types of conduct which not constitute assaults. It provides:

Section 22.01. Assault

1. A person commits an offense if he
    a. Intentionally, knowingly, or recklessly causes bodily injury to another; or

b. intentionally or knowingly threatens another with imminent bodily injury; or
c. intentionally or knowingly causes physical contact with another when he knows or should reasonably believe that the other will regard the contact as offensive or provocative.

Although intent to injure is still included in the express description of the type of assault covered by subparagraph a. so far as it condemns intentionally causing bodily injury, the same is not true with respect to recklessly causing bodily injury. Nor is the intent to cause bodily injury a requirement under subparagraph c. of the statute. The offense condemned by that subparagraph is complete when the actor intentionally causes physical contact when he knows or should know that the victim will regard that contact as offensive or provocative. By instructing the jury, over appellants' objection, that "intent to injure is the gist of an assault," the trial court unduly restricted the type of conduct which could be considered as an assault, and in effect deprived appellants of the right, under their pleadings, to recover for other types of conduct condemned by the statute. The instruction was undoubtedly harmful to appellants because appellee's main defense was that he did not intend to injure the boy, and the instruction was calculated to lead the jury to believe that such a lack of intent would be a complete defense. The charge should have simply defined assault in the terms of Section 22.01. The first point of error is sustained.

Appellants also contend that the trial court erred in submitting, over their objections, Special Issue No. 2 and its accompanying instruction which read as follows:

SPECIAL ISSUE NO. 2

Do you find from a preponderance of the evidence that any contact, if there was, between Defendant Gary L. Williams and Plaintiff Rory Melvin Hogenson was done for instruction and encouragement and without any intent to injure or harm him?

ANSWER: *We do.*

You are further instructed that you may take into consideration that a teacher of a physical contact sport would not commit an assault where he makes physical contact with a student for the purpose of encouragement and instruction and without any intent to injure him. In determining whether or not there was such an intent, you may take into consideration the relative size and strength of the parties and the amount and degree of force and violence, if any, used. Any force or violence used under such circumstances other than that necessary for instruction and encouragement, taking into consideration the relative size and strength of the parties, would be an assault if the other conditions under the definitions thereof are present.

Appellee argues that the issue and instruction were proper under the general rule that school teachers have the right to discipline their pupils, and the use of reasonable force or physical contact to accomplish that purpose is privileged and does not constitute an assault. Although appellee testified that the physical contact he used was not for the purpose of disciplining the child, he stated it was administered for the purpose of "firing him up" or "instilling spirit in him." He thus contends the phrase "for the purpose of instruction and encouragement," as used in the instruction at issue, properly applied the law to the facts of this case. We do not agree. The wording of the issue and the instruction gives an incorrect and incomplete statement of the law of privileged force. The phrase "for instruction and encouragement" comes close to expressing the legitimate purposes of privileged force, but it is neither entireley accurate nor complete, and in our opinion it is conducive to misunderstanding. Moreover, the instruction repeated the error of requiring that an intent to injure be present in order for the physical contact to constitute an assault.

Reversed and Remanded

Defamation

Within the last decade there has been an increase in the number of defamation cases involving athletes and sports. This may be attributed to a recognition by those sports and public figures that publishers have no right to be as critical of their actions as they might have been. It is not only a criticism of their actions but what might also be inferred. As with most legal discussions of recreation and sports, while the facts and circumstances are unique to that field, the defamation rules of law transcend the diversity of factual patterns in recreation and sports.

A statement is considered to be defamatory if it causes damages to one's interest in a good name, reputation, or business and is false. This tort is based on the policy that people should be able to enjoy their good name free from false and malicious statements. Defamation is a generic word describing the twin torts of libel and slander. If the communication is verbal it is slander, and if in writing or printing it is libel. The form of the statement is not as important as the effect which must diminish the esteem, goodwill, or confidence in a person or excite adverse or derogatory opinions. Thus, defamation may occur in the report of rumors, gossip, ridicule, or sarcasm. The communication of a false statement must be to a third person or must be overheard by the third person. It is not defamation to utter a false and defamatory statement only to the defamed person. A person repeating defamatory statement is generally liable even if that person identifies the source of such statement.

Proof of actual damage is required in libel and slander actions unless the statement contains an imputation of a communicable disease, unchastity of a woman, allegation of commission of a serious crime, or affects the defamed person's business, trade, or profession. If the statement falls in one of these categories the plaintiff doesn't have to prove any special damages. The *Moresi* v *Teche* case shows that statements which reduce business income may generate a lawsuit.

Certain communications, even if defamatory, are absolutely privileged and therefore are not subject to action. Statements made during judicial and legislative proceedings, executive communications, and husband and wife discussions enjoy this status. A qualified privilege extends to statements made about public figures and since many athletes, sports personalities, and program administrators are public figures they have greater potential for being the recipients of defamatory statements. In *New York Times Co.* v *Sullivan*, 376 U.S. 254 (1970), the court held that a "public official" could not recover for a defamatory falsehood unless he could prove the statement was made with "malice," which would require publication with the knowledge that the statement was false. The classification of "public official" and "public figure" do not include individuals who have achieved no general fame or notoriety in the community. Thus it is easier to defame a private person than a public figure.

Where unreasonable conduct on the part of the publisher is present, the public figure may recover for defamatory statements. The prime case allowing recovery is *Curtis Publishing Company* v *Butts*, 388 U.S. 130 (1967), where the athletic director of the University of Georgia brought suit against a national weekly magazine, alleging that he had been defamed by an article which reported that he participated in fixing a college football game. The evidence at trial indicated that the magazine, interested in cultivating a "sophisticated muckraker" image, had ignored even the most elementary precautions to insure publication of the truth and established that the allegations in the article were not supported by credible evidence. This, the Court said, was sufficient to establish the presence of "highly unreasonable conduct" which would constitute the requisite publication with reckless disregard for the truth to satisfy the constitutional malice standard.

Truth is generally an absolute defense to defamation. Thus, a person may communicate to another a harmful true statement about an individual and commit no tort, even if the recipient of the statement loses esteem. Although usually not called a complete defense, a retraction of a statement may mitigate damages.

Recreation and sports enterprise employees are subject to liability for slanderous and libelous statements. Casual conversations about an individual that an employee may have observed in a park area noted as a lover's lane may result in an embarrassing slander suit. Employees should be admonished that casual conversation or loose talk may result in liability.

MORESI v TECHE
PUBLISHING CO.
Court of Appeal of Louisiana,
Third Circuit 298 So.2d 901 1974

Watson, Judge

Plaintiff, George Moresi, Sr., d/b/a Cypremort Point Campground, is the owner of that compground and the lessee of Cypremort Point Beach in the St. Mary and Iberia Parishes of Louisiana. He filed this suit, contending that he was damaged by articles which appeared in the Daily Iberian newspaper on Sunday, June 24, 1973, and Friday, June 29, 1973, concerning Cypremort Point Beach and by a UPI wire service report. Defendants were: Teche Publishing Company, Inc., d/b/a/ The Daily Iberian, a Louisiana Corporation; United Press International, a foreign corportion, which allegedly stated in a story on its service wires that Cypremort Point Beach would be closed on July 4, 1973, because of water pollution; Woody Baird, the reporter who wrote the news articles; and M. A. Wolcott, the managing editor of the Daily Iberian.

Plaintiff stated in deposition that he had operated the Cypremort Point campground for two years commencing in May of 1972. The campground and a store operated by plaintiff are located on property leased for $3,000 a year from the Bourgeois family. Plaintiff also has a concession from the State of Louisiana to operate the Cypremort Point Beach. The concession from the state provides for a rental of $100 per month and requires plaintiff, as concessionaire, to keep the beach open to the public for twelve months a year and to operate and maintain rest rooms, utilities, and a water well on the property. The concession agreement grants plaintiff the right to charge $1 per person per day as an entrance fee for the use of the beach. The property and facilities are under the jurisdiction of the Louisiana Parks and Recreation Commission. Plaintiff stated that he had spent between fourteen and fifteen thousand dollars improving and cleaning up the beach. Plaintiff admitted that the articles published in the Daily Iberian on June 24 and June 29, 1973, did not defame him personally but said that they hurt his business. The portion of the article of June 24 objected to by plaintiff is worded as follows:

"Moresi, however, said that the condition of the beach is getting better and people are commenting on it to him. But now, another problem is showing itself. "According to the Iberia Parish Health Unit, the water at the beach is polluted. A spokesman for the health unit said that they could not recommend water contact sports at the beach area." Mr. Moresi stated in his deposition that he felt the article made it appear that he, Moresi, was saying that the water was polluted.

Mr. Moresi also complained that, as a result of a UPI wire service story, KFRA radio and KIFY, Channel 10 TV, on Monday, July 2, 1973, broadcast a story that the Cypremort Point Beach was closed indefinitely because of pollution. As a result of these reports and those carried by the Daily Iberian newspaper, Mr. Moresi stated that his business deteriorated, resulting in only six people being in his campground the Fourth of July and 115 people on the beach, an incredibly small number for that holiday. Mr. Moresi contrasted his business of the previous year, his only other year of operation, as being a good crowd consisting of two or three thousand people on the beach and fifty or sixty people at the campground. In the deposition of Woody Baird, a reporter for the Daily Iberian, he stated that Leonard LeBlanc, the executive editor, assigned him to do a series of articles on Cypremort Point a week or ten days before the Fourth of July. He stated that Leo Thomas of the Iberia Parish Health Unit told him that there were E. Coli bacteria in the water at Cypremort Point and therefore Thomas could not recommend swimming or water contact sports. On the basis of this and other information, he wrote the article of June 24 stating that the water was polluted. In deposition, M. A. "Red" Wolcott, publisher and editor of the Daily Iberian, stated that he was in Mexico at the time the articles in question were published and was not aware that the articles were published.

A motion for summary judgment was filed on behalf of defendants, Teche Publishing Company, Inc., M. A. Wolcott, and Woody Baird. Attached to the motion were the three depositions and three sworn affidavits; one by A. Leo Thomas, Chief Sanitation of the Iberia Parish Health Unit, stating that he had examined the June 24, June 29, and July 3, 1973, editions of the Daily Iberian and the articles therein by Woody Baird concerning coliform bacteria in the waters of Vermillion Bay off Cypremort Point and the statements in the articles that he could not recommend water contact spots represent a true and accurate representation of what he said to Woody Baird; another, by John Koury, regional engineer for the Louisiana Department of Health in the Lafayette region, stating that he had examined the edition of the Daily Iberian for July 3, 1973; and the article concerning coliform bacteria in the waters of Vermillion Bay off Cypremort Point and that the article is true and accurate to the best of his knowledge; and a third by Ben Potier, Chief Sanitarian in the St. Mary Parish Health Unit, stating that he had read the articles in the Daily Iberian on June 24, June 29, and July 3, 1973 concerning coliform bacteria in the waters of Vermillion Bay off Cypremort Point, that tests by the St. Mary Parish Health Unit show the presence of such bacteria, that he discussed the water quality of the area with Woody Baird prior to June 29, 1973, and stated to Mr. Baird that, although the samples indicated the water would not be dangerous for swimming, he could not recommend swimming and water contact sports in Vermillion Bay at that time.

An opposition to the motion for summary judgment was filed by attorney for plaintiff, accompanied by an affidavit from Ben Potier stating that coliform bacteria are found in every natural body of water and an affidavit from Mr. Moresi stating that Mr. Baird's articles hurt his business, that the water adjacent to the beach is safe for swimming, and that Mr. Baird's articles were not based on proper research. The trial court granted the motion for summary judgment on behalf of defendants, Woody Baird, M. A. Wolcott, and Teche Publishing Company, Inc.

The trial court stated in its reasons for judgment that, in order to prevail in an action for defamation, plaintiff must show that the stories were untrue, the stories were defamatory, and the stories were written with a reckless disregard for their truth. The trial court concluded that the affidavits showed that the newspaper articles were based on facts and investigation and that nothing in the articles of June 24 or June 29 was personally defamatory, libelous, or insulting to plaintiff, as he admitted in his deposition. The trial court stated that the articles were published in connection with a public beach and a public body of water and that the newspaper had a right, if not a duty, to inform the public of the condition of the beach and water. The trial court found that there was no genuine issue as to material fact between plaintiff and defendants.

We have studied the newspaper articles on which plaintiff bases his claim. We have concluded that they are not defamatory; indeed, some expressions are complimentary to plaintiff. We agree with the trial court's observation that the articles are " . . . in no way, shape, or form derogatory or uncomplimentary toward Mr. Moresi with regard to his business activities and conduct."

Affirmed

Invasion of Privacy

A person's right to be free from unwanted publicity is protected by the tort of invasion of privacy. The right of privacy includes four different areas recognized by courts. It is the right to be free of

1. Intrusion to solitude or seclusion,
2. Public disclosure of private facts,
3. Publication of information that places a person in a false light, thereby resulting in public ridicule, and
4. Use of a person's name or picture for commercial purposes without permission.

An obvious form of invasion of privacy is the intrusion into a person's home or property. Thus, a Peeping Tom peering into the windows of a home or business is subject to liability. Generally, a person has no right of privacy when on a public street or in a public place such as a park. However, there are public facilities, such as bath houses and restrooms, that are intended to be private. An employee who uses a peek hole in a women's locker room may be subject to liability. In a classic case involving a commercial recreation enterprise, a court recognized that even in a public place there can be some things which are still private. The plaintiff in that case believed that it was an invasion of her privacy to be photographed with her dress unexpectedly blown up.[7]

False Imprisonment

An intentional, unlawful detention, or confinement of persons against their will is false imprisonment or false arrest. Imprisonment does not mean incarceration but is akin to restricting freedom of movement. Restrictions of movement can be attained not only by physical barriers but also by threats of physical force intimidating a person into compliance. The restraint must be against a person's will or wishes and any voluntary agreement to the restraint invalidates the claim. A person need not risk personal injury seeking escape.

In recent years, a substantial number of lawsuits have been instituted against businesses and law enforcement agencies based on claims of false imprisonment. Merchants often face false imprisonment lawsuits after they have detained a suspected shoplifter for questioning only to discover that no theft occurred. A number of states have modified the common law rules on false imprisonment by enacting so called *shopkeeper-privilege* legislation. A merchant is generally immune from false arrest or imprisonment claims under these statutes if the following conditions are satisfied:

1. The merchant had reasonable grounds to suspect the detained person,
2. Detention was in the store or in the immediate vicinity (parking lot),
3. Only reasonable force was used in the detention, and
4. Detention was of a short time duration.

This immunity extends to the merchant or employees even though the person detained was innocent of any wrongdoing. Public park and recreation agencies generally do not qualify for shopkeeper immunity.

Confinement may also be imposed by the assertion of legal authority. If a person is taken into custody or detained by an official without proper legal authority or probable cause, a claim of false arrest or false imprisonment is usually asserted. Park and recreation law enforcement officials, supervisors, or administrators may be named in false arrest lawsuits.

Established defenses to false imprisonment claims are consent, privilege, and shopkeeper's immunity. There is no false imprisonment if a plaintiff voluntarily submits to the confinement or agrees to surrender freedom of movement by accompanying an official to clear up any suspicion. Law enforcement officials are privileged to make an arrest when acting upon reasonable grounds to suspect a person has committed a felony.

It is for this reason that an action for false arrest as a remedy is fairly ineffective in instances where an officer acts upon probable cause and in a reasonable manner. As identified earlier, merchants and employees are privileged to detain a customer on or near the premises for a brief time when there is reasonable belief that the person is a shoplifter.

SUMMARY

Comprising a small but significant body of case law, intentional torts in recreation and sports is a potential area of legal liability for the agency, its employees, participants, and spectators. Where negligence is concerned with involuntary actions, intentional torts focus on voluntary acts. The potential for liability arises primarily though actions based on assault and battery, defamation, invasion of privacy, and false arrest, and although agency-employers are not liable for the intentional torts of their employees there are exceptions to this rule. When the employer encourages and supports the tortious conduct of an employee or when the act is committed in conformance with the employer's directives, the agency may be liable.

When a person commits an assault and battery on another the wrong-doer is personally liable for the tort. This rule was seldom applied to recreation and sports and until recently very few participant v participant lawsuits were successful. The *Hackbart* and *Tomjanovich* cases changed this rule and extended the recognized legal principles to sports by holding that the intentional infliction of an injury by one player upon another can give rise to tort liability. Thus the tort law principle for assault and battery applies to all employees, participants, and spectators.

DISCUSSION QUESTIONS

1. In what ways may an agency be liable for intentional torts committed by employees?

2. Based on the *Hogenson v Williams* case, how much physical abuse may a coach give to a player and still call it instructional?

3. What technique will bring about quicker results if the goal is to reduce sports violence, self-policing by the league or player v player lawsuits for assault and battery?

4. Does a criminal conviction for assault and battery preclude an injured player from suing the tortfeasor for damages in a civil lawsuit? Why?

5. What should be the policy of an agency regarding the physical removal of boisterous and unwanted users from recreation and sports events? Who should be responsible for removing those guests?

6. Under what circumstances may an employee of a private recreation enterprise detain a visitor suspected of stealing recreation equipment? If the visitor refuses to be searched must the employee allow the visitor to leave?

NOTES

[1]V.A.T.S. art. 6252-19 §14(10).
[2]*Stockwell* v *Gee*, 249 P. 389 (OK 1926).
[3]*Nielson* v *Eiler*, 227 N.W. 688 (MT 1929).
[4]*Townsdin* v *Nutt*, 19 Kan. 282 (KN 1887).
[5]WEISTANT, "Athletics," *Law and Contemporary Problems* 38:2 (1973).
[6]KUHLMANN, "Violence in Professional Sports," *Wisc. Law Rev.* 771 (1975).
[7]*Daily Times Democrat* v *Graham*, 162 So.2d 474 (AL 1964).

nine

strict liability in recreation and sports

Major developments have occurred over the last two decades to shift the burden of cost of serious injuries from the injured person to the enterprise responsible for the injury, irrespective of the party's fault. This shift has evolved as the law of strict liability. Historically, liability was based on the failure to live up to a standard of conduct, a concept legal writers referred to as fault. Strict liability, as the term is used by the courts and in this book, imposes liability on a party without proving fault. The rationale of strict liability is to discourage dangerous activities while not entirely prohibiting any social benefit the activities offer. For example, a keeper of wild animals has been held to be absolutely liable for injuries caused by wild animals. Although the mere keeping of wild animals is not unlawful, the owner is under a duty to exercise the highest degree of care to protect the public.[1] In some cases, economic factors have weighed heavily on court decisions. When both parties are blameless, courts, under the guise of social and economic justice, determine who can best bear the risk of loss and then shift the burden of loss to the solvent party. As one commentator noted, an entire field of workman's compensation legislation is based on that principle.[2]

Strict liability is not a major concern to the recreation and sports field unless it deals with injuries caused by animals, defective equipment, or tainted food. Nuisance is related to strict liability and although there is some dispute within the legal profession on its classification it is not included in this chapter for the reader's understanding of the subject.

CATEGORIES OF STRICT LIABILITY

Wild Animals

One of the earliest applications of strict liability was associated with the keeping of certain species of animals which involve obvious dangers to the public even if they are kept with the utmost care. Those who keep or own such animals are required to protect the public from harm. The failure to provide protection results in liability. Most authorities hold that the owner or keeper of a wild animal, *ferae naturae*, is strictly liable for injuries caused by the animal, regardless of the victim's contributory negligence.[3] According to the strict liability rule, the basis of liability is not the manner of keeping the wild animal, but the mere possession of it with the knowledge of its wild characteristics.[4] No allegations are needed beyond the fact that the animal is wild and by nature dangerous. Under such circumstances the owner is presumed to have knowlege of its wild and dangerous nature.[5]

Two factual questions frequently arise in strict liability. Is the animal in question a wild animal and what is the effect of taming or domestication? A wild animal is generally defined as a beast of a savage nature or disposition and so requires to be reclaimed and made tame by art, industry, or education, or else must be kept in confinement to be brought within the immediate power of the owner.[6] The common theme in this definition is a beast of a known savage and vicious nature and not by custom devoted to the service of mankind. Size is also a factor, the larger the animal the stronger the tendency for a finding of savage and vicious nature. Generally, bears, lions, bobcats, coyotes, apes, chimpanzees, buffaloes, and elephants are classified as wild animals.

Taming or domestication of wild animals to remove their savage tendencies is a second issue frequently raised by defendants. The authorities are not in agreement on the effects of taming as a defense to strict liability.[7] One line of cases recognizes that, to a certain extent, some wild animals can be tamed, but nevertheless holds that domestication is not a defense.[8] The contrasting line of cases holds an owner/keeper of a domesticated wild animal liable only upon a showing that the owner had knowledge of its vicious propensities. Thus, in *Swain* v *Tillett*, 152 S.E.2d 297 (NC 1955), a case involving injuries inflicted by a tame buck deer, the court ordered a new trial when the defendant contended lack of knowledge that the deer had developed dangerous propensities. The court recognized that certain classes of animals such as deer may be domesticated; that the plaintiff must prove the animal as vicious or mischievous; and that the owner "knew or should have known of the animal's vicious propensity character and habits." The difference between these two rules concerns the defendant's knowledge regarding the animal's vicious tendencies. The former rule does not impose a knowledge condition while the latter rule does.

A minority view rejects the strict liability doctrine and imposes liability based on the negligence of the owner or keeper of the wild animal. States adopting the negligence rule impose liability based on failure to warn of the dangers or to restrain or confine the animal.[9] There is a split of authority for user injuries in public zoos. The majority rule follows strict liability and minority rule bases liability on negligence. Complicating many of the cases under either line of authority are questions of governmental tort immunity. These cases have dubious authority value since the governmental immunity doctrine has been abolished or modified in most jurisdictions. The trend to abolish or modify the tort immunity of the governmental agency and place it on the same footing as the private corporation has implications for future liability. Following this trend and without a legislative mandate imposed on the public agency to maintain a zoo, the majority rule imposes strict liability on a public zoo for injuries caused by wild animals. This rule also applies to privately owned and operated zoos, wildlife parks, and wild animal exhibits.

LEWIS V GREAT SOUTHWEST CORPORATION
Court of Civil Appeals of Texas
473 S.W.2d 228 1971

Langdon, Justice

Suit for injuries sustained by plaintiff as a result of being butted by domestic goat owned and exhibited by defendants in their amusement park. The District Court, Tarrant County, Harold Craik, J., directed verdicts for defendants, plaintiff appealed.

Ruby Mae Lewis, a feme sole, the plaintiff, sued Great Southwest Corporation and Six Flags Over Texas, the defendants, for damages for personal injuries sustained by her as the result of being struck (butted down) by a domestic goat which was owned, maintained, and exhibited by the defendants in a petting zoo or amusement park owned by them.

The plaintiff's suit is founded upon strict liability for breach of implied warranty of safety of defendants' product, its goat exhibit; and strict liability for the keeping and maintenance of animals of dangerous propensities.

Plaintiff purchased a ticket and entered the premises of defendants' place of amusement on July 21, 1966, accompanied by her son, A.C. Lewis, and her grandchildren. All of them entered the Animal Kingdom, or petting zoo exhibit. The plaintiff was pushing a baby stroller containing her two year old grandson. The petting zoo contained approximately forty animals including goats, sheep, and pigs. No signs posted warning of any dangerous animals, nor were there signs warning patrons that they entered at their own risk. There was an attendant in the petting zoo. His sole purpose was to pick up trash and to keep children from mistreating the animals. "He has a little broom and a dust pan." All of the animals in the petting zoo are raised by the defendants. On July 21, 1966, all of the goats (with the exception of two females of three years of age) were not older than six months of age. All male goats in the exhibit were castrated at birth. Patrons of the exhibit are encouraged to touch, feed, and pet the animals. Plaintiff, a fifty-seven year old woman, was knocked down by one of the goats in the petting zoo when it struck her in the knee. She was knocked loose from her hold on the baby stroller and fell to the concrete floor. One of her shoes fell off at this time. The goat was standing over the plaintiff and was moved away or shooed by plaintiff's son and another person. Immediately prior to the incident, there had been no harassment of the animals and nothing had occurred which would be calculated to cause excitement to the animals. Plaintiff was raised on a farm and was familiar with the nature and habits of goats. She had observed others feeding the goats in the petting zoo, but she had not been feeding them. The goat of its own volition, without any warning or indication of its intentions, butted the plaintiff. There was no time element involved because there was no previous indication of what was to happen.

By her third point of error, appellant charges that the defendants are strictly liable for keeping and exhibiting such an animal "with the natural propensity to butt and do harm." under this record there is no evidence that any of the goats in the petting zoo had ever evidenced any dangerous propensity prior to the incident in question.

In 4 Am. Jur. 2d, Animals, Sec. 2, page 251, it is said:

"Generally, the present day classification of animals, and one which has been recognized from the earliest date of recorded history, is twofold: wild or ferae naturae, and domestic or domitae naturae. Animals ferae naturae are such as are of a wild nature or disposition and so require to be reclaimed and made tame by art, industry, or education, or else must be kept in confinement to be brought within the immediate power of the owner. Animals domitae naturae, on the other hand, are those which are naturally tame and gentle or which, by long continued association with man, have become thoroughly domesticated and are now reduced to such a state of subjection to his will that they no longer possess the disposition or inclination to escape. The class of domestic animals includes cattle, horses, sheep, goats, pigs, poultry, cats, and all other animals which by habit or training live in association with man."

Under the record in this case we are dealing with a plain ordinary goat which is classified as a domestic animal and comes under the following rule:

"With regard to an animal not naturally vicious, the general rule, in the absence of statute, is that the owner of the animal is not answerable for injuries done by it when in a place where it had a right to be, unless it was, in fact and to the owner's knowledge, vicious or dangerous. If being theretofore of a peaceable disposition, it suddenly and unexpectedly, while in the charge of its owner or his servants, inflicts injury on another, neither, if at that time due care was exercised, is answerable." 4 Am.Jur.2d, Animals, 86, p. 332.

In the present case there is no evidence that any of the goats in the petting zoo were frightened, tormented, or infuriated. The evidence is quite clear that there was no harassment of the animals and that nothing whatsoever occurred unexpectedly or otherwise to excite the particular goat involved or any other goat, and that nothing was seen or heard which would indicate that the animals had been aggravated, teased, or molested.

Appellant argues that, based on her previous farm knowledge, she would not have gone into the petting zoo had she known that the animals were not all females, since billy goats are known to butt people. It was established by the testimony that all males in the herd had been castrated at birth. It follows that a castrated male goat is no longer a billy goat. Further, the evidence is clear that appellant was struck by "one of the relatively larger goats in the pen." The particular goat involved in this case was never identified. The record reflects that there were only two large goats in the exhibit at the time in question and they were both females.

We find and hold that under the evidence in this record viewed in the light of prevailing authority that, as a matter of law, no rule of strict liability may be applied against the defendants in this case because there is no evidence of prior knowledge on the part of appellees as to danger, appellees should have been on notice of danger, and the domestic goats in question were not by law naturally dangerous.

Aside from the logic of the law, we agreed with the appellees that from the standpoint of public policy the continuation of an exhibit such as the petting zoo is beneficial to inhabitants of all ages who reside in thickly populated metropolitan areas. Everyone is entitled to a touch of farm life. Without such exhibits and petting zoos many children and adults might not otherwise ever see, much less touch, feed, and pet an actual living and breathing farm animal. Such a benefit must of necessity outweigh the risk that a lively and frolicsome animal might, by sheer unprovoked accident, do injury to a bystander. Further, the absolute necessity for survival of humankind by the keeping of herd animals reflects the propriety in this present day of the continuing wisdom of the common law. "The timorous may stay at home" and by doing so be denied down-to-earth bucolic adventures.

Affirmed

Recreation and Sports Equipment

The phrase product liability is a generic term that includes liability based on negligence, breach of warranty, fraud, and misrepresentation. A new basis of liability has been added to this list—the principle of strict liability in tort for a defective product. This concept came to the forefront in the mid 1960s in a California case and has been refined in recent court cases. It is now applied to impose liability on a manufacturer, wholesaler, retailer, or supplier for a defective product placed on the market that causes injury to a person.[10] The doctrine, also referred to as *enterprise liability*, is said to insure that the cost of injuries resulting from defective products are born by the parties who put such product on the market rather than by the injured persons.[11] The concept has received approval in Restatement (Second) of torts 402A. The Restatement provides

1. One who sells any product in a defective condition unreasonably dangerous to the user or consumer or to his property is subject to liability for physical harm thereby caused to the ultimate user or consumer or to his property if
    (a) the seller is engaged in the business of selling such a product, and
    (b) it is expected to and does reach the user or consumer without substantial change in the condition in which it is sold.
2. The rule used in Subsection a. applies although the seller has exercised all possible care in the preparation and sale of the product.

Liability under this theory is strict in the sense that an injured party does not have to establish negligence. In brief, strict liability requires proof of a product defect and its unreasonably dangerous condition but does not make the manufacturer or seller an insurer that no injury will result from the product's use. Lack of such proof will prevent recovery by the plaintiff.

Since strict liability is not based on negligence the contributory negligence of the plaintiff is not a defense. Assumption of risk is a defense when the seller can show that the product user recognized the dangerous or defective condition of a product and voluntarily proceeded to use it with disregard for the known dangers. Knowledge of the defect by the user is the key to this defense. Misuse, or improper or abnormal use of a product by a user is a recognized defense available to the seller. Product misuse occurs when a plaintiff does not follow stated directions or knowingly violates product directions or warnings. Additionally, the defendant may show a lack of causal connection between the product and the injury to the user or that a product was substantially or materially altered by the user.

Manufacturers, distributors, retailers, and users of athletic, sports, and recreation equipment have been at the cutting edge of the development of the product liability doctrine. Product liability has drastically changed the recreation equipment industry in several areas. Consider, for example, football helmet manufacturers.

In 1978, football helmet manufacturers faced between $116 million and $150 million in pending product liability and negligence claims, such potential exposure representing approximately five to six times the industry's annual gross sales of $24 million and 100 times its annual profits. Not surprisingly, where 14 football manufacturers could be found in the United States in 1976, only seven remain today.[12]

Balanced against the cost of litigation on manufacturers is the positive effect litigation has on the safety of future products. The Federal Consumer Products Safety Council and other industry groups have instituted product safety standards hearings which will ultimately benefit the manufacturer and the consumer.

Recreation and sports equipment litigation often involves several parties including manufacturers, suppliers, and program sponsors. The injured plaintiff will join all parties in the lawsuit and may rely on different legal theories to impose liability. The *Sanchez* v *Espanola* case illustrates that recreation and sports enterprises may become defendants in such litigation.

SANCHEZ V CITY OF ESPANOLA
New Mexico Court of Appeals
615 P.2d. 993 1980

Lopez, Judge

The city of Espanola appeals from the apportionment of a judgment on a crossclaim requiring it to pay one half of the total amount of damages awarded plaintiffs in a suit by them against three defendants wherein all three defendants were found jointly and severally liable for the injuries of plaintiff, Peggy Sue Sanchez. We reverse the trial court on the apportionment of contribution between the three defendants. Peggy Sue Sanchez and her mother sued the City of Espanola, Aalco Manufacturing Company and Tiano's Sporting Goods Store for damages arising from an accident in which a volleyball standard fell and severely injured Peggy Sue's foot, eventually resulting in the amputation of two of her toes. The standard, manufactured by Aalco, had been purchased by the City from Tiano's and was being used in a recreation center under the City's supervision when the accident occurred. A jury found the City liable for the injury under a negligence theory whereas Tiano's and Aalco were found liable under strict products liability. The total award was for $96,000. A judgment holding the three defendants jointly and severally liable for that amount was accordingly entered.

As between the defendants, the court found that the City and Aalco should each pay one half of the judgment and that Aalco should indemnify Tiano's for any costs. The basis of this apportionment was the court's judgment that Tiano's was not negligent but was only a party in the chain of supply, and was therefore not active tortfeasor as were the City and Aalco. The court, claiming it should be required to pay only one third of the damages since there are three tortfeasors, appeals the court's allocation of damages. Aalco has not appealed the decision that it should indemnify Tiano's, and, therefore, that issue is not before us.

The sole question on appeal is whether, under the Uniform Contribution Among Tortfeasors Act which New Mexico has adopted, damages awarded against three tortfeasors, two of whom are liable under strict products liability and one of whom is liable for negligence, should be split equally three ways, or whether the tortfeasors liable under strict product liability should be considered as one tortfeasor in assessing the amount of contribution between the parties. We hold that, in these circumstances, each defendant should be required to contribute one third of the total damages. Since the trial court's judgment that Aalco indemnify Tiano's has not been challenged, our decision in this case will result in the City of Espanola paying one third of the damages and Aalco paying two thirds.

Espanola is required to pay only one third of the judgment. The propriety of the indemnity awarded Tiano's as against Aalco not having been appealed, Aalco will pay the remaining two thirds. The order of the trial court is reversed with respect to the apportionment of contribution among the three defendants and the case is remanded for proceedings consistent with this opinion.

Reversed

Food Services

Service of tainted food has such a negative impact on normal sensibilities that public policy requires a standard of care close to strict liability for a seller of foodstuffs. A vendor or seller of food served to the public for immediate consumption impliedly warrants that the food is fit for human consumption and is of merchantable quality. Liability for service of unfit food is based on breach of warranty, and for the injured person to recover it is not necessary to prove negligence.[13] Thus a food vendor, particularly a restaurant owner, is an insurer of the food served and is strictly liable for injuries. The Uniform Commercial code, a statute adopted by all states, provides that a sale of food by one who normally engages in food sales gives rise to an implied warranty of merchantability.[14]

Today's park and recreation department and most athletic associations provide food services to program participants and spectators. What duty do these organizations owe consumers of food articles? They owe the same duty of any food vendor—an implied warranty that the food is fit for human consumption. They may be liable for any breach of such warranty.

If an agency has an agreement with an independent contractor to provide food services as any sponsored activity, the agency is not exposed to this warranty liability but it is imposed on the independent contractor. An agency could be liable under a negligence theory if it knew or should have known that a particular food vendor served tainted food.

SUMMARY

Some prognosticators have forecast the demise of many recreation and sports programs due to changes in the law of product liability and indeed recreation and sports equipment manufacturers have been at the cutting edge in the evolution of product liability. Product liability notwithstanding, liability based on the concept of strict liability in tort applies but is of minor concern to recreation and sports agencies and its employees. Strict liability in recreation and sports applies to injuries caused by wild animals in the possession of the agency, defective recreation equipment, and food services.

One of the earliest applications of strict liability was associated with injuries caused by wild animals. The rule has evolved that the owner is strictly liable irrespective of knowledge or lack of it regarding the animal's vicious propensities. The rule does not apply to domestic animals but only to wild animals. Municipal and educational institutions are subject to this rule just as if they were a private person. To reduce the possibility of injury and resulting liability, owners of wild animals should keep larger and potentially dangerous animals physically separated from visitors.

Although the number of product liability cases involving an agency and its employees are not as voluminous as negligence cases, employees are listed as defendants in about one third of the product liability lawsuits involving recreation and sports equipment.[15] Since the emphasis in product liability is on the manufacturer this area does not directly apply to the recreation and sports agency and its employees. Product liability is imposed on the manufacturer for any injury caused by a defect in the product at the time it was manufactured or distributed. Direct involvement of an agency or its employees is possible if they are connected with the selling, advertising, or representing of a product, but most often they are named as a codefendant because the attorneys are following court rules to join all possible defendants in the lawsuit.

DISCUSSION QUESTIONS

1. Based on the *Lewis* v *Great Southwest Corp.* case what types of animals are subject to the rule of strict liability?

2. What is the difference between taming and domestication of wild animals and how does this affect strict liability?

3. To recover under the theory of strict liability for a defective product what must the injured person prove?

4. What is product misuse and how does it affect liability?

5. How does strict product liability differ from negligence?

NOTES

[1]*Vaughn* v *Miller Bros. "101" Ranch Wild West Show,* 153 S.E. 289 (WV 1931).
[2]WILLIAM PROSSER, *The Law of Torts,* 4th ed. (St. Paul: West Publishing Co.) 1971, p. 494.
[3]See 21 A.L.R.3rd 603 for annotation of cases.
[4]*Hayes* v *Miller,* 43 So. 818 (AL 1907).
[5]*Collins* v *Otto,* 369 P.2d 564 (CO 1962).
[6]4 Am.Jur.2d Animals. §2.
[7]See 3A C.J.S. Animals §176. Contrast 21 A.L.R.3d §13.
[8]*Vredenburg* v *Behan,* 33 La. Ann. 627 (LA 1881); *Newman* v *Cleveland Museum of Natural History,*
    55 N.E.2d 575 (OH 1933); *Tonkawa* v *Danielson,* 27 P.2d 348 (OK 1933).
[9]Del: *Barclay* v *Hartman,* 43 A. 174; MA: *Bottcher* v *Buck,* 163 N.E. 182 (1928); Mont: *Hansen* v
    Brogan, 400 P.2d 265 (1965); N.H.: *King* v *Blue Mountain Forest Assoc.,* 123 A.2d 151
    (1956); CA: *Lindley* v *Knowlton,* 176 P 440 (1933); D.C.: *Jackson* v *Baker,* 24 App D.C. 100
    (1904); KY: *Lehnard* v *Robertson Admrx,* 195 S.W. 441 (1917); N.Y.: *Hyde* v *Utica,* 20
    NYS2d 335 (1940).
[10]*Greenman* v *Yuba Power Products, Inc.,* 377 P.2d 897 (CA 1963).
[11]Ibid.
[12]TERRI PETERSON AND SCOTT SMITH, "The Role of the Lawyer on the Playing Field," *Barrister,*
    Vol. 7, No. 3, 1980, p. 10.
[13]See 35 Am.Jur.2d Food §85 for an extensive listing of cases for this proposition.
[14]Uniform Commercial Code §2-314 to §2-317.
[15]DON ARNOLD, "Sports Product Liability," *Joper,* November–December 1978, pp. 25–28.

ten

nuisance law and recreation and sports facilities

Although recreation and athletic facilities are likely subjects for nuisance lawsuits these actions represent a small percentage of the cases filed in the recreation and sports field. Nuisance actions are generally instituted when there is a claim that a park or athletic facility interferes with the living conditions of neighbors surrounding the facility. Even though the number of cases involving parks and recreation and sports facilities is small, a current finding that a facility is a nuisance creates major problems for the owner. Under these circumstances, courts are reluctant to close the facility but they are willing to restrict the hours of operation, minimize noise and traffic, or order other accommodations between the parties. For these reasons a discussion of nuisance law and its impact on recreation and sports is warranted.

The term *nuisance* has come to have a variety of meanings in the law. It is often associated with loud noises, objectionable odors, highway traffic, bright lights, public parks, fireworks, liquor establishments, or conditions which endanger public health and safety or impinge on use and enjoyment of land. As was stated by the court in *Antonin v Chamberlin*, 78 N.E.2d 752 (1947)

> The law of nuisance plays [sic] between two antithetical extremes: the principle that every person is entitled to use his property for any purpose that he

sees fit, and the opposing principle that everyone is bound to use his property in such a manner as to not injure the property or rights of his neighbor.

In legal terminology, the term nuisance applies to a class of torts arising from an "unreasonable or unlawful use of property that endangers life or health, gives offense to the senses, violates laws of decency, or obstructs the reasonable and comfortable use of property."[1] Numerous definitions appear in textbooks, legal encyclopedias, treatises, and in statutes but all generally apply the term to a condition of property or an activity that causes a substantial and unreasonable interference with the use and enjoyment of property or physical injury to a person or to the public.[2] Nuisance as a tort is not based on tortious conduct but on the type of interest invaded, although the cause of the nuisance may be intentional or negligent based on conduct that is out of place in its surrounding.[3]

TYPES OF NUISANCES

Generally, nuisances are categorized as either public or private in character. These categories are based on the parties affected by the nuisance and the particular types and circumstances of the nuisance.

A public nuisance refers to a group of criminal offenses interfering with the rights of the public. It is usually defined as an act or condition that injuriously affects public health, safety, welfare, or morals or constitutes an obstruction of public rights and order.[4] The Restatement of Torts defines a public nuisance as "an unreasonable interference with a right common to the general."[5] Public nuisances arise out of unlawful acts and an act cannot be a nuisance if it is lawful.[6] An act may be unlawful if it violates common law, a state statute, or a municipal ordinance. A public nuisance includes interferences with public health, as in the case of a swimming pool with a high fecal coliform in the water; with public welfare, as in the case of operating a house of prostitution,[7] illegal liquor establishments,[8] public profanity,[9] loud noises from a ballgame,[10] or a rock festival,[11] with public safety, as in the case of the transportation, sale, and shooting of fireworks in the streets.[12] The remedy for abating a public nuisance is exclusive to the state or municipality.

A private nuisance is a civil wrong based on a disturbance of rights in land.[13] It is an act, activity, or condition that causes a substantial and unreasonable interference with the use, enjoyment, and comfort of real property.[14] In a private nuisance the rights of one or a few persons are affected and the remedy for it lies in the hands of the individual(s) whose rights have been disturbed.

The fundamental difference between public and private nuisances are the parties affected—general public v individuals. A public nuisance may also be a private nuisance when it interferes with a person's use and enjoyment of land. Beyond this distinction the two have almost nothing in common.

Modern remedies for a party injured by a nuisance are derived from common law and are supplemented by statutes in many states. The legal options available to an injured party are to seek monetary damages, an injunction abating the nuisance, or criminal prosecution for a public nuisance. An injured party may seek both damages and an injunction to abate a nuisance. The remedies are concurrent, not exclusive, and the injured party may pursue either or both. Criminal prosecution is available only to public agencies and only to abate a public nuisance.

As a general rule, courts are reluctant to close down a recreation facility or business in nuisance cases, preferring instead to mitigate or remove the offending conditions. If this is not possible, a permanent injunction closing down the facility will be the final resort. The injunctive form of relief is available to and against public agencies, private corporations, and individuals in nuisance ligitation.

In the case of public nuisance, the usual remedy is for a public official to seek criminal prosecution for a misdemeanor violation. This prosecution is based on state statute or municipal ordinance describing the nuisance and providing for criminal prosecution. An alternative remedy is an injunction, although its use is somewhat complicated by the traditional rule that equity will not enjoin a crime.

NUISANCE LAW
APPLIED TO FACILITIES

Generally parks, recreation, and sports facilities are not nuisances but may become such if not properly planned, located, or managed according to recognized standards. Courts have uniformly recognized these facilities as places of wholesome recreation and advantage to the health and well-being of a community and have exhibited great reluctance in finding them to be nuisances.[15] In an exhaustive inventory and analysis of park and recreation court cases, van der Smissen found that approximately 15 percent of the cases in twenty-nine states involved allegations of nuisance, with the plaintiff recovering only about 25 percent of the time.[16] Two types of nuisance cases are filed against public and private recreation enterprises. The first type is filed by a facility user against public enterprises for personal injuries sustained in a park. As will be explained these cases are based on exceptions to the doctrine of governmental immunity. The second type of case is filed by property owners adjoining recreation and sports facilities as a land use control method. The intent is to regulate and control the location of facilities and to regulate the method and manner of operating the facility.

Generally public park and recreation injury cases have been filed under a nuisance theory because the claimant cannot recover from the public agency under the doctrine of governmental immunity. An exception to this doctrine provides that a governmental agency has no right to maintain a nuisance and where it is maintained the agency will be liable for injury and damages. *Sparks* v *Pella*, 137 N.W.2d 909 (IA 1965). Attorneys have used this loophole with mixed results as a means to circumvent the immunity defense. In *Kilbourn* v *Seattle*, 261 P.2d 407 (WA 1953), the court recognized this when it said

> In recent years there has been a great increase in the number of personal injury actions brought against municipalities on the theory that the city had created, maintained, or permitted a nuisance. It was said . . . that where negligence is present but the defense of governmental functions subsists, a wise advocate may seek to present his case upon the theory of public nuisance. There are many cases involving the claimed exception to the governmental immunity rule; and we are impressed by the aptness of a statement found in *Ramirez* v *Cheyenne*, 34 Wyo. 67, 241 Pac. 710 (WY 1925), that nuisance is a good word to beg a question with.

With the decline of governmental immunity the majority of park user lawsuits involve negligence rather than nuisance claims. Although reliance on the nuisance exception has been reduced it still remains viable in many states and for this reason it is important to review some of these cases.

Personal injury nuisance cases affecting public park and recreation agencies generally involve playgrounds, fireworks, pools, beaches, and a miscellany of other facilities. With few exceptions, defective playground equipment has been held not to be a nuisance.[17] Claims for injuries caused by defective or improperly used fireworks have been more successful from a claimant's perspective.[18] The majority of these cases, however, are from Ohio and have not been universally adopted by other jurisdictions.[19]

Pools and beaches generated a substantial number of cases alleging nuisance based on shallow water, cloudy water, design defects, and broken glass.[20] As with playgrounds, recovery by the claimant was the exception rather than the rule. In *Sansone* v *Cleveland*, 31 Ohio L. Abs. 246 (OH 1940), the court found that the maintenance of a fifteen foot diving platform with a sign affixed thereto advising that the water was ten feet deep, when it was only four and one half feet deep, constituted a nuisance to give the administratrix of a deceased pool patron a cause of action against the city. However, in *Seldon* v *Cuyahoga Falls*, 6 N.E.2d 976 (OH 1937), no nuisance condition was found in the maintenance of a two foot diving board over a water depth of three feet. Improper placement of drainage pipes in pools or open drains were held not to be a nuisance in three cases.[21] The lack of notice of broken glass was crucial in a finding of no nuisance in *Clark* v *Seattle*, 102 Wash. 228 (WA 1918). Evidence indicated the pool was drained and cleaned each Friday and there was no nuisance condition to allow recovery for a child cut by the broken glass during a swimming period on the following Sunday. The result might have been different, the court reasoned, if the city had notice of the existence of broken glass on the pool bottom.

Nuisance law has been used by adjoining property owners as a legal tool to resolve facility use conflicts. Courts have not exhibited the same reluctance in adopting nuisance theory as a means to resolve land use conflicts as they have in awarding damages to injured park patrons. In resolving these conflicts, courts follow the general proposition that a resident adjacent to a recreation and sports facility must accept a reasonable amount of noise, traffic, light, and litter but that excessive interference with the peace, enjoyment, and use of adjacent residences will be enjoined as a nuisance.[22] Basically the court must decide whether the facility is properly planned and operated. If the court finds that a recreation and sports facility is not properly designed and operated it may require that the facility be relocated or that it be operated to avoid unreasonable interference with adjoining property. In some cases, this means the enterprise must have fences to prevent park users from trespassing on adjoining property or that baseball or softball games on lighted fields must conclude by 10 P.M. or that the volume of sound systems at swimming pools must be lowered.

Almost any type of recreation facility is subject to a nuisance claim, however swimming facilities, sports fields, golf courses, racetracks, and rifle ranges have generated the substantial body of case law.[23] Most of the cases have turned on a claim of noise, dust, traffic, lights, or trespass as constituting an unreasonable interference with the use and enjoyment of property rather than on the facility location. The problem is one of cause and effect—a poorly planned and sited facility generates maintenance and operation problems which generate political and legal problems.

Swimming Pools

Among the conditions examined by courts in swimming pool nuisance cases are excessive noise,[24] lighting,[25] traffic conditions,[26] and diminishment of property values.[27] Noise from loudspeaker systems as a nuisance was a contention in *MacArthur* v *Graylyn Crest III Swim Club Inc.*, 187 A.2d 174 (DE 1963), and *Liddell* v *Swathmore Swim Club*, 2 PaD &C2d 468 (PA 1954). In both cases, the court refused to enjoin the pools from operating but included requirements in the decree that volume controls be placed on the equipment to prevent loud noise. Although the claimants in pool cases are generally not successful in closing down a facility, they frequently obtain a modicum of relief when conditions are placed on operation of the pools.

Sports Fields

Adjoining landowners have relied upon combinations of noise, dust, traffic, lights, and trespass as a basis in seeking to enjoin the operations of playgrounds. In the few cases in which these contentions have been accepted, the courts have indicated a preference to eliminate the particular annoyance and have rejected the request for total closure of the playground. By de facto limiting baseball diamond lighting to the hours between 7 A.M. and 10 P.M., the court in *Corporation of Presiding Bishop of Church of Jesus Christ of Latter Day Saints* v *Ashton*, 448 P.2d 185 (UT 1968), minimized the impact on the neighbor's property. In refusing to stop the use of a little league ballfield in *Lieberman* v *Saddle River*, 116 A.2d 809 (NJ 1955), the court did require the defendants to move a parking lot in the park so that it was not adjacent to the plaintiff's residence. With regard to allegations of noise in the park, the court said that persons living next to a park must accept some noise and that the noise in question was not excessive and unreasonable.

Trespass upon adjoining land by persons retrieving foul balls may be grounds for injunctive relief. Something more than an occasional foul ball is required before relief is granted. The usual remedy is a fence or screen to be built by the park owner. A factual finding in *Hennessy* v *Boston*, 164 N.E. 470 (MA 1929), of repeated trespass and substantial property damage justified, in the court's opinion, a requirement of city fencing. It appeared that many balls were hit or thrown onto the plaintiff's land; that windows in plaintiff's garage were broken; that there was apprehension the balls would damage autos in the garage, injure customers and employees; and that property would be further damaged when the ball players retrieved the balls. On those facts, the court found substantial injury.

Target Ranges

Although a target, rifle, or skeet range may be found to be a nuisance *per accidens* under selected circumstances, the rule seems to be that such a facility is not a nuisance per se.[28] The conditions giving rise to a nuisance claims involve noise and danger from bullets. To constitute a nuisance, noise must be continuous and recurring. There must be a clear and present actual danger from bullets and not merely the possibility of bullets striking or passing over adjacent land. Without evidence that bullets have struck persons, property, or buildings, courts have refused to enjoin the operation of target ranges.[29]

In reviewing the circumstances when noise may constitute a nuisance, the courts have considered factors such as the character, volume, time duration, and locality of the noise in arriving at a decision.[30] Noting that shooting matches are not nuisances per se, the court in *Schneider* v *Waters*, 52 Lanc. L. Rev. 113 (PA 1950), found that two championship matches held annually only on Sunday would not constitute a nuisance even though the noise produced during a match was unusual. As with other recreation cases, anticipation of a nuisance is not sufficient for a finding of a nuisance.

Thus the court in *Brenner* v *Melrose Ganders, Inc.*,63 Dauph Co. 33 (PA 1952), refused to enjoin the construction of a shooting range based on the plaintiffs allegation of apprehension. As noted by the court, the plaintiffs could file a nuisance action if, upon construction and operation of the range, it turned out to be a nuisance.

Golf Courses

Six cases were found on the topic of golf courses as a nuisance to adjoining property owners.[31] In all but one case, the alleged nuisance condition involved golf balls landing or striking an adjoining property. Where there was more than an occasional hook, slice, or mishit ball from a tee that landed on plaintiff's property, the court required relocation of the tee box or screening of the adjacent property.

The following case illustrates the importance of facility planning and prudent operation. It is indicative of the athletic field nuisance cases.

KASALA v KALISPELL PEE WEE BASEBALL LEAGUE
Montana Supreme Court
439 P.2d 65 1968

John C. Harrison, Judge

This appeal results from a finding by the trial court, sitting without a jury, that the Pee Wee Baseball League as conducted in Kalispell was a nuisance, and from an injunction that not only would prevent the use of a playground for baseball, but also would order the removal of all light poles, backstops, and other baseball paraphernalia from the playground.

In 1936, the City of Kalispell purchased a vacant city block located in the residential section of the city, referred to as "Thompson Field." Throughout the ensuing years, the field has been used for football, softball, and the Pee Wee baseball since 1952.

The Pee Wee Baseball League in the city is an unincorporated association of parents imbued with the idea that the all-American game of baseball is important to a growing boy. Lights were installed at Thompson Field in 1963 so that the Pee Wee League could play ball into the summer evenings up until 10:00 P.M. According to the testimony this was necessary because the fathers who served as team coaches did not get off work early enough to have their teams play daylight games. During the 1964 season over 400 boys between eight and twelve years of age participated in the program and used the field, during a seven week period in June and July, and in which months, between twenty-three and thirty evening baseball games were played.

The respondents Collier, whose home was located in the northeast corner of the block just west of the field, purchased their property in 1952; the respondents Carlson, whose property adjoins the Colliers, purchased their property in 1950; and the respondents Kasala, whose property was located in the block northwest of the field, purchased their property in June 1964.

Two of the respondents, the Colliers and the Carlsons, testified that they did not object to the use of the field for baseball, but did object to the lights and the noise and increased traffic at the time of the games. The respondent Kasala testified in support of their request for an injunction that

1.   The bright lights bothered them at night;
2.   Noise from the attending crowd bothered them;
3.   That heavy traffic created a hazardous condition;
4.   That when the field was dragged the dust bothered them;
5.   That some children used foul language;
6.   Balls were hit into their yard and their lawns and flowers were damaged; and
7.   Games were played after 10:00 P.M.

Needless to say, at the time the matters were heard, public interest was in evidence. The appellants had some twenty-seven witnesses, twenty-four of whom lived either across from the field or within one half block of it. Some sixteen of these witnesses' testimony was stipulated to at the time of the hearing, but without question the majority of the property owners, whose property surrounded the field disagreed with the respondents and testified that there was little or no interference with the comfortable use of their property. City officials testified that they were familiar with the area, had received requests and complaints from the respondents, and had tried to rectify their complaints. The chief of police testified that special measures were taken on the nights of ballgames to control traffic; testimony was given indicating that the public officials, when informed that debris from the field blew onto respondents' lawns, made special efforts thereafter to see that the area was policed, and in addition, upon learning of respondents' objections to the lights, efforts were made to have the games end before 10:00 P.M., so that the lights could be turned off.

In spite of all this testimony the court found:

1.   The property of the plaintiffs (respondents) and each of them is continually trespassed upon;
2.   The plaintiffs (respondents) and each of them, including their friends, families, and guests live in fear of injury to their persons and property from flying balls;
3.   That by reason of the playing of baseball games, the quiet and enjoyment of the plaintiffs' (respondents') property has been seriously interfered with by reason of the excessive noise caused by the attending public and the

participants; that the attending public, on many occasions disorderly, congregates in the area; that obscene language is used publicly;

4. That a large part of the attending public arrives by private automobile, causing serious congestion in the immediate vicinity of the plaintiffs' property, thereby creating a serious traffic hazard;

5. That the Kalispell Pee Wee Baseball League, without the consent of the City of Kalispell, and other persons, erected light poles, flood lights, backstops, screens, fences, and other structures on said real estate which items detract from the value and enjoyment of plaintiffs' property; and

6. That these circumstances and conditions created undue interference with the plaintiffs' peaceful quiet use and enjoyment of their property.

The court then went on to its conclusions of law, finding that the circumstances clearly set forth facts describing a nuisance within our statute.

This, in spite of substantial evidence that no nuisance existed. (The court reviewed other nuisance cases and concluded.)

. . . The case differs fundamentally from other cases, all typical cases of nuisance, in that light is not a noxious, but is, in general, a highly beneficial element. The development of parks and playgrounds equipped for the enjoyment of the working public, whose recreation is necessarily taken after working hours, and frequently after dark, is a significant phenomenon in thousands of urban communities. The court takes judicial knowledge that many lighted parks and fields are located adjacent to residential property and must to some extent interfere with the full enjoyment of darkness (if desired), by the residents.

"We do not say that the shedding of light upon another's property may never under any conditions become a nuisance, but we do say that extreme caution must be employed in applying any such legal theory. The conditions of modern city life impose upon the city dweller and his property many burdens more severe than that of light reflected upon him or it."

The respondents contend that the case resolves itself to one of property rights versus the national sport, baseball, and that historically, when this national sport is involved, prejudice and passion overrule reason and law. To this argument we must answer that property rights were long recognized and established before the advent of our national sport, however, the law does not in every instance provide directly for compensation or fiscal redress for every damnum a person may sustain as a member of an organized society. It is established law that even an intentional interference with the use and enjoyment of land is not actionable unless the interference be both substantial and unreasonable. Restatement of Law of Torts, Vol. 4, 822.

The respondents claim that traffic hazards and the improper use of streets and driveways for parking creates a public nuisance. These are matters subject to local police regulation and do not constitute a public nuisance.

(The Court disagreed with the trial court.) Clearly no facts were shown that the maintenance of the Pee Wee ballgrounds resulted in conditions which were injurious to health, or indecent, or offensive to the senses, or were obstructions to the free use of property, nor were there interferences created with the comfortable enjoyment of life or property.

It should be noted in considering the court's actions in this case that if a nuisance is private and arises out of the particular manner of the operation of a legitimate enterprise the court should have done no more than to point to the nuisance and decree methods of adoption calculated to eliminate the injurious features. Here it was possible to have eliminated the objectionable features which were alleged to have infringed upon the ordinary rights of the respondents, for equity may so decree, instead of compelling, as the trial court did here, the abatement of the use of the baseball field. However, in a case such as this, where there is little or no conflicting credible evidence, and where no substantial evidence has been furnished for a basis for the findings of the trial court, this court will not hesitate to finally determine the rights of the parties.

Therefore, in the spirit of "Casey at the Bat," Oh, somewhere in this favored land dark clouds may hide the sun. And somewhere bands no longer play and children have no fun. And somewhere over blighted lives there hangs a heavy pall. But in Kalispell, hearts are happy now, for the Pee Wee can play ball.

Reversed

SUMMARY

Due to the noise, traffic, lights, and crowds associated with recreation and sports facilities complaints from surrounding landowners often raise questions regarding these facilities as a nuisance. As a general rule, every landowner has the right to use his or her property as may best suit the landowner's purposes, so long as it does not interfere with public rights and the use of private lands. In determining whether a particular use of property is a nuisance the court will balance the utility of the conduct against the gravity of harm that it produces. If the harm outweighs the benefits the use may be declared a nuisance.

The law of nuisance is divided into public and private nuisance. A public nuisance is an activity or use of land in such a way that it interferes with the health, safety, welfare, or morals of the general public. Activities subject to allegations of public nuisance have included automobile races, prize fights, gambling, prostitution, and nude dancing. A private nuisance is an activity or use of land in such a manner that it creates a substantial and unreasonable interference with the use and enjoyment of privately owned lands. It is within this context that recreation and sports facilities have been alleged to be a nuisance.

In resolving conflicts between owners of recreation and sports facilities and neighboring landowners the courts have followed the general proposition that a resident adjacent to such a facility must accept a reasonable amount of noise, traffic, light, litter, and crowds. It is when this condition become unreasonable that the court have formulated remedies to remove the conflict. This is especially difficult when the remedy sought is injunctive relief which would cause the offending party to cease a worthwhile and beneficial use of land. In these cases the courts balance the benefit of the use of land for recreation and sports against the harm caused to neighbors. Generally, courts have exhibited a reluctance to close a recreation and sports facility, preferring instead to minimize one of the offending conditions. Thus courts have restricted the hours of operation of recreation and sports facilities or have required modification of the physical facility to minimize the conflict. To avoid court ordered sanctions the following points should be considered when planning and operating recreation and sports facilities:

1. Locate major athletic facilities in community parks rather than in neighborhood parks.
2. Avoid lighting ball diamonds located in neighborhood parks when surrounded by single family residences.
3. Provide adequate buffer between major recreation facilities and adjacent residences.
4. Be a good neighbor—prevent or minimize the impact of park users trespassing on adjoining private property.
5. Do not locate parking lots immediately adjacent to adjoining residential property.
6. If substantial unregulated park use continues past 11 P.M. consider park hours of operation.
7. Be prepared to offer alternatives and mitigation measures to minimize or remove alleged nuisance conditions.
8. Involve adjacent property owners in facility planning prior to construction of facilities.

DISCUSSION QUESTIONS

1. How do public and private nuisances differ?
2. Why is the doctrine of nuisance significant to parks, recreation, and sports enterprises?
3. What conditions in a park are most likely to result in nuisance allegations? What can a manager do to minimize these allegations?
4. Why do users injured in a park or at a facility claim that these were nuisances?

NOTES

[1]66 C.J.S., Nuisance, §1; 58 Am.Jur.2d Nuisance §1—citing a long line of cases.

[2]58 Am.Jur.2d., Nuisance §3.

[3]WILLIAM PROSSER, *Law of Torts*, 4th ed. (St. Paul: West Publishing Co., 1971), p. 574.

[4]*State v Turner*, 18 S.E.2d. 372 (SC 1972), *Parker v Ft. Worth*, 282 S.W.2d 721 (TX 1956), Am.Jur.2d Nuisance §7, 8 Am.Jur. Proof of Facts, 527, Nuisance.

[5]Restatement (Second) of Torts §821B.

[6]58 Am.Jur.2d, Nuisance, §28.

[7]*Wilcox v Ryder*, 147 N.W. 953 (MN 1914).

[8]*Steinberg v People*, 390 P.2d 811 (OR 1963).

[9]*Wilson v Parent*, 365 P.2d 72 (OR 1961).

[10]*McMillan v Kuehnle*, 73 A. 1054 (NJ 1909).

[11]*Town of Preble* v. *Song Mountain, Inc.*, 308 N.Y.S. 2d 1001 (NY 1970).

[12]*Straughton v Ft. Worth*, 277 S.W.2d 150 (TX 1954), *Parker v Ft. Worth*, 282 S.W. 2d 721 (TX 1955).

[13]PROSSER, Torts, p. 572.

[14]Restatement (Second) of Torts 821; 8 Am.Jur, Proof of Facts 527; 68 A.L.R. 2d 1323.

[15]*Casteel* v. *Afton*, 287 N.W. 245 (IA 1939).

[16]Betty van der Smissen, *Legal Liability of Cities and Schools for Injuries in Recreation and Parks* (Cincinnati: W.H. Anderson Co., 1968), p. 103.

[17]*Anderson v Board of Ed.*, 190 N.W. 807 (ND 1922), *Berstein v Milwaukee*, 149 N.W. 382 (WI 1914), *Fowler v Winfield*, 286 F.2d 385 (KS 1960), *Grinde v Watertown*, 288 N.W. 196 (WI 1939), *Malchow v Leoti*, 149 P.687 (KS 1915), *Piaseeny v Manchester*, 136 A. 357 (NH 1926), *Royston v Charlotte*, 270 N.W. 288 (MI 1936) *Stuver v Auburn*, 17 P.2d 614 (WA 1932). Exceptions: *Lubbock v Green*, 201 F.2d 146 (TX 1953), *Ford v City of Detroit*, 283 N.W.2d (MI 1979), *Schmitt v Cheviot*, 31 Ohio NP 12 (OH 1940).

[18]*Cleveland v Ferrando*, 150 N.E. 747 (OH 1926), *Harris v Findlay*, 18 N.E.2d 413 (OH 1938), *Schwartz v Cincinnati*, 9 N.E.2d 3 (OH 1936).

[19]*Hassett v Thurston*, 110 A. 394 (RI 1920), *Pope v New Haven*, 99 A. 51 (CT 1916), *Whittaker v Franklinville*, 191 N.E. 716 (NY 1934).

[20]49 A.L.R.3d 652.

[21]*Shoemaker v Parsons*, 118 P.2d 508 (KS 1941), *Johnson v Alcoa*, 145 S.W.2d 796 (TN 1940), *Madlin v Havener*, 98 S.W.2d 863 (TX 1936).

[22]*Casteel v Afton*, 287 N.W. 245 (IA 1939).

[23]For a listing and discussion of cases see, Public Swimming Pools, as Nuisance, 49 A.L.R. 3d 1127.

[24]*MacArthur v Graylyn Crest III Swim Club, Inc.*, 187 A.2d 417 (DE 1963).

[25]*Liddell v Swathmore Swim Club*, 42 Del. Co. 69 (DE 1954).

[26]*Hood v Winding Vista Recreation, Inc.*, 149 S. E.2d 784 (G. A. 1960).

[27]*Marco v Swinnerton*, 171 A.2d 418 (1960).

[28]*Silverman v User*, 147 A. 421 (ME 1929), *Smith v Western Wayne County Conservation Assoc.*, 158 N.W.2d 463 (MI 1968), *Gundel v Kemmick*, 60 Lanc. L. Rev. 116 (PA 1966), *Larson v Calder's Park Co.*, 180, p. 599 (UT 1919).

[29]*Wolcott v Doremus*, 101 A. 868 (DE 1817), *Smith v Western Wayne County Conservation Assoc.*, 158 N.W.2d 463 (MI 1968), *Digiralamo v Philadelphic Gun Club*, 89 A.2d 357 (PA 1952).

[30]*Roberts v Clothier*, 37 Montg. Co. LR 165 (PA 1920).

[31]*Drennan v Mason*, 133 So. 689 (AL 1930), *Sans v Ramsey Golf and Country Club, Inc.*, 149 A.2d 599 (NJ 1959), *Waters v McNearney*, 168 N.E.2d 255 (NY 1959), *Nussbaum v Lacopo*, 265 N.E.2d 762 (NY 1970), *Patton v Westwood* 247 N.E.2d 761 (OH 1969), *Sierra Screw Products v Azusa Greens Inc.*, 151 Cal. Rptr. 799 (CA 1978).

eleven

risk management concepts

It is clear that exposures to tort risk and liability are inherent in the operation of park, recreation, and sports enterprises, public or private, large or small. Employees of these enterprises are exposed to many legal liability risks which could result in a devastating personal loss. The preceding chapters have classified and analyzed liability exposures for the enterprise and employees from a legal perspective. This chapter outlines a management process for handling liability exposure through the practice of risk management.[1]

For many recreation and sports administrators this may be their first exposure to the term and concept of risk management. Although the management of liability risks for public agencies is of recent origin, the practice has been used in the private sector for many years.[2] The earliest organizations to practice risk management were insurance companies whose techniques have been modified and applied by hospitals, public schools, and universities. The size, type, and complexity of an organization dictates the internal emphasis on a risk management program. Some organizations have a staff devoted exclusively to risk management and in others it may be an adjunct duty of a business manager or financial officer.

Risk Management Process

The objective of risk management is to efficiently conserve the assets and financial resources of the organization and to achieve financial stability by reducing the potential for financial loss. Financial stability is especially important to public and private recreation enterprises during periods of inflation and stable or declining revenues. An unplanned financial loss could have significant consequences for their programs. As outlined in Fig. 11.1, the risk management process encompasses *identification, evaluation, selection,* and *implementation.* The elements in the process are the same regardless of the recreation organization, although the type of organization and the diversity of recreation facilities and programs will affect the risks to which they may be exposed.

Risk identification   The exposure identification phase of risk management is crucial since it is not possible to treat the risks faced by the agency and its personnel prior to loss without this identification. Risk may be defined as uncertainty as to the occurrence of a financial loss, that is, the likelihood of a loss from exposure to a peril. Thus a risk manager is con-

FIGURE 11-1 Risk Management Process.

cerned with efficient minimizing of financial loss associated with legal liability.

Recreation enterprises are exposed to a host of financial and legal risks. While this book examines tort liability, the reader should recognize there are risks associated with property loss, contractual liability and fidelity losses. These losses may or may not be associated with tort liability, nevertheless they are significant to the enterprise. As owners and operators of recreation buildings, equipment, and vehicles, enterprises are exposed to financial losses if these assets are destroyed or damaged from fire, floods, vandalism, wind, hail, rain, or explosion. Most private enterprises manage this risk through purchase of property insurance, while public agencies act as self-insurers.

All public and private enterprises enter into contracts with a variety of vendors. As described in Chapter 4, a contract is a binding agreement that may expose the enterprise and vendor to legal liabilities if contract terms are not fulfilled. Thus an agency may be liable for damages when it fails to meet its contract obligations. Conversely an agency may seek damages for vendor breach or nonperformance of contract obligations.

Fidelity risks are those associated with employee dishonesty in the handling of funds and merchandise. Examples of these risks are (1) misappropriation of petty cash or other funds, (2) loss of cash due to theft, fire, or other human or natural calamity, (3) forgery of a check, draft, or other financial instrument, or (4) loss through employee failure to perform accounting or other financial duties.

Two options are available to identify the tort liability risks confronting the enterprise and its personnel. The administrator may retain the services of an insurance consultant to identify risk or may undertake this process with existing staff. Risk analysis questionnaires are available from individual insurance companies, insurance publishing houses, or the Insurance Division of the American Management Association to assist the manager with self analysis. These questionnaires must be structured to meet individual agency needs. Once the survey is completed, it may be helpful to list the risk exposure into property, contract, fidelity, and tort categories. After this listing phase is complete, the evaluation phase can begin.

Risk evaluation   Measurement techniques vary depending on whether the risk involves property or tort losses. They range from simple evaluations to very complex statistical equations. Regardless of the formula or technique all involve the determining of the probability of a loss occurring, maximum and minimum severity of such loss, predictability of a loss in a given time period, and financial resources available to meet such losses.

This process applied to a playground and a swimming pool illustrates the varying risks associated with these two facilities. Statistics suggest that there are far more accidents and injuries on playgrounds than at swimming pools. The severity of playground injuries, however, is lower than at pools, that is, broken bones v drowning. It is reasonable to expect that more accidents will occur at the playground than at a pool during a year allowing for prediction of a loss in a given time period. The resources available to meet the financial loss will determine a risk management option. The one in a million accident at a pool that may cost the agency a million dollars demands a different approach than ten playground accidents resulting in $5,000 in losses.

Risk treatment measures   After the risk exposure has been identified, the agency must decide on the options available to protect against losses. The options available to the park and recreation agency are: (1) risk avoidance, (2) risk reduction, (3) risk retention, and (4) risk transferance. The characteristics and application of each of these methods to the recreation enterprise is discussed in greater detail in the next section of this chapter. Selection of the single best method cannot be predicated on a precise mathematical model. Subjective evaluations must be made in the process. The attributes of the agency and its financial status must be matched with the types and frequency of risks to which it is exposed. It is possible however to outline several rules of thumb for selecting a method. These rules are incorporated in Fig. 11.2.

FIGURE 11-2 Risk Measures Matrix

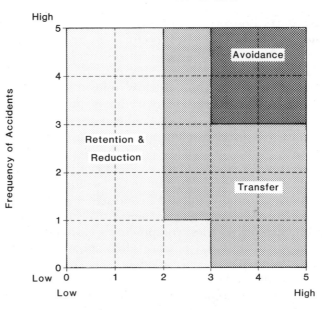

Implementation   The implementation of a risk management plan involves a policy commitment from the agency's governing board coupled with establishment of the necessary administration procedures. Necessary forms and documents must be prepared and distributed to all levels within the organization. The administrative ingredients are similar to other programs, namely a trained and motivated staff.

Risk Treatment Methods

Several tools are available to the agency to *avoid, reduce, retain,* or *transfer* the tort risks identified through the management process. Selection of a method is based on the frequency of the occurrence and severity of loss. (See Fig. 11.2.)

Risk avoidance   The complete elimination of a risk is certainly a management option. It requires the cancellation of an activity or program so that the possibility of loss becomes nonexistent. Many recreation professionals and educators prefer not to exercise this option. As noted by van der Smissen, avoidance is an unacceptable approach to risk management for physical education and athletics.[3] Nevertheless, a number of schools, municipal parks, and recreation programs have employed this technique. For example, consider the demise of the trampoline in many school physical education classes or the removal of the mechanical bucking bull in many bars and nightclubs. In removing this type of equipment, the sponsors weighed the advantages of such equipment against undesirable results and possible losses.

Risk reduction   Loss prevention and reduction measures attack risk by lowering the chance that a loss will occur or by reducing its severity if it does occur. Even those recreation enterprises that have opted to purchase insurance for risk protection may use this technique to reduce costs. Many insurance policies leave a portion of a loss uninsured through either a deductible amount or policy exclusion. By reducing the chance that a loss will occur, the agency reduces costs from uninsured coverage.

Controlling risk involves interference with accident occurrence frequency and minimizing the dollar amount of the loss associated wth the accident. Lowering the chance of an accident can be accompanied by: (1) developing safety rules for the operation of facilities and equipment and diligently adhering to those rules; (2) conducting periodic safety inspections for all facility and equipment; (3) aggressively using preventive maintenance techniques on vehicles, equipment, areas, and facilities; and (4) training all employees in safety practices, first aid, emergency procedures, and preventive maintenance. Since accidents related to facilities and equipment account for the majority of injuries in parks, recreation, sports, and athletics, the safety of equipment and facilities must be a regular focus of the risk management program. Other examples of accident frequency reduction programs include periodic physical examinations for employees, immediate first aid for persons injured on the premises, fire alarms, speed limits for vehicles, transfer of accident prone employees, and prohibiting employees with poor driving records from operating vehicles.

Minimizing the amount of dollar loss from accidents is a second alternative in risk reduction. These programs take effect in advance of the loss, while it is occurring, or shortly thereafter. Automatic sprinklers in community centers, for example, are designed to minimize a fire loss. Public relations programs may also be used to minimize dollar losses from accidents. The intent of such a program is to convey to an injury victim that the agency and its staff acted as responsible prudent professionals in minimizing risks of harm and that unpreventable accidents sometimes occur.

Risk retention Retention is a form of self-insurance whereby the enterprise assumes a certain level of losses. Retention may be passive or active. When an agency is not aware of the risks and consequently doesn't attempt to manage them, this is a form of passive retention. The old adage "ignorance is bliss" aptly describes this form of retention. Passive retention may be a good approach to a particular risk by chance, but it is not a rational and prudent way of managing risks. For example, many administrators, believing that public park and recreation agencies cannot be sued under the doctrine of governmental immunity, are using passive retention.

Active retention occurs when the agency identifies the risk, considers other methods of handling it, and decides to pay any losses out of its own resources. This form of risk management, when coupled with a loss prevention and insurance program, has the greatest potential for recreation agencies when at least one of the following conditions exist:

1. It is impossible to transfer the risks to another or to prevent the loss from occurring.
2. The maximum possible loss is so small that the agency can absorb it in the operating budget.
3. The probability of a loss is so low that it can be ignored, and
4. The cost to transfer the risk is so high that it would cost almost as much as the worst loss that could occur.

The success of a risk retention program depends to a large degree on the ability of an agency to control losses and to maintain fiscal stability. Staff must be trained in loss control techniques and must be motivated to follow those techniques. An effective loss control program is only wishful thinking without a significant commitment from administrators and staff.

Risk transfer Shifting risk to another party provides the recreation enterprise with protection from financial loss. Transferring risks should be considered if the financial capability of the agency cannot support a given amount of loss. Thus, risks associated with high frequency and large losses are candidates for transfer. Shifting the risk may be accomplished by transferring the property or activity generating the risk to another, or by transferring the risk of loss but not the property or activity. For example, an agency that leases a golf course to someone else transfers the facility and correspondingly the risk. A transfer of just the risk of loss may be accomplished by purchasing an accident insurance policy covering loss associated with the operaton of the golf course. A variety of methods under either approach are available. Some of the commonly used methods include leasing land or facilities to others, contracting and subcontracting the performance of certain services and programs to independent contractors, purchase of liability insurance, use of surety bonds to guarantee performance, and the use of liability waivers, hold-harmless clauses, and subrogation clauses in contracts.

Liability Insurance

Insurance is the keystone of most risk management programs. Through the purchase of insurance, a recreation enterprise transfers to the insurance company the risks it can't afford for a price it can afford. Purchase of an insurance policy does not protect the insured from the occurrence of an injury or damage, nor can it protect against personal anxiety and professional embarrassment. Insurance only protects the insured from the financial loss arising from the covered peril. Determining the insurance needs of a recreation enterprise is a complex and difficult task.

Insurance protection can be purchased to cover virtually all recreation enterprises and employees. All states have enacted statutes authorizing municipalities, schools, and other public entities to carry insurance covering the agency. Some states allow the public agency to extend this coverage to employees. In considering the purchase of insurance, it is important that the administrator determine the liability potential for the agency and employees. Among the many guidelines that must be answered are those concerning the extent to which the agency and employers may be liable for various types of injury to persons or property, the extent to which protection may be secured by insurance, the effect of such insurance on governmental immunity and the use of tax revenues to purchase insurance. A minority of states follow the rule that the purchase of an insurance policy constitutes a waiver of immunity, at least to the extent of the insurance. The majority hold that immunity is not waived by the purchase of insurance. No general statement can cover all of these variables and the administrator would be well advised to seek the assistance of an attorney and an insurance consultant prior to any insurance decision.

Analyzing insurance needs and contracts can be a complex and arduous task. Insurance policies may be standardized or personalized and usually contain language that is highly technical. The administrator must learn how to analyze policies in order to make insurance purchase decisions. It is helpful to understand the structure of a typical insurance policy, and be aware of the types of insurance policies.[5]

Structure of an insurance policy The provisions in an insurance policy can be classified as declaratons, insuring agreements, exclusions, and conditions. Although not all contracts will have such neat labels, all policies whether standardized or personalized have these components.

1. *Declarations.* This is the *preamble* of the policy describing the property or activity being insured, types of coverage purchased, policy limits, deductibles, time period of coverage, and premium paid for each coverage. The purpose of the declaration section is the disclosure of sufficient information by the insurer (seller) to the insured (buyer) to allow for the sale and purchase of a desired contract at a proper price.

2. *Insuring Agreements.* The agreements indicate the obligations of the insurer including the events and perils covered under the contract.

3. *Exclusions.* This section outlines the limits of coverage under the insuring agreements for such things as perils, property, sources of liability, persons, losses, locations, deductibles, and time periods. The exclusions serve to exclude losses that the insurer considers to be uninsurable, to exclude losses covered by the contracts, to eliminate losses that are the result of ordinary wear and tear, to exclude losses that are incurred by a few people, and to produce a limited coverage at a reasonable premium rate.

4. *Conditions.* The conditions section describes the procedures, rights, and obligations of the parties after a loss. Certain terms used in other parts of the contract are defined as well as conditions that must be met before the insurer is liable under the contract.

Analyzing an insurance policy In reviewing an insurance contract the reader should review the contract several times to gain an understanding of format and content. After this review, the reader should seek answers to the following checklist of questions:

1. What events are covered?
2. What property or activities are covered?
3. What persons are covered?
4. What losses are covered?
5. What locations are covered?
6. What time period is covered?
7. What special conditions are excluded?
8. What amount of loss will insurer pay?
9. What steps must the insured take following a loss?

Although these are not all of the questions to be asked about an insurance policy, they can assist the administrator in evaluating a specific policy.

Types of policy coverage   Liability insurance contracts are written to cover a specific hazard or a comprehensive range of hazards. Losses covered by insurance include buildings and facilities, motor vehicles, recreation and sports activities, and acts or conduct of employees. Not surprisingly, insurance policies have been written to cover each of these areas. Some of the policies only protect the enterprise, while others extend coverage to employees of the enterprise.[6]

1. *Owners', Landlords', and Tenants' Liability Coverage.*   This type of policy covers the losses arising from claims on account of bodily injury or property damage caused by an accident arising out of the ownership, maintenance, and use of parks and recreation facilities. Principal exclusion from this policy include bodily injury of property damage liability (1) arising from automobiles, watercraft or aircraft away from the premises, (2) liquor liability, and (3) contamination or pollution of land, air, or water.

2. *Automobile Liability Coverage.*   Losses covered by these policies may include damage and destruction of the vehicle itself and injury or damage to the property of others. Usually this coverage is limited to only the insured vehicles but a nonownership endorsement can be added to protect all vehicles owned by others but operated on behalf of the insured. Thus insurance protection may be extended to employees' vehicles if used in the course of employment. An employee should inquire about this coverage as a condition of employment. Whenever possible the insured should purchase a comprehensive liability policy rather than a specific perils in conditions policy.

3. *Products Liability Coverage.*   This is specialized insurance covering losses associated with the possession, use, or consumption of products manufactured, sold, handled, or distributed by the insured. It is insurance protecting manufacturers and sellers of recreation products from losses associated with product defects.

4. *Professional Liability Coverage.*   Commonly called malpractice insurance, these policies protect the enterprise and/or professional against liability for damages based on professional mistakes. Originally drafted for doctors and dentists, the coverage is made available for accountants, architects, attorneys, brokers, corporate directors, engineers, and other professionals for injuries arising out of the rendering of professional services.

5. *Theft and Dishonesty Coverage.*   Losses of money and securities from employee dishonesty and theft are covered by this type of policy. In addition, protection can be extended to losses associated with robbery, burglary, or other types of risk.

6. *Participant Accident Coverage.*   This policy protects the individual or participant who is injured by accident while participating in a recreation and sports program. Student accident insurance is an example of ths type of coverage. Most accident benefit plans cover financial loss from medical and hospital bills. They also make the program sponsor and participant safety conscious and are a good public relations device.

7. *Contractual Liability Coverage.*   The insured is protected against losses assumed through contractual arrangements such as hold-harmless agreements in land and facility leases. Coverage may be extended to losses from damages to the leased premises as well as to personal injuries associated with the use of the facility.

8. *Errors and Omissions Coverage.*   Originating in the early seventies, this form of

insurance coverage protects the enterprise, its officers, and employees against losses arising from claims based on misfeasance and nonfeasance and other acts not covered by a general liability policy. It is supplemental to existing policies and covers errors and omissions in duties of employees. A unique feature of this coverage is that it protects the enterprise, its corporate directors, and designated employees. When purchasing comprehensive liability insurance the administrator should ask the insurance consultant or attorney about this type of coverage.

All of the foregoing types of insurance policies cover specific conditions and perils. These types of policies offer the advantage of structuring loss protection for known risks at a lower premium cost. A second option is to provide a *comprehensive liability policy* covering claims and losses arising from all of these perils. Many insurance professionals believe that this approach provides the best form of tort liability protection for the enterprise, professional, and employees. It is customary for these policies to provide first dollar coverages of defense costs and damages but to incorporate a deductible arrangement in the policy. Deductibles can be arranged in almost any amount, generally the higher the deductible the lower the premium. In reality, a deductible is a form of self-insurance and the insured should consider the degree of predictability of the occurrence and available resources when establishing a deductible limit.

Personal liability insurance Employees of public or private recreation enterprises may be individually liable for torts they commit, notwithstanding the fact that the enterprise is also sued and carries insurance. A prudent professional must seek adequate insurance against financial loss from a tort lawsuit. Employees may add insurance liability coverage through their personal or homeowners liability policy or through the purchase of a group insurance policy. When adding coverage under a homeowner policy a specific endorsement is needed. Personal liability protection for professionals is available from a number of professional organizations. Members of the American Alliance for Health, Physical Education, and Dance and the National Recreation and Parks Association can purchase this coverage at a nominal premium cost. Both policies cover losses and costs associated with investigation and defense of claims involving alleged negligence by the insured arising out of the performance of duties in connection with gainful employment in the fields of health, recreation, parks, and physical education.

DISCUSSION QUESTIONS

1. What are the objectives of risk management and why are they important to a public agency?
2. What are the elements of a risk management program?

3.   Under what conditions should a public agency adopt a risk retention program?

4.   Purchasing liability insurance is one method of risk management. Under what circumstances should an agency purchase insurance?

5.   What are the types of insurance coverages that a park, recreation, and sports agency should consider?

NOTES

[1] This chapter draws heavily upon a presentation of the subject in Arthur Williams and Richard Heins, *Risk Management and Insurance* (NY: McGraw-Hill Book Co., 1971); Ray Aikens, John Adams, and John Hall, *Legal Liability in Higher Education: Their Scope and Management,* Association of American Colleges, 1976.

[2] NESTOR ROOS and JOSEPH GERBER, *Governmental Risk Management Manual* (Tucson: Risk Management Publishing Company, 1968).

[3] BETTY VAN DER SMISSEN, "Could You Pay a $147,000,000 Settlement," *AAHPER Convention,* March, 1979.

[4] JAMES DOOLEY, *Modern Tort Law* (Wilmette: Callaghan and Co., 1982), p. 416.

[5] This discussion on the structure of an insurance policy is adapted from Arthur Williams and Richard Heins, *Risk Management and Insurance* (New York: McGraw-Hill Book Co., 1971), pp. 254–265.

[6] This discussion of types of insurance policy is drawn from Ray Aiken, *Legal Liability in Higher Education: Their Scope and Management,* Association of American Colleges, 1976.

twelve

transferring legal risk by leasing and contracting

Leasing of facilities and contracting for services are not new concepts for public agencies but they are receiving renewed emphasis under the euphemism of *privatization*. Under this concept, public services are provided by the private sector under the rubric of public sponsorship. Historically, these techniques were used when the public agency had neither resources or expertise to provide the service, but today they can also be used to transfer the legal risk of liability for user injuries to third parties.[1] An example of the historical use of leasing and contracting is the National Park Service. Concessionares have constructed and operated recreation facilities for over 100 years in some national parks. The system of using private concessionares goes back to the Yellowstone Park Act, which among other things provides that the Secretary of Interior may

> grant leases for building purposes for terms not exceeding ten years, of small parcels of ground, at such places in said park as shall require the erection of buildings for the accommodations of visitors.[2]

State and local park and recreation agencies have similar authority to enter into contracts with private entrepreneurs for the leasing of land or facilities. Depending on the circumstances the public agency may be a landlord or tenant of a premises. With the recent upturn in privatization the following section has special meaning for parks, recreation, and sports enterprises.

FACILITY LEASING

The general rule of law respecting an owner's liability to third parties is that an owner, out of possession and control of the premises, is not liable for the condition of the premises. Thus the owner is not subject to liability for physical harm sustained as a result of a condition of the premises even though that condition existed before the tenant took possession.[3] During the time of the lease the tenant/lessee becomes the owner and is entitled to exclusive possession and control with all of the responsibilities for normal repairs and maintenance. Given this strong recognition to the possessory interest of the lessee, the law imposes no liability upon the lessor for negligent actions of the lessee or for defective conditions of the premises at the time of the lease.

As with any general rule of law there are a number of exceptions. To this nonliability of the owner rule four exceptions are recognized and are applicable to recreation enterprises. Under these exceptions the owner may be liable to third parties where (1) latent hazards known to him caused the injury, (2) the premises are leased for admission of the public, (3) the lessor retained control over the premises, or (4) there was an agreement to repair the premises. Each of these exceptions are outlined in the following sections. Application of the general rule of nonliability to the lessor is outlined in the following case.

GEORGE v CITY OF FORT WORTH
Court of Civil Appeals of Texas
434 S.W.2d 903 1968

Renfro, Justice

A.S. George, joined by Florence George, his wife, sued Gerard W. Purcell Associates, Ltd., a corporation, and The City of Fort Worth for damages for personal injuries sustained by Mrs. George when she dropped or slipped off the edge of the bottom step of a stairway in a city-owned building. Will Rogers Coliseum, City owned, was under written lease to Purcell on the night in question. For convenience we refer to Mrs. George as plaintiff.

Purcell sponsored a concert by Liberace on November 10, 1966. Plaintiff pleaded that she paid an admission fee, went to her seat, and enjoyed the concert, and "at the conclusion of the concert, but during the Grand Finale, Mrs. George descended the stairs in the upper part of the Coliseum in a careful and prudent manner. She negotiated all the steps without incident until she reached the bottom step where she was caused to fall."

She alleged the defendants were negligent, and such negligence was a proximate cause of her injuries in the following particulars: (1) in failing to maintain enough light on the bottom step on which plaintiff fell to properly illuminate such step, (2) in failing to properly design the bottom step on which plaintiff fell so that it did not blend in with the walkway area, (3) in failing to properly maintain the bottom step on which plaintiff fell so that it did not blend in with the walkway area and created an optical illusion, (4) in failing to warn plaintiff that the steps on which she fell blended with the walkway area and created an optical illusion.

The City denied any negligence whatever, and plead five specific acts of contributory negligence on the part of plaintiff, and, in the alternative, unavoidable accident. The City also pleaded the lease contract between City and Purcell, alleging that under the terms thereof Purcell becomes bound to indemnify the City for any damages arising out of use of the Coliseum.

On appeal plaintiff contends she presented a controverted fact and there the court was in error in granting defendants' motions for summary judgment.

The City established without dispute that there were no cracks, defects, or broken places on the step; there were no foreign objects or substances on the steps or on the landing in the vicinity of the steps.

D. Don Magness, Managing Director of the Will Rogers Memorial Center for the City, by affidavit in support of the motion for summary judgment, and by deposition, swore and testified: All the steps by the portals are the same. During a performance the steps are lighted by lights in the walk around which comes through the portals, and a certain amount of light "bleeds" back from the stage lighting. He sees that all lights in the Coliseum are reglobed prior to a show. There have never been any complaints from patrons concerning inadequacy of lighting. No one has ever fallen on the steps or stairways. He has never seen or heard of anyone stumbling on the steps, either before or after plaintiff's fall. The steps are raw concrete, dark gray. The face of the steps are painted yellow.

On the occasion of the Liberace concert more light was used than usual.

The overhead lights were on before the concert started, but turned off just prior to the start of the performance. The lights were turned on during intermission. The lights had not been turned on when plaintiff descended the steps. They are turned on after a performance. He has never received any complaints of the condition of the steps in the Coliseum.

The mere fact that plaintiff fell on the step did not establish negligence on the part of the defendants. In our opinion plaintiff's own testimony failed to raise any issue as to negligence on the part of defendants. She does not contend that she could procure and introduce any such evidence in a trial.

We affirm the trial court primarily upon the basis that there was no evidence, or, at the most, a mere scintilla of evidence of negligence on the part of defendants.

The judgment for the City of Fort Worth was proper for a third reason. Purcell occupied the Coliseum on the date in question as a tenant under a written lease agreement wit the City. It was agreed in the written lease that Purcell would provide ticket sellers, ticket takers, ushers, floor managers, stage crews, electricians, technicians, and all help necessary.

We find nothing in the lease agreement, or in the record before the trial court, which would have the effect of taking the arrangement between the City and Purcell out of the normal landlord and tenant relationship. The general rule then applies that "Where there is no agreement by the landlord to repair the demised premises and he is not guilty of any fraud or conceal- ment by failing to disclose hidden defects of which he has knowledge, the tenant takes the risk of their safety and the landlord is not liable to him."

Affirmed

Latent Hazards

The rule of *caveat emptor* (let the buyer beware) applies to a lease of real estate. It is the duty of the lessee to inspect the premises to ascertain whether it is safe and adaptable for the purposes required. Where neither party has knowledge of hidden dangers, the responsibility for discovery falls on the lessee, but where the lessor has knowledge of the hidden dan- ger, the duty to disclose is on the lessor. This rule applies only to hidden defects; a lessor is not liable for an obvious and open defects. This rule is incorporated in the Restatement (Second) of Torts §358 as

> A lessor of land who conceals or fails to disclose to his lessee any condition, whether natural or artificial, which involves unreasonable risk or physical harm to persons on the land, is subject to liability to the lessee and others upon the land . . . for physical harm after the lessee has taken possession, if (a) the lessee does not know . . . of the condition or risk involved, and (b) the lessor knows or has reason to know of the condition.

The rule is applicable to recreation enterprises operating a facility as a landlord or tenant. As a precaution the enterprise should always inspect a facility prior to leasing it. Correspondingly, when acting as a lessee the en- terprise should also conduct facility inspections prior to admitting the pub- lic to the facility.

THOMPSON v UNITED STATES
United States Court of Appeals
592 F.2d 1104 1979

Hug, Circuit Judge

Gary Thompson, through his guardian ad litem, brought an action against the United States under the Federal Tort Claims Act, 28 U.S.C. 1346(b), for injuries he received in the course of a motorcycle race on federal land. The Bureau of Land Management (BLM) had granted a permit to Ronald Vincellette, on behalf of the Sportsman Racing Association (Association) to conduct the race. The appellant contends that the injury resulted from the negligent marking of the race course or the failure to properly control the spectators and that the United States owed a duty to appellant to assure the race was conducted safely. The district court entered a summary judgment for the government, from which Thompson appeals. We affirm.

On September 18, 1972, the Riverside, California office of the BLM received a Special Land Use Application from the Association, for permission to conduct a European-style scrambles motorcycle race on October 1, 1972. The BLM issued the permit on September 29. As a special condition to the permit, Ronald Vincellette, on behalf of the Association, agreed to assume responsibility for public safety at the event. The Association laid out a race course through the hilly desert near Adelanto, California, on United States government land. The course was marked with colored ribbons tied to bushes, and the spectator area near the finish line was sectioned off for several hundred feet by a rope with colored pennants. Three races had been run prior to the 250 cc motorcycle novice race in which Thompson participated. Thompson commenced the fourth race and, when approaching the finish line at the end of his third and final lap, he crashed and was struck by oncoming racers, causing his injuries.

The only real dispute concerning the facts is whether the accident happened as a result of spectators being allowed to walk in the path of the appellant driver, causing him to swerve to miss them, or whether it resulted merely from his own carelessness in attempting to pass another motorcycle at the end of the race. In reviewing this summary judgment, we must assume the facts to be as stated by the appellant and determine whether the government is entitled to a judgment as a matter of law. We must therefore assume that the injury resulted from a negligent failure to mark the race course properly or to control the spectators so as to avoid interference with the racers.

There is no evidence that there was any hidden peril or inherently dangerous condition existing on the property when the permittee took possession. It is clear that any negligence claimed resulted from the faulty design of the race course or the lack of control of the spectators, after the lessee took possession. There is thus no basis for finding negligence on the part of any federal employee because of failure to warn of a hidden peril or a known hazardous condition on the land.

Generally, it has been an accepted rule of common law that the lessor of land (no matter how long or short the period) is not subject to liability to his lessee, or others upon the land with the consent of the lessee, for physical harm caused by any dangerous condition which comes into existence after the lessee has taken possession, with certain defined exceptions. None of these exceptions applies to the case at hand. Under the general common law rule, a landowner would not be found to have a duty under the circumstances of this case.

Appellant next argues that the BLM assumed a duty to supervise the safety of the race by virtue of its own internal regulations, and that having undertaken the responsibility to supervise the race, it must carry it out? . . . In this case, the BLM did not supervise the race. It was clear from the provisions of the permit that the Association had the full responsibility for public safety and supervision of the race. Neither the participants nor the spectators relied upon to BLM employees to supervise the race. No BLM employees were even present.

Appellant cites an internal instruction memorandum from the state director of the BLM to the regional offices, which was to take effect on September 18, 1972, the day the application was received, and which provided in part:

"(1) On-site inspections should be made by BLM before events to be sure that all pre-event is in progress."

"(2) Inspection for compliance with permit stipulations should be made while the event is in progress."

This regional office instruction could not constitute an assumption of liability or responsibility by the government for injury to participants, as this would conflict with 43 C.F.R. 2920.3(d), which states:

"(d) Liability. The applicant shall agree and stipulate that the Federal Government, Department of the Interior, and the Bureau of Land Management and its representatives shall not be responsible for damage or injury to persons and property which may occur during the permitted use period or as a result of such use."

Furthermore, the mere provisions for government safety inspections, or the ability to stop an activity for failure to comply with safety standards, does not impose liability on the government for failure to do so. A government safety manual or safety program does not impose a special duty on the government.

Affirmed

Public Admission

When property or a facility is used for public recreation or entertainment, it is universally agreed that the lessor has a duty to exercise reasonable care to inspect for and remedy unreasonably dangerous conditions existing when possession is transferred.[4] Of course this rule is limited to those parts of the premises which will be open to the public. A lessor is not liable for an area not open to the public.

In cases involving athletic facilities, fairgrounds, beaches, pools, and bathing facilities the courts have imposed liability on the lessor of the facilities for injuries resulting from defects existing in the leased premises at the time of the lease.[5] In a case indicative of this trend, recovery was allowed against the lessor of a baseball park in an action by a spectator who was injured when the bleachers on which he was seated broke and fell to the ground. The court held in *Tulsa Entertainment Co. v Greenlees,* 205, p. 179 (OK 1922) that it was incumbent on the owner (lessor) to put the bleachers in safe repair before the public was permitted to occupy them.

Given the long line of cases upholding this public use exception, it is incumbent on the lessor to inspect the premises and facilities for dangerous conditions and to remedy those conditions prior to leasing. A lease agreement whereby the lessee agrees to repair the defect does not bar landlord liability unless the lessee agreed not to admit the public until repairs were made.

Retention of Control

Although the majority of cases justifying this exception deal with office buildings and apartments, the concepts are applicable to a recreation facility lease. When the lessor retains control over a portion of a facility, the lessor will be liable for user injuries within that area of control. Typically in recreation facility leases the lessor may lease only a portion of a building, retaining control over hallways, stairwells, basements, bathrooms, parking areas, or maintenance facilities. In those instances, the lessor may be liable for visitor injuries regardless of the fact that the visitor was an invitee to an activity sponsored by the lessee. The greater the degree of control over a premises in a lease, the greater the potential for landlord liability.

AASER v THE CITY OF CHARLOTTE
Supreme Court of North Carolina
144 S.E.2d 610 1965

Lake, Justice

The plaintiff alleges that on December 6, 1963, she was a spectator at an ice hockey game played in the Coliseum owned by the city of Charlotte, and administered for it by its agency, the Auditorium-Coliseum Authority, hereinafter called the Authority, having purchased a ticket entitling her to admission thereto. She sues the city, the Authority and the Charlotte Hockey Club, Inc., the promoter of the hockey game, for injuries she sustained when struck by a hockey puck while walking in a corridor of the Coliseum. She alleges that a group of young boys were playing in the corridor, knocking the puck back and forth with hockey sticks and, in their play, struck the puck and drove it against her ankle. She further alleges that the defendants had prior knowledge of such play in the corridors by groups of children and were negligent in failing to use due care to stop it, thus failing to exercise reasonable care to keep the premises in a safe condition for use by their invitees, including the plaintiff.

The defendants in their respective answers deny all allegations of negligence and deny that they had any knowledge of such acts and conduct by any group of children, including the group alleged to have been so playing at the time of the plaintiff's injury. At the close of the evidence offered by the plaintiff the court entered judgment of nonsuit as to the defendant Charlotte Hockey Club, Inc., but denied the motions therefore by the city and the Authority. The jury rendered a verdict in favor of the plaintiff, finding her damages to be $2,500 and judgment was rendered thereon.

The plaintiff's own testimony is to the effect that: She and her husband, having purchased tickets entitling them to admission, went to the Coliseum on December 6, 1983, to witness the hockey game being played there that evening. During an intermission she left her seat and went to a hospitality room maintained by the Hockey Club for the entertainment of holders of season tickets, such as the plaintiff. Leaving the hospitality room, she was walking in the corridor toward the ladies' rest room when she was struck upon her right ankle with a hockey puck, resulting in a fracture of the ankle. As soon as she was struck she looked to her right and observed eight or ten young boys about fifty feet from her, running away and carrying hockey sticks. Upon her return to the hospitality room she saw therein Police Officer Zagar and R. H. Gilland, a director of the Hockey Club and told them what had occurred. Gilland replied that "they had been playing in the hallways before with hockey pucks and sticks." As she walked initially along the corridor to the hospitality room the plaintiff did not observe any children playing with hockey sticks or pucks. She stayed in the hospitality room above five minutes, then went back out into the corridor to go to the rest room. She walked some twenty-five feet along the corridor on this occasion but did not observe the children until after she was struck. She had never before observed or heard of such playing in the corridors.

The lease from the Authority to the Hockey Club granted the latter "the right to use (the Coliseum) . . . together with the usual entrances and exits to the same . . . and such additional space as the Lessor in its discretion shall allocate to the Lessee to be used for the purpose of thirty-six Hockey Games . . . exclusive of lobbies, general offices and all space in halls, corridors, basements, grounds, and so forth, used by the Lessor for concessions . . . all of which . . . are hereby expressly reserved by Lessor to its own use, with the privilege of occupying and using same at any and all times during the term of this agreement." The agreed rental was a share in the gross box office receipts. Free access at all times to all space occupied by the Lessee was reserved to the Authority and its officers and employees.

Upon this appeal it is not necessary for us to determine the duty owed to a ticket holder by the owner of an arena who has leased it to the promoter of an athletic exhibition so as to divest the owner of all control over the building. Here, by the terms of the lease, the city, through the Authority, retained a substantial measure of use of and control over the corridors of the Coliseum, even while the lessee was using it for its hockey games. The mere execution of such a lease does not free the city and the Authority from liability to a ticket holder injured in the corridor while in the Coliseum to attend a hockey game.

One who purchases a ticket and, pursuant thereto, enters such an arena is an invitee of the operator of the exhibition. While in a corridor providing access to portions of the building which his ticket entitles him to enter, he is also the invitee of the owner of the building who has retained the right to control the corridors. No appeal having been taken from the judgment of nonsuit as to the Hockey Club, we are not here concerned with the liability of the promoter-leasee to a ticket holder injured in the corridor which the owner has retained the right to use and control. Nor are we concerned here with the right of the ticket holder against the owner of the building for injury received in the portion of the Coliseum in which the hockey game is actually played. The plaintiff was injured in a corridor where she had a right to be as the holder of a ticket to the hockey game. The city and the Authority had the right to control the corridor. As to her use of and injury in this corridor, the relation of the plaintiff to them and their duty to her are the same as if the city were a private corporation both owning the building and promoting the hockey game therein.

One who, expressly or by implication, invites others to come upon his premises to view, for a price, an athletic event being carried on therein has the duty to be reasonably sure that he is not inviting them into danger and must exercise reasonable care for their safety. He is not an insurer of their safety and is liable only for injuries proximately caused by his failure to use reasonable care to discover and remove, or otherwise protect against, dangerous conditions, activities, or occurrences upon his premises.

The evidence offered by the plaintiff is not sufficient to justify a finding that a condition precedent to her right to recover from the city or the Authority existed. Therefore, the motions of the city and the Authority for judgment of nonsuit should have been granted.

Reversed

Agreement to Repair

When the lessor fails to keep the premises in good repair for the benefit of the lessee as required by the lease, then the lessor may be liable in tort when a lessee or a visitor is injured. In recreation leases, responsibility for repairs to the premises are often not adequately addressed. With the potential for liability, this question should be carefully reviewed by the enterprise prior to executing any lease.

Reversed. Judgment for City

CONTRACTING SERVICES

As with facility leasing, public recreation and sports agencies often contract to provide activities and programs through the private sector. Often the reason given for this practice is the lack of resources and expertise in the public sector with both being available to the private sector. Again there may be a third advantage to such a practice—transferring to the private sector the liability risks associated with the program.

Various doctrines in the law hold individuals, organizations, agencies, and enterprises responsible for the negligent conduct of others. The doctrine of *respondeat superior* provides that the employer is responsible for the tortious acts of employees or agents while acting in the course and scope of their employment. Thus a recreation enterprise may be liable for the negligent conduct of employees. Other forms of vicarious liability are (1) *dram shop* laws whereby the tavern owner may be liable for injuries caused by an intoxicated customer, (2) *incorrigibility statutes* whereby parents are liable for damages caused for the negligence of their children, and (3) *auto-owner responsibility laws* whereby the owner is liable for injuries caused by the negligence of the driver.

It is well established that a party who has entered into a true independent contractor relationship is not generally liable for the wrongs of that contractor, its employees or any other subcontractor employed. An independent contractor is typically defined as one who undertakes a specific job and the person who engages him does not have the right to direct and control the method and manner of doing the work. A caveat must be given regarding total reliance on this as a means to transfer risk. The doctrine of nonliability for the conduct of independent contractors has become suspect due to the large number of exceptions fabricated by the courts. Transfer of risk is not effective where

1. The employer fails to exercise reasonable care in selecting an independent contractor,
2. The work is inherently dangerous,
3. The work involves portions of premises retained by the lessor,
4. The employer fails to inspect the completed work, and
5. The employer retains the right to control the work of the contractor.

Under any of these exceptions the protection afforded to the employer of an independent contractor may be lost. Whenever using independent contractors, a careful analysis should be made to determine whether any aspects of the relationship fall within any of these exceptions.

Beyond the legal issues, a number of policy and economic realities must be addressed by the recreation and sports agency prior to entering into the contract. Although the agency may be seeking to transfer the legal risk to the performing party this may not be possible if the program is not profitable to the performing party. In that case the sponsoring party will have to balance the benefits of transferring the legal risks against a guarantee of profitability to the performing party. When the benefits exceed the costs the decision is easier than when the contrary is true. Under these circumstances the decision is a business question and not a legal question.

DOCKERY v WORLD OF MIRTH SHOWS
Supreme Court of North Carolina
142 S.E.2d 29 1965

Moore, J.

Action to recover damages for personal injuries suffered by plaintiff when she fell from a "ride" operated at the Dixie Classic Fair.

The evidence favorable to plaintiff tends to establish these facts: The Dixie Classic Fair is an unincorporated association, is operated by a commission appointed by the Winston-Salem Foundation and has a manager in charge. The Fair was held in 1961 during the period October 10 to October 14. It entered into a contract with defendant, World of Mirth Shows, Inc., in which it was provided that Mirth should furnish certain amusements (fifteen major rides and fifteen major shows), from the operation of which the Fair would receive specified percentages of gross receipts and Mirth would indemnify the Fair for any loss or liability which might arise from the operation of the amusements.

Mirth provided the amusements in accordance with the contract. One of the rides furnished was the "Scrambler." Mirth contracted with Michael Dembrosky, doing business as M.D. Amusement Company, to provide and operate the Scrambler and Dembrosky, through his employees, "installed and operated the Scrambler and invited the public to ride on it by paying an admission charge." The Manager of the Fair had no contacts with Dembrosky; all of his dealings were with Mr. Bergen, an official on Mirth. An employee of Mirth took the accounting and receipts of all amusements each day to the Superintendent of Admissions, who handled all the financial matters for the Fair. In the event of any complaints from members of the public, or anyone else, as to the operation of any activity of the Fair, the complaint was taken up with Mr. Bergen. Mirth advertised through the Dixie Classic Fair. The Fair gave out "news releases, picture of attractions, and so on" through its advertising agents.

About 4:30 in the afternoon of October 11, plaintiff, a twelve-year-old child and three companions bought tickets and were admitted. They attempted to occupy a single seat but it was too crowded. Plaintiff and one of her companions went to another seat. The ride was about to start and they had to hurry. Plaintiff got in first and was on the left or inside portion of the seat. They tried to close the bar but the latch would not catch and the bar would not close. The attendant did not check the seats to see that the bars were closed. The ride started and plaintiff rose to her feet in a crouched or squatting position to call to the attendant. She shouted, "Stop! The door won't shut." She was shouting in a loud voice; she was frightened. The attendant paid her no attention. The ride was moving faster and faster. She had her hand on the bar but it was moving back and forth. About the time the ride reached its maximum speed, the centrifugal force of the circular action threw her across the legs of her companion in the bucket in front of the seat, the seat jerked inward and she was thrown through the open end of the bucket and fell out. The ride made two revolutions before it stopped. She was injured both internally and externally. A kidney was injured to such extent it had to be removed; she has several permanent scars. Other persons who rode the Scrambler at other times during the same day had difficulty in closing the bars; the attendant made no effort to see that the bars were closed and the riders were secured.

Plaintiff alleges that defendant Mirth "assumed responsibility for the operation of all . . . rides at the fair and exercised supervision and control over them," the Scrambler "was an inherently dangerous device capable of inflicting serious injury . . . unless maintained in good operating condition, and unless operated with care and caution," Mirth well knew the Scrambler was inherently dangerous and it had the "obligation to inspect and maintain the Scrambler in good and safe operating condition for the protection of the . . . public," the duties and obligations of Mirth "in these respects were nondelegable to concessionaires and others," and Mirth was negligent "in failing to have the bar across the front of the Scrambler seat in which the plaintiff was riding securely fastened and in failing to inspect the same and to see that it was securely fastened, in failing to inspect the same and to maintain it in good safe working condition in view of the hazardous nature of the ride, and such negligence . . . was the proximate cause of" plaintiff's injuries.

Defendant Mirth, answering, avers that the bar attached to the seat in which plaintiff was riding and the latch on the bar were not defective and were "more than adequate to secure the plaintiff in her seat and remained latched and secured" during her ride, the attendant "checked all seats including plaintiff's seat and after seeing that plaintiff was safely seated and that the bar was latched and secured, started the ride," plaintiff "continued to stand up in the face of obvious . . . danger to herself and negligently and carelessly disregarded the warnings and appeals made to her to sit down," plaintiff's fall and injury were solely caused by her negligence, if defendant was negligent in any manner the negligence of plaintiff was a contributing cause of her injury, and Dembrosky, owner and operator of the Scrambler, was an independent contractor and not an agent of Mirth, and Mirth is not responsible for negligence on the part of Dembrosky. Dembrosky could not be located and no process was served on him. The action proceeded against Mirth as the sole defendant.

Defendant Mirth asserts that the negligence, if any, giving rise to plaintiff's fall and injuries consisted of acts and omissions of Dembrosky, an independent contractor, and the conduct of plaintiff in standing while the Scrambler was in motion. In response to an issue submitted by the court, the jury determined that Dembrosky was not an agent or employee of Mirth. An employer is not ordinarily liable for injury resulting from dangerous conditions collaterally created by the negligence of an independent contractor. But where it is reasonably foreseeable that harmful consequences will arise from the activity of the contractor unless precautionary methods are adopted, the duty rests upon the employer to see that these precautionary methods are adopted, and he cannot escape liability by entrusting this duty to the independent contractor. The contractor may be liable for the same want of due care in not taking the necessary precautions, for the omission of which the employer is liable; but as to the employer, the liability is direct, and not derivative, since public policy fixes him with a nondelegable duty to see that the precautions are taken.

It is generally held that the owner of a place of amusement having a variety of attractions and devices or a general concessionaire actually engaged in the conduct of such place of amusement cannot avoid liability for injuries to patrons resulting from the defective or dangerous condition of the premises or from defective amusement apparatus or devices on the ground that such premises or devices are under the control of and used by a subconcessionaire. Liability of such owner or general concessionaire is predicated either upon his nondelegable duty to maintain a reasonably safe place for the patrons, in accord with which he must answer for the negligence of the latter's employees in rendering the premises and devices unsafe, or merely upon the general ground that such owner or general concessionaire is responsible for his breach of duty to keep the premises, including the devices, reasonably safe, without reference to any separate act or omission of the subconcessionaire. While there are some decisions to the contrary, the greater weight of authority is that such owner or general concessionaire will not be relieved from responsibility because the amusement or device is provided and conducted by the subconcessionaire, provided it is of a character that would probably cause injury unless due precautions are taken to guard against it; and this duty applies not only to the condition of the premises and device, but also the management and operation where the device is of a character likely to produce injury unless due care is observed in its operation. The duty is a continuing one.

The evidence in the instant case is sufficient to permit the jury to find these facts: Mirth, general concessionaire, agreed to provide rides and shows for the Dixie Classic Fair. It provided these amusements, among them the Scrambler which was operated by an attendant, an employee of the owner thereof, Dembrosky, subconcessionaire. Mirth by contract assumed responsibility for the amusements and agreed to indemnify the Fair for any liability incurred by reason of the operation thereof. Inspections were advertised by the Fair and the public was invited to attend. Mirth gave attention to all complaints, and daily reported and delivered all admission receipts of the amusements to the Superintendent of Admissions, an agent of the Fair. The Fair received a percentage of receipts; Mirth looked to the amusements for its compensation. Many, if not most, of the patrons of the Scrambler were children. The Scrambler was inherently dangerous if precautions were not taken to assure the safety of the riders. The bars on the seats of the Scrambler, designed to secure the safety of riders, were difficult to fasten. The procedure of the attendant was to leave to the riders the closing and latching of the bars and to start the motor and operate the ride without ascertaining that the bars were closed and latched and the riders secure. Reasonable inspection and oversight of the Scrambler while in operation would have disclosed the condition of the bars and the attendant's method of operation. Mirth failed to perform its duty of inspection and supervision, or, if it performed the duty, it failed to take precautions for the safety of riders. The difficulty in closing the bars and the neglect of the attendant to see that riders were secure proximately caused the injury to plaintiff. In the operation of an amusement "ride," it is the duty of the operator to be alert and to see that the riders are safe during the operation.

We have carefully considered all assignments of error and we find nothing sufficiently prejudicial in the conduct of the trial and the charge of the court to warrant a new trial.

Affirmed

SUMMARY

Facility leasing and contracting for services are common business practices for park, recreation and sports agencies in the public and private sectors. Aside from the business considerations, transfer of legal risks is an option offered by both practices. Although this may be a benefit it is not failproof.

As a general rule, when a landlord transfers exclusive possession and control of a facility to a tenant the tenant assumes the liability for injuries remains with the landlord where: a hidden defect, known to the landlord but not the tenant, caused the injury; the landlord retained significant control over the operation of the facility; the landlord agreed to repair any defects but failed to do so and the public was expected to use the facility and the risk of injury was great. In these instances the injured party may look to the landlord for relief rather than to the tenant.

When entering into leases recreation and sports enterprises should consider these points to deal with legal risk:

1. Legal restrictions on the powers of public agencies to lease land and facilities. Review these legal technicalities with your attorney.
2. Provision by the tenant of adequate insurance to protect the landlord during the life of the lease. Require that the tenant furnish proof of insurance.
3. Above and beyond the insurance requirements insert a clause that the tenant will be responsible for injuries and damages and will indemnify the landlord for any losses suffered.
4. Insert lease clause that tenant takes the premises as is with all known and reasonably discoverable defects.
5. Minimize landlord control of operations through provision of performance standards and provide means to deal with noncompliance.

In contracting services and programs with third parties, transfer of legal risk is an option that should not be overlooked by the sponsoring agency. As a general rule, the sponsoring party transfers the legal risk to the performing party for any injuries that occur in the program if the performing party is in the status of an independent contractor. An independent contractor is a person who undertakes a specific task and the person who engages him does not have the right to direct and control the method and manner of doing the work. Where the performing party is not classified as an independent contractor the sponsoring party retains liability for user injuries.

As with facility leasing there are a number of points the contracting parties should consider prior to entering into any agreement for services and programs. The sponsoring agency should review:

1. Its legal powers and duties with respect to contracting for services and programs,
2. Statements identifying whose insurance coverage will handle user injuries,
3. The insurance policy of the performing party when one is required to determine the extent of coverage,
4. All performance standards in the contract to insure that the performing party retains the status of independent contractor, and
5. The qualifications and expertise of the performing party.

DISCUSSION QUESTIONS

1. When a lease is silent as to property damage who bears the loss for property destruction—the landlord or the tenant?
2. Should a tenant always purchase insurance coverage for user injuries?
3. How much control may a lessor retain over the operation of a facility and still transfer liability to the tenant?
4. Where a lease does not specify control over an area between the landlord and tenant which party bears the legal risk for an injury in that area?
5. Under what circumstances is the transfer of legal risk to the performing party not effective when contracting for services and programs?

NOTES

[1]See generally, RONALD PAIGE, "Contracting for Services—A Valid Response to Fiscal Conservancy," *Parks and Recreation,* November 1982, p. 30, and JAMES KOZLOWSKI, "Statutes Dictate Public Contracting Requirements," *Parks and Recreation,* October 1982, p. 28, and RODNEY WARNICK, *The Scope, Nature, and Effect of Contracting Public Recreation and Park Services to the Private Sector in the Northeastern United States,* The Pennsylvania State University (unpublished M.S. thesis), 1982.
[2]16. U.S.C. 21.22, 17 Stat 32 (Act of March, 1872).

³Restatement (Second) of Torts §§355, 356, 64 A.L.R.3d 339. See also Prosser, p. 100, citing a
  long line of cases.
⁴Restatement (Second) of Torts §359.
⁵Athletic facilities: *Gibson* v *Shelby County Fair Assoc.*, 44 N.W.2d 363 (IA 1950), *Lush* v *Peck,* 93
  N.E. 377, *Williams* v Strickland, 112 S.E.2d 533 (NC 1960), *Faukman* v *Lauer,* 91 A.218
  (PA 1914). Swimming facilities: *Ward* v *U.S.,* 208 F. Supp. 118 (CO 1962), *Martin* v
  Ashbury Park, 168 A. 612 (NJ 1933), *Larson* v *Calders Park Co.,* 180 P. 599 (UT 1919), 17
  A.L.R.3d 872.

appendix

**GOVERNMENTAL IMMUNITY
FOR STATE AND LOCAL GOVERNMENTS**

(Restatement (Second) of Torts §895B, Reporter's Note)

Alabama

State—Constitutional provision against suit. Ala. Const. art. I, §14. Legislature cannot consent to suit.

Local—Judicially abolished. Statute remains unchanged and allows suit. Ala. Code, titl. 11, §11-47-190 (1975.)

Alaska

State—Constitutional provision allowing legislature to establish procedures for suits against state. Alaska Const. Art. 2, §21. Statutory authorization with exceptions for discretionary functions and intentional torts. Atty. Gen. may settle claims. Alaska Stat. §§09.50.250 to 09.50.300.

Arizona

State—Judicially abolished. Statutory exception for discretionary functions. Ariz. Rev. Stat. §26-314.

Arkansas

State—Constitutional provision against suit. Ark. Const. Art. 5, 20. Applies to agencies, cannot be waived. Statutory establishment of State Claims Commission, with exclusive jurisdiction and no judicial review. Ark. Stat. Ann. §§13-1401 to 13-1406.

Local—Statutory provision that political subdivisions are immune for torts, but procedure authorized for handling tort claims. Requires motor vehicle insurance coverage. Ark. Stat. Ann. §§12-2901 to 12-2903.

California

State—Judicially abolished. Presently a detailed Tort Claims Act. West's Ann. Cal. Gov. Code §§815-996.6.

Local—Same.

Colorado

State—Judicially abolished. Colo. Rev. Stat. 1973, §§24-10-101 to 24-10-117. Insurance waives immunity to extent of coverage.

Local—Same.

Connecticut

State—Conn. Gen. Stat. Ann. §§4-141 to 4-165b. Judicial refusal to abolish sovereign immunity.

Local—Suit against employee, with payment by municipality, subject to certain limitations. Conn. Gen. Stat. Ann §7-465 (Supp. 1983). If not within statute liability only for ministerial acts.

Delaware

State—Constitution authorizes suits against the state, subject to lawful regulation. Del. Const. Art. I, §9. Statutory authorization with usual exceptions. 10 Del. Code Ann. §§4001-4005.

Local—Same.

Florida

State—Constitution allows provision to be made for suit against State. Fla. Const. Art. 10, §13 (1970). Statutory waiver of sovereign immunity in tort

with exceptions. West's Fla. Stat. Ann. §768.28.
Local—Same.

Georgia

State—Constitution authorizes legislature to create a Court of Claims for tort claims against the state, but does not waive immunity. Ga. Const. art. 6, sec. 5. This court has not been established, but the constitutional amendment authorizing it means that sovereign immunity has constitutional status and cannot now be judicially abrogated. Insurance for motor vehicles does not waive immunity. Ga. Code Ann. §89-932.
Local—Traditional position for municipalities. Ga. Code Ann. §69—301. Counties are not liable for suit unless made so by statute. Ga. Code Ann. §23-1502. All political subdivisions may procure insurance for motor vehicles, which waives immunity to the extent of the coverage. Ga. Code Ann. §89-932.

Hawaii

State—State Tort Liability Act waives immunity with exceptions, like discretionary duties and intentional torts. Hawaii Rev. Stat. §§662-1 to 662-16.
Local—Same.

Idaho

State—Judicially abolished. Tort Claims Act abolishes the government/proprietary distinction, provides for indemnification of employee, and excepts intentional torts, discretionary functions, etc. Idaho Tort Claims Act. §§6-901 to 6-928.
Local—Same.

Illinois

State—Constitution waives immunity. Ill. Const. Art. 13, §4. Ill. Ann. Stat., ch. 37, §439.8.
Local—Judicially abolished. Statutory restoration of exceptions, Ill. Ann. Stat. ch. 85, §§1-101 to 10-101.

Indiana

State—Tort Claims Act. §§34-4-16.5-1 to 34-4-16.5-17.
Local—Same.

Iowa

State—Tort Claims Act. Iowa Code Ann. §§25A.1-25A.22.
Local—Abolished by statute with limitations and exceptions. Iowa Code Ann. §§613A.1 to 613A.13.

Kansas

State—Proprietary immunity judicially abolished. Insurance authorized, with waiver of immunity of extent of coverage. Kan. Stat. Ann. §§74-4701 to 74-4707.
Local—Insurance authorized.

Kentucky

State—Immunity unless waived by legislature. Ky. Rev. Stat. Ann. §§44.055 to 44.160.
Local—Judicially abolished.

Louisiana

State—Constitution abolished tort immunity. La. Const. Art. 12, §10A. Statutory procedure for suing State or political subdivisions. La. Rev. Stat. 24:152.
Local—Legislative authority to be sued apparently abolishes immunity.

Maine

State—Judicially abolished. Tort Claims Act. 14 Me. Rev. Stat. Ann. §§8101 to 8118.
Local—Same.

Maryland

State—Immunity retained; abrogation said to be up to the legislature.
Local—Insurance for counties authorized, with corresponding waiver. Md. Code Ann. 1978, Art. 25A, §5.

Massachusetts

State—Statutory provision for liability with exceptions for discretionary functions, intentional torts, etc. Mass. Gen. Laws Ann., c. 258, §§1 to 8.
Local—Same.

Michigan

State—Judicially abolished. Mich. Stat. Ann. §§3.996(101) to 3.996.
Local—Judicially abolished. Restored by statute as to governmental functions. Mich. Stat. Ann. §§3.996(107) (1977, Supp. 1979).

Minnesota

State—Statute abolished immunity with exceptions including discretionary functions. Minn. Stat. Ann. §3.736.

Local—Judicially abolished. Minn. Stat. Ann. §§466.01 to 466.15 (1977, Supp. 1978).

Mississippi

State—Immunity retained, with some exceptions when there is insurance.
Local—Same.

Missouri

State—Judicially ajbolished. Vernon's Ann. Mo. Stat. §226.092.
Local—Same.

Montana

State—Constitutionally abolished. Mont. Const. Art. 2, §18, State Comprehensive Insurance Plan and Tort Claims Act. Mont. Rev. Codes Ann. 1977, §§82-4301 and 82-4327.
Local—Same.

Nebraska

State—Constitution held to abolish immunity but leave to legislature to ide for suit. Neb. Const. Art. 5, §2. State Tort Claims Act. Neb. Rev. Stat. 1977 Supp. §§81-8, 209, to 81-8, 239.
Local—Judicially abolished. Followed by Political Subdivisions Tort Claims Act, which retains immunity for discretionary functions, intentional torts, and the enforcement of invalid statutes using due care, but gives the governing body authority. Neb. Rev. Stat. §§23-2401 to 23-2410.

Nevada

State—Statutorily abolished. Nev. Rev. Stat. §§41.031 to 41.039 (1979).
Local—Judicially abolished. Followed by statute above.

New Hampshire

State—Insurance authorized waives immunity to extent of coverage. N.H. Rev. Stat. Ann. §412:3. Immunity retained otherwise, unless state has consented to suit.
Local—Judicially abolished. Insurance authorized. N.H. Rev. Stat. Ann. §412:3.

New Jersey

State—Judicially abolished. Followed by New Jersey Tort Claims Act, providing for immunity with exceptions. N.J. Stat. Ann. §§59:1-1 to 59:12-1.
Local—Same.

New Mexico

State—Judicially abolished. Followed by Tort Claims Act, which provides for immunity unless specifically excepted, like claims arising from motor vehicles, streets, facilities. Insurance required for excepted areas. N.M. Stat. Ann. 1978, §§41-4-1 to 41-4-25.
Local—Same.

New York

State—Statutory waiver of immunity. Tort Claims Act. Gen. Mun. §50-a to 52.
Local—Same.

North Carolina

State—State Indus. Comm'n. hears claims against state dep'ts. and agencies. N.C. Gen. Stat. §§143-291 to 143-300.6 (1978).
Local—Insurance authorized for cities, with waiver of immunity. N.C. Gen. Stat. §§160A-485.

North Dakota

State—Insurance authorized for state agencies, with waiver of immunity to extent of policy. N.D. Cent. Code §39-12.1-15. Insurance also authorized for motor vehicles. N.D. Cent. Code §39-01-08.
Local—Judicially abolished. Statutory waiver of immunity for negligence actions. N.D. Cent. Code §§32-12.1 to 31-12.1-14.

Ohio

State—Constitution held to abolish immunity, but to require legislative consent for suit. Ohio Const., Art. I, §16. Statutory waiver of immunity, suit in court of claims with right of appeal and limitations. Ohio Rev. Code §§2743.01 to 2743.20.
Local—Waiver in Court of Claims Act held not to apply to political subdivisions.

Oklahoma

State—Immunity waived only to insurance coverage. 47 Okl. Stat. §158.1.
Local—Political Subdivisions Tort Claims Act provides for liability.

Oregon

State—Abolished by statue, with usual exceptions. Or. Rev. Stat. §§30.260 to 30.300.
Local—Same.

Pennsylvania

State—Judicially abolished.
Local—Judicially abolished. Statutorily reinstated, with exceptions for certain negligent acts of employees. Pa. Cons. Stat. Ann. §§53-5311.802.

Rhode Island

State—Abolished by statute. R.I. Gen. Laws 1978, §§9-31-1 to 9-31-7.
Local—Judicially abolished. Followed by statute, supra.

South Carolina

State—Traditional immunity retained.
Local—Permitted to procure insurance. S.C. Code Ann. §1-11-140.

South Dakota

State—Office of Commissioner of Claims makes advisory findings to legislature, which determines whether to award relief. S.D. Comp. Laws §§21-32-1 to 21-32-7.
Local—Insurance authorized. S.D. Comp. Laws §9-12-7.

Tennessee

State—Constitution requires legislative consent for suit against state. Tenn. Const. Art. I, §17. Reinforced by statute depriving courts of jurisdiction over suits against state unless legislature has consented.
Local—Abolished by Governmental Tort Liability Act, applicable to all political subdivisions. Tenn. Code Ann. §§23-3301 to 23-3331.

Texas

State—Abolished by Texas Tort Claims Act, but many exceptions. Retains governmental/proprietary distinction. Vernon's Tex. Ann. Civ. Stat. art. 6252-19.
Local—Same.

Utah

State—Immunity retained for governmental functions subject to exceptions in act. Utah Code Ann. 1978, §§63-30-1 to 63-30-34.
Local—Same.

Vermont

State—Abolished by statute, subject to usual exceptions. 12 Vt. Stat. Ann. §§5601 to 5605.

Local—Insurance authorized and immunity waived for municipalities. 24 Vt. Stat. Ann. §1092.

Virginia

State—Retaining immunity.
Local—Governmental/proprietary distinction.

Washington

State—Abolished by statute for both governmental and proprietary functions. West's Wash. Rev. Code Ann. §§4.92.090 to 4.92.170.
Local—Statute to abolish. West's Wash. Rev. Code Ann. §§4.96.010 to 4.96.030.

West Virginia

State—Constitutional provision that state cannot be a defendant in a suit. W. Va. Const. Art. 6, §35.
Local—Judicially abolished for municipalities.

Wisconsin

State—Legislature to determine consent and method for suit. Wis. S.A. Const. Art. 4, §27. Immunity judicially abolished.
Local—Judicially abolished. Wis. Stat. Ann. §895.43. Insurance authorized.

Wyoming

State—Constitution allows legislature to provide for suits against the state. Wyo. Const. Art. 1,§8. Govt. Claims Act. §§1-39-101 to 119.
Local—Same.

Glossary

Action A lawsuit; a court proceeding to enforce a legal right.

Adjudication A judicial action leading to a judgment.

Adhesion Contract Standard form contracts whereby the stronger party dictates the terms.

Affirm The decision of an appellate court to ratify or confirm the judgment of a lower court.

Affirmative Defense A response to a claim which challenges the plaintiff's legal right to bring an action.

Allegation An assertion of a fact which the person making it intends to prove.

Answer The defendant's written response to the complaint.

Appeal An application to a higher court to correct or modify the judgment of a lower court.

Appellant the party who initiates the appeal from one court to another; sometimes called a petitioner. Either plaintiff or defendant at trial court may be termed an appellant.

Appellee The party against whom an appeal is taken; often called a respondent.

Assumption of Risk An affirmative defense in a negligence action; a person who voluntarily exposes himself to a known and obvious danger may not recover for the injury.

Battery The unprivileged intentional touching of another.

Breach of Contract Failure, without legal excuse, to perform the obligations and terms of the contract.

Burden of Proof The duty of proving or disproving facts disputed at trial.

Case Law Judicial precedent created by court decisions; court or judge made laws.

Cause of Action A legal right of redress against another; it includes the right to sue and the right to recover in court.

Caveat A warning.

Civil Action A lawsuit instituted to protect a private right as contrasted with a criminal action which protects the rights of the state.

Claim for Relief A short statement in the complaint requesting a remedy.

Common Law The law developed from decisions in American and English courts, not an action of the legislature.

Comparative Negligence The relative degree of negligence on the part of the plaintiff and defendant with damages awarded on a basis proportionate to each person's carelessness.

Compensatory Damages Money awarded equivalent to the actual value of damages or injury.

Complaint The initial pleading in a civil action filed by the plaintiff; also called the petitions.

Contributory Negligence Conduct on the part of the plaintiff falling below that required for his protection which contributes to the plaintiff's injury.

Crime An act that is a violation of law punishable by the state or nation.

Defamation Anything published or publicly spoken causing injury to a person's good name, reputation, or character.

Defendant The party against whom the lawsuit is brought.

Demurrer A pleading of defendant admitting to the plaintiff's allegation of facts but asserting that the plaintiff's claim fails to state a cause of action.

Deposition A written record of verbal testimony in the form of questions and answers made before a public officer for use in a lawsuit.

Discovery The process by which opposing parties obtain information in preparation for trial.

Discretionary Duty A responsibility carried out by a public official while setting policy as contrasted with a ministerial duty which is established for and carried out by employees.

Directed Verdict A determination made at the direction of the judge in cases where there has been insufficient evidence to meet a party's burden of proof.

Duty A flexible term describing a legal obligation.

Equity Fundamental fairness; a type of justice that developed separate from the common law in England.

Exemplary Damages A monetary award above and beyond actual damages intended to punish the defendant for intentional torts.

Felony A type of crime for which the penalty is imprisonment in a state penitentiary or death.

Foreseeability An occurrence which a reasonable and prudent person would perceive and anticipate under existing conditions.

Good Samaritan Laws Statutes designed to protect a person who in good faith assumes a legal duty to provide medical assistance to a person in peril.

Governmental Function A term for various activities of a political entity carried out for the protection and benefit of the general public.

Guest Passenger Laws Statutes prohibiting a person riding as guest in the automobile from suing the driver or owner unless the injury resulted from more than ordinary negligence.

Indemnify To compensate one for a loss or to reimburse one for expenses incurred.

Injunction A court order requiring a person to act or refrain from acting in a certain manner.

In Loco Parentis Acting as a parent with respect to the care and supervision of a child.

Invitee A person who goes upon the land or premises of another by express or implied invitation.

Judgment N.O.V. (Non Obstante Veredicto) A judgment entered by the court for legal reasons that is contrary to verdict rendered by the jury.

Jurisdiction The authority of the court to hear and decide a lawsuit.

Laches A doctrine preventing a party from recovering a judgment due to their delay in bringing the lawsuit.

Liability A legal responsibility, duty, or obligation.

Libel A written defamation of one's character or reputation.

Licensee A term for a social guest.

Liquidated Damages The amount of money which the parties agree to in the contract as the compensation to be paid if the contract is breached.

Litigation A lawsuit.

Malfeasance In negligence law it refers to the commission of an illegal act.

Misfeasance The improper doing of an otherwise proper act; a negligent act.

Misdemeanor The lessor crime punishable by a fine or imprisonment in a city or county jail for less than one year.

Negligence   Conduct falling below the standard of care exercised by a reasonable and prudent person in relation to the protection of others.

Nominal Damages   Money awarded by the court for a technical infraction of a duty when there has been no actual loss or injury from the breach of duty.

Nuisance   An act which causes a substantial and unreasonable interference with a person's use and enjoymr inference drawn from the proven instance of some fact.

Procedural Law   Rules of law which deal with the mechanics of court procedure.

Proprietary Function   Acts which are performed by political entities for a pecuniary benefit.

Proximate Cause   Something which produces a result and without which the result could not have occurred.

Remand   The action of an appellate court sending a case back to a trial court for further action.

Respondeat Superior   A legal rule that holds an employer liable for the negligent acts and actions of employees.

Respondent   A party against whom a motion is filed in an appellate court; analogous to an appellee.

Risk   A specified contingency or peril.

Slander   Verbal communication of defamatory statements.

Sovereign Immunity   A rule of law that a nation, state, or local unit of government cannot be sued without its consent.

Stare Decisis   A court doctrine recognizing the value of prior decisions (precedent) and requiring that courts follow the decisions in resolving similar disputes.

Statute of Limitations   Statutes of the federal and state governments setting maximum time periods for the filing of lawsuits.

Summary Judgment   A decision of a court on the merits of a lawsuit when the pleading's and other documents reveal there is no genuine issue as to any material facts and the party who sought the judgment is entitled to it as a matter of law.

Tort   Civil wrongs (as opposed to criminal) not arising from a breach of a contract.

Tortfeasor   One who commits a tort; a wrongdoer.

Ultra Vires Act   An action of a person which is outside the scope of authority granted them by law.

Unenforceable Contract   A contract having no legal effect or force in a court action.

Vicarious Liability   Substituted or indirect responsibility for someone else's actions arising out of a legal responsibility (see respondeat superior).

Waiver   An intentional release of a known legal right.

Writ   A written court order or a judicial process.

Wilfull/Wanton Conduct   Behavior that manifests a disposition to perversity.

index